THE WORLD OF
GHOSTS
AND THE
SUPERNATURAL

RICHARD CAVENDISH

First published 1994

Published in Great Britain by Waymark
Publications, an imprint of AA
Publishing (a trading name of
Automobile Association Developments
Limited, whose registered office is
Norfolk House, Priestley Road,
Basingstoke, Hampshire RG24 9NY.
Registered number 1878835).
© The Automobile Association 1994
Maps © The Automobile Association 1994
The Automobile Association retains the
copyright in the original edition © 1994
and in all subsequent editions, reprints and
amendments.

Mapping produced by the Cartographic
Department of The Automobile
Association

ISBN 0 7495 0710 1

A CIP catalogue record for this book is
available from the British Library.

The contents of this publication are
believed correct at the time of printing.
Nevertheless, the publishers cannot be
held responsible for any errors or
omissions or for changes in the details
given in this guide or for the
consequences of any reliance on the
information provided by the same.

Colour separation by Daylight Colour Art
Pte Ltd, Singapore

Printed and bound by Dai Nippon Printing Co.
(Hong Kong) Ltd.

Text compiled and written by
Richard Cavendish

Edited by Rebecca King

*Title page: an Indian mask
from Brazil.
This page: a representation of
the Hawaiian god Ku.*

CONTENTS

INTRODUCTION

Everywhere on earth, and all through history, people have believed that there is more to the world than meets the eye. Behind the outward, material appearance of things there is sensed something inward, immaterial and usually invisible.

Probably the most widespread and popular religion that has ever existed is animism – belief in the existence of a spirit, or unseen force, in everything that is, animate and inanimate.

In this animistic view of the world, everything in existence is sacred, which tends to induce a perspective on nature radically different from the superior and exploitative attitude too characteristic of the modern West. The permeation of everything by spirit means that all things are linked together in a network of relationships. Human beings move in this network with cautious care for everything around them. It makes sense, for instance, to propitiate the spirit of a wood before felling a tree or the spirit of a mine before digging out its ore – indeed it would be dangerous not to, and thoroughly impolite.

✣

SPIRITUAL SPECIALISTS

✣

Another principle of animism is that since all things, including human beings, contain spirit, it is possible for human beings and spirits to communicate. Not

Ouija boards and small wheeled boards called planchettes are used during seances. When the participants rest their fingers on the board, it spells out messages – from spirits?

often for most human beings, perhaps, who are of too coarse a clay, and not usually in any normal state of mind, but for some specially gifted human beings and in abnormal states of mind. Societies the length and breadth of the world have felt the need of specialists in the sacred – shamans, priests, spirit mediums, magicians, 'masters', 'clever men', medicine men, conjure doctors, healers, diviners – who are skilled in communicating with spirits and acting as go-betweens with them.

Many of these specialists put themselves or others into trance – often assisted by hypnotic drumming, dancing and chanting – in which they are believed to become possessed by a

supernatural being, who 'mounts' them like a rider on a horse. They behave in the spirit's characteristic fashion and they speak with the voice of the spirit.

In these possession cults, when a god or a spirit seems to descend and become visible in someone, it naturally has a potent effect in reinforcing beliefs.

Possession can also be an effective therapeutic technique for people with emotional and psychological problems, who are believed to be possessed by a spirit, for either the entity is successfully exorcised or they have to come to terms with the 'spirit', which is an aspect of themselves.

Trances and visions have played a vital role in religion, in inspiring or reinforcing faith, from visions of the Virgin Mary at Lourdes or Medjugorje to the visions which inspired the Ghost Dance religion of the North American Indians. Unusual mental states are also believed to lead to the acquisition of extraordinary physical powers, as among shamans in Siberia, dancing dervishes in Turkey, holy men in India, lamas in Tibet or Taoist sages in China.

✣

SUPERNATURAL APPROACHES

✣

Many societies and cultures acknowledge the existence of powerful deities who are in charge of the various departments of nature and life, but these formidable beings are often thought of as too high and mighty to bother about the ordinary person's needs and concerns. To gain happiness, success and good fortune, or ward off disease and the bad things of life, people turn to lesser supernaturals, local spirits and intermediaries who are more likely to pay attention.

Christians from Mexico to Rome to the Philippine Islands turn to the Virgin Mary or to a favourite saint with petitions which they would not bother God or Christ with, while all through the Muslim world sincere believers in Allah take offerings and prayers to the tomb of a local holy man when they need help.

There are places on the earth's surface where the realms of the human and the sacred are felt to be specially close, places with a powerful atmosphere of sanctity or evil, or where it is believed that mysterious currents of energy can be discerned and put to use, as at Stonehenge and other prehistoric sites in Europe.

✜

THE UNCANNY DEAD

✜

As well as the nature spirits of widespread belief, there are evil spirits, too – bringers of disease and misfortune, horrible menacing things that live on the threshold between the human world and the spirit plane, from vampires and zombies to the sly and sinister familiars of witches and sorcerers, and the nightmare creatures vividly represented by masks in Africa, Asia and the Pacific.

Uncanny, too, are the spirits of the dead – ancestors and ghosts. In much of the world to this day veneration is paid to the ancestors of the family, the clan,

In the Middle Ages, Christian authors developed a hierarchy of evil spirits, of which Beelzebub, Lord of the Flies, was one of the most powerful.

the village, the tribe, who are believed to take a continuing interest in the welfare of their descendants. In households from Brazil to India to China there are little shrines where the family's ancestors are, not worshipped exactly, but remembered, saluted, given little tokens of affection and asked for help in time of need.

Ancestors are usually regarded as benevolent, but ghosts are a different matter. They may be well disposed, but they may be souls that have failed to make the proper transition from the human world to the spirit plane, in which case they can be intensely dangerous. There are stories of hideously malignant and murderous entities infesting houses, like the famous Amityville Horror of Long Island.

Stories and experiences of ghosts have only been collected and analysed to any great extent in the West, which is also the arena in which psychical

research societies and university parapsychology departments have been most active. Reports of ghosts elsewhere have a different flavour and people in other parts of the world generally do not take the detached attitude of liberal Western intellectuals to ghosts and 'paranormal' phenomena.

✜

CLOSE ENCOUNTERS

✜

Particularly interesting are the poltergeist cases, where a 'noisy spirit' starts throwing things at people, smashing plates, starting fires, scrawling messages on walls or disrupting the electricity or telephone systems. More often than not, these outbreaks often seem to be connected with a disturbed person on the scene ('the poltergeist personality'), who is apparently causing the phenomena unconsciously, or sometimes with a severe state of strain present in the household as a whole ('the poltergeist family'). However, some investigators have found themselves driven to think that a 'spirit' or 'entity' – whatever that may mean – has fastened on someone on the scene, whose energy it uses to cause the disturbances. In either case, the implications for the human mind's ability to affect matter are fascinating.

Many supernatural beings are believed to intervene in the world from distant realms in the sky. They range from the angels of Jewish, Christian and Muslim tradition to the aliens from outer space reported since 1945 in the Americas and Europe (and to a lesser extent from other areas of the world), who arrive in spacecraft and take humans prisoner as specimens for examination.

To what extent spirits and supernatural beings are real is a disputed question, but even in the materialistic, supposedly sceptical modern West, they still seem to be needed.

EUROPE

Europe is full of ghosts, and has been throughout the centuries. They materialise disconcertingly in corridors or on staircases. They shimmer through library walls, challenge diplomats on Norwegian ski slopes, glide across the lawns of English rectories in full sunlight or embarrass people in German bathrooms. The more sensational of them stalk grim castle battlements with their heads tucked underneath their arms or career along lonely roads at midnight in spectral coaches drawn by headless horses.

Above: the demure spirit of 'Katie King', materialised by a medium and photographed in 1874. When a rich American admirer gave 'Katie' jewellery, she took it away with her to the spirit world. Left: spirits have long haunted the European mind. This demon supports a holy water stoup in a church in Rennes-le-Château, France.

At haunted places scenes and moments from the past are played over again as if a film was being run through. Phantom armies fight their battles over once more. An elderly woman runs terrified and screaming round the headsman's block in the Tower of London: she has been dead more than 500 years. The disastrous 1942 Allied raid on Dieppe is heard happening all over again nine years afterwards.

It is a very ancient belief that human beings cut off before their time – executed, murdered, killed in battle or in an accident – are left with a powerful store of unused life-energy and a burning resentment, which may enmesh them in the world of the living when in the natural course of things they should go away to the realm of the dead where they belong.

Reports of ghosts and spectral encounters have continued to accumulate all through this century, in what is supposed to be an age of materialism and disbelief: except in the former Communist countries, where ghosts were politically incorrect. The best ghost sightings – the most dramatic and neatly turned ones – are the least believable. More persuasive are the everyday, casual encounters with entities which are not spine-chilling at all. Like President Paasikivi of Finland, seen in 1957 by two ladies in an apartment

remember he had died four months before, and only then did they feel frightened. Experiences like this raise the question, do we all encounter far more ghosts than we realise?

Poltergeist cases are among the most impressive, where crockery flies off the shelf and smashes, objects are flung about, people are thrown bodily out of bed or scratched, anguished messages appear on the walls. In one recent outbreak, when the exasperated human beings started chucking stones at the 'spirit', or whatever it was that was annoying them, it promptly threw them back.

Cases of this kind, too, are very old and in the past they aroused intense fear – of the unruly dead and of uncanny and sometimes malignant spirits, which hovered on the edges of the human world and threatened to invade it. They could be drawn into the human sphere by witches or they might need human blood to survive – like the vampires that terrified eastern Europe.

These old bugbears still linger, not far below the surface rationality of the European mind.

building in Helsinki. He was waiting for the elevator, joined them in it when it came, smiled politely at them and got off at the fourth floor – though no one had pressed the fourth-floor button. Only afterwards did they

Left: one very old way of harming an enemy by supernatural means is to make a doll to represent the victim and injure it. Here the doll is speared to a tree so that the victim will die in agony. Fastened to the doll is a piece of paper bearing the victim's name.
Above: Abandon hope. Traitors' Gate yawned for many a state prisoner at the Tower of London, which today harbours a legion of unquiet phantoms.
Below: a 12-year-old is tied to the bed to stop any trickery during the investigation of a poltergeist case in England in 1945.

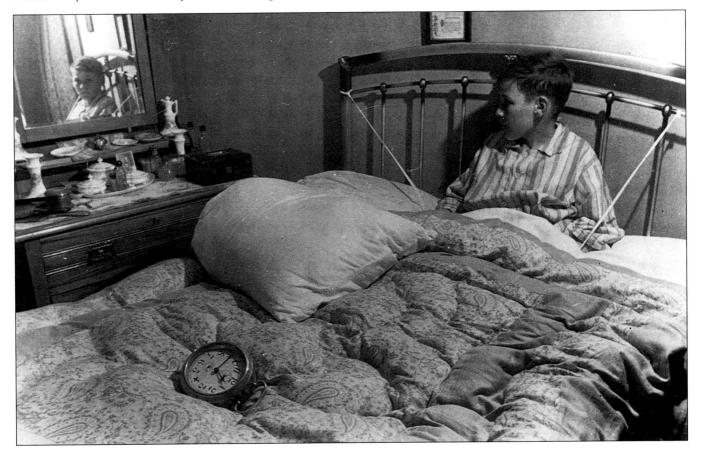

SEE INSET

Oslo

Stockholm

Helsin

Gurre ● Helsingor
Copenhagen

Schiedam

Berlin

Warsaw

Brocken

Bedburg

Dieppe ● Mons

Pointe
du Raz ● ● Mont-St-
Michel

Paris

Bingen

Île du Loch ●

Carnac ●

Combourg
Castle

Versailles
Chartres

Orléans

Ujazd

Wildenstein
Castle

Braunau am Inn

Strasbourg

Carpathian

Dole

Vienna
Mayerling
Rosenheim

Lockenhaus

Rattenburg Mariazell

Geneva

Lyon

Luggau

Toresz

Vallensages

La Salette

Varazdin

San Sebastián
de Garabandal

Eugénie-
les-Bains

Avignon

Belgrade ● Meduegna

Ituren ●

Toulouse

Aix-en-
Provence

Sujos
Sarajevo

Lourdes

Medjugorje

Avila

Assisi

Fatima

Rome

Monte
Gargano

Bélmez de
la Moraleda

Lake
Averno

Kostaritsa

Levàdh

Cape
Tainaron

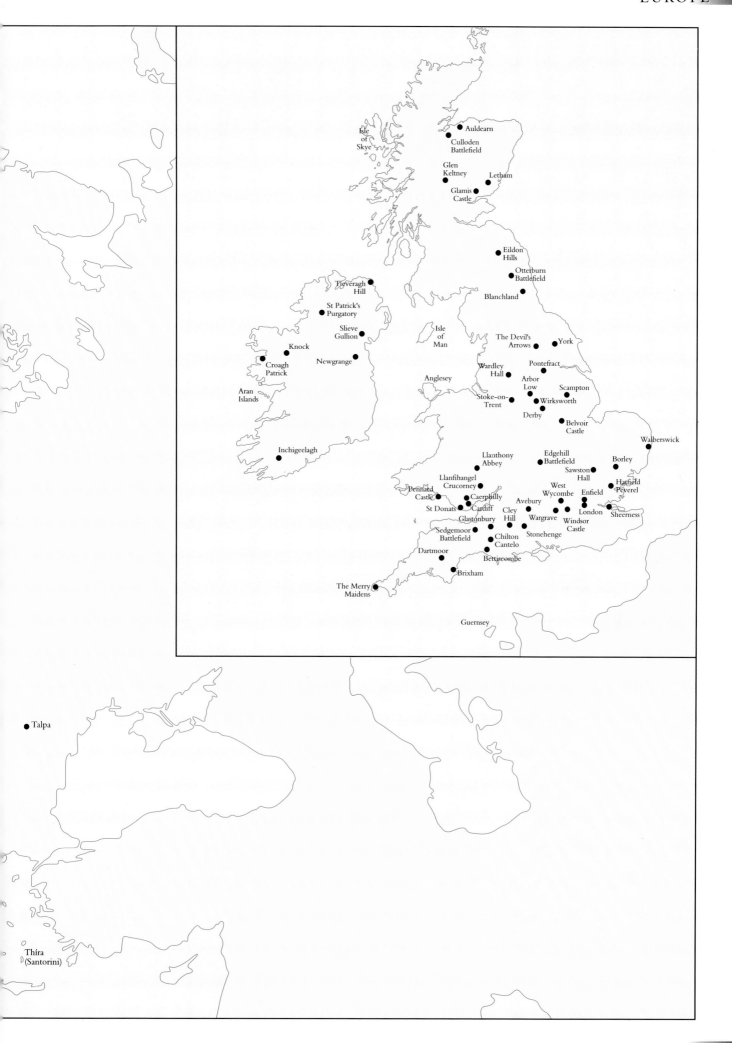

Auldearn

Culloden
Battlefield

Isle
of
Skye

Glen
Keltney
Letham

Glamis
Castle

Eildon
Hills

Otterburn
Battlefield

Tieveragh
Hill

Blanchland

St Patrick's
Purgatory

Slieve
Gullion

The Devil's
Arrows
York

Isle
of
Man

Knock

Newgrange

Wardley
Hall

Pontefract

Croagh
Patrick

Arbor
Low
Scampton

Anglesey

Stoke-on-
Trent
Wirksworth

Aran
Islands

Derby

Belvoir
Castle

Walberswick

Inchigeelagh

Llanthony
Abbey

Edgehill
Battlefield
Borley

Sawston
Hall

Llanfihangel
Crucorney

Hatfield
Peverel

West
Wycombe
Enfield

Pennard
Castle

Caerphilly

Avebury

St Donats
Cardiff

Cley
Hill
Wargrave
Windsor
Castle

London

Sheerness

Glastonbury

Sedgemoor
Battlefield

Chilton
Cantelo
Stonehenge

Dartmoor

Bettiscombe

Brixham

The Merry
Maidens

Guernsey

Talpa

Thíra
(Santorini)

OF ROYAL BLOOD

Anne Boleyn, King Henry VIII's second wife, was not yet 30 when she was accused of adultery and incest. She had a swarthy complexion and a long, slender neck, which a French executioner cut through with a sword on Tower Green in 1536. Circling her neck with her fingers, she herself had bravely joked beforehand that the headsman would have an easy task.

When a prisoner was beheaded, the corpse was taken away for burial with the head tucked tidily under the arm, which accounts for the many stories of phantoms cradling their severed heads. Poor Anne has been seen many times gliding through the precincts of the Tower of London – a figure in white, with her head on her shoulders or off them – among that grim prison-fortress's shadowy retinue of spectres. Not surprisingly in view of its long history of bloodshed, torture and fear, it is the most haunted place in London.

Margaret, Countess of Salisbury, an elderly, harmless lady in her sixties, was sent to the block in 1541. Panicking, she ran about shrieking in terror before being caught and forced to the block. There are reports of her phantom repeating the terrible moment long afterwards and running screaming round Tower Green. Sir Walter Raleigh was incarcerated in the Bloody Tower for 12 long years, and still he cannot escape, for his ghost walks the battlements by moonlight. He was seen, looking quite solid, in 1983 and again in 1985. Two ghostly children sighted walking hand in hand are thought to be

✣

It was dangerous to be on or close to the throne. Many who succeeded or climbed ambitiously to power paid for it with their lives, and places linked with Britain's royalty have more than their fair share of restless, reproachful ghosts.

✣

Top: ominous and uncanny, the Tower of London glistens by night. Above: the ill-fated Anne Boleyn.

the two little murdered Princes in the Tower.

The unfortunate Lady Jane Grey, only 16 when her head was taken off in 1554, haunts the fortress, too – two guards saw her in 1957. And shadows from the past crowd the chapel of St Peter ad Vincula, where many of the executioner's prey were hastily interred. 'In truth,' Lord Macaulay wrote in a famous passage, 'there is no sadder spot on the earth than that little cemetery. Death is there associated...with whatever is darkness in human nature and human destiny, with the savage triumph of implacable enemies, with the inconstancy, the ingratitude, the cowardice of friends, with all the miseries of alien greatness and of blighted fame.' The weight of accumulated misery in the atmosphere can affect even the most briskly insensitive observer.

✣

SCREAMING FOR MERCY

✣

Perhaps wistful memories of a happy childhood tugged Anne Boleyn's spirit back to youthful scenes. She has been seen standing on the bridge over the River Eden at Hever in Kent, where she grew up. At another of her childhood homes, Blickling Hall in Norfolk, she arrives in a spectral coach on the anniversary of her execution. Her severed head lolls in her lap and her coachman has no head.

Another of Henry VIII's queens accused of adultery was Catherine Howard, whose unquiet ghost clings to Hampton Court, the royal palace on the

Thames south-west of London. In desperation, knowing what fate awaited her, she shrieked out appeals for mercy to her royal husband as he prayed in the chapel royal. She beat frantically on the closed door, but he turned a deaf ear and she was dragged away. Her terrible, anguished screams are still heard sometimes echoing in the gallery outside the chapel.

Henry VIII himself has been sighted occasionally at Hampton Court, and limping on his ulcerated legs along corridors at Windsor Castle. In the Queen's Gallery there, the ghost of Elizabeth I has been seen, ashen-faced. George III, who greatly loved Windsor, is unable to tear himself away from the royal library, where his typical muttering 'What! What!' has been heard.

✢

THE TAPESTRY ROOM

✢

Mary I, better known as 'Bloody Mary', has been seen in the much-haunted Tapestry Room in Sawston Hall in Cambridgeshire, where she was given shelter when Lady Jane Grey's partisans were hunting her. There is a portrait of her in the house, so she is easy to recognise. Few people have slept in the Tapestry Room twice.

Mary, Queen of Scots, also highly recognisable, was executed at Fotheringhay Castle in Suffolk, which was afterwards demolished.

The headsman's axe severed many a noble neck in the Tower, hence the stories of headless spectres.

The Monster of Glamis

Glamis Castle in Scotland, the Queen Mother's family house and the home of the Earls of Strathmore, is famous for supernatural appearances. The ominous reputation of Macbeth, Thane of Glamis, clings to its fairytale towers and turrets, and the chapel is haunted by the Grey Lady, who is thought to be the Lady Glamis who was burned alive as a witch in 1540. A less alarming White Lady is supposed to flit about outdoors.

Legend has it that one more window (bricked-up and barred) can be counted on the outside of Glamis Castle than the rooms inside account for. The extra room is said to be a secret chamber, the lair of a hideous semi-human monster who was, in fact, a deformed son of one of the earls. A story goes that a workman who, having discovered a secret passage in the house which led to a concealed room, was quietly persuaded to emigrate. There is also talk of the eldest son of the family being told on his coming-of-age of some dread ancestral secret. The 2nd Lord Halifax, author of a famous 'ghost book', gathered material about the tale from friends of the 13th earl, who succeeded to the title at that time. He said that the new Lord Strathmore had been initiated into the secret by the family lawyer and the factor, and was afterwards 'quite a changed man, silent and moody, with an anxious scared look on his face'. Such was the effect on him that when his eldest son came of age, the boy refused to be told the secret, while the factor, a notably shrewd and hard-headed Scot, could never be induced to spend a night in the castle.

VERSAILLES
AND SPECTRAL ENCOUNTERS

The supremely elegant Petit Trianon in the grounds of the magnificent royal palace of Versailles, outside Paris, was built in the 1760s for King Louis XV, who gave it to his mistress, Madame du Barry. Later it was much loved by Marie-Antoinette, the ill-fated queen of Louis XVI.

Years afterwards, in 1901, the grounds of the Petit Trianon were explored by two English ladies of high intelligence and impeccable reputation – Miss Charlotte Moberly, who was principal of a women's college at Oxford, and Miss Eleanor Jourdain, her deputy. They found themselves seeing people and features which at the time seemed real though rather odd, but which afterwards turned out to have belonged not to 1901, but to the 18th century.

It was a hot day in August and, according to Miss Jourdain's account, the two ladies were walking towards the Petit Trianon when they turned off down a side path, having asked the way from two men oddly attired in green clothes and three-cornered hats. She sensed 'a feeling of depression and loneliness' about the place and 'a heavy dreaminess' which was oppressive. 'I

✛

At Versailles in 1901 two visiting English ladies apparently stepped back 130 years in time. In other cases, too, people and scenes from the past seem to repeat themselves in the present, as if a video film was somehow unrolling on the screen of today's world.

✛

Above: stately fountains helped to make Versailles a fitting palace for the gilded royalty of France in days which seem to have left a ghostly imprint on the sands of time.
Below left: the rustic watermill.
Below right: the Salon de Mars.

began to feel as if I were walking in my sleep.' Presently they saw a building in front of them, and seated on the steps was a man with a heavy black cloak round his shoulders, wearing a slouch hat. 'At that moment', Miss Jourdain wrote, 'the eerie feeling which had begun in the garden culminated in a definite impression of something uncanny and fear inspiring. The man slowly turned his face, which was marked by smallpox, his complexion was very dark. The expression was very evil and though I did not feel he was looking particularly at us, I felt a repugnance to going past him.'

✛

IN THE CHINESE GARDEN
✛

The ladies saw other figures, including a woman and a little girl at a cottage, and a woman in a shady white hat with sketching paper at the Petit Trianon itself. Afterwards discussing what had happened, they were slowly driven to the conclusion that they had somehow seen and spoken to people who had been alive more than 100 years before. They subsequently wrote a brief account of

what had happened, which was published ten years later as 'An Adventure'.

The ladies assumed that the scenes they saw must have dated from Marie-Antoinette's time. However, subsequent detailed analysis of plans and pictures identified eight features that were not there in 1901, or in Marie-Antoinette's time either, but they had been there earlier still. Who the people the ladies encountered were, no one has been able to establish, but they apparently saw features of the 'Anglo-Chinese garden' as it existed there in 1770.

It has been sceptically suggested that what the ladies really saw was Count Robert de Montesquiou and friends holding a costume party, in 1901, but Miss Moberly and Miss Jourdain were not fools, and it seems unlikely that they would both so easily have mistaken a fancy-dress occasion for the real thing. Nor does this explanation account for the garden features the ladies described, while other reports have come of figures in 18th-century dress being seen by other people in the same area in 1910, 1938, 1949 and 1955. Eleanor Jourdain also claimed to have seen visions of the past in Oxford, including one of people cheering and dancing as they accompanied a condemned prisoner on his way to the gallows to be hanged.

Similar experiences have been reported elsewhere. In 1916, for instance, the writer Edith Olivier, passing by the stone circles at Avebury in Wiltshire on a rainy evening, saw a crowded fair going on with swings and coconut shies and so on, lit by torches and flares. She only discovered afterwards that no fair had been held at Avebury since 1850 and that some of the standing stones she had noticed had vanished from view 50 years or more before that.

Right: German troops examine one of the Canadian tanks used at Dieppe. Below: first reports of the raid in the British press presented it as a success.

ECHOES OF DIEPPE

A more recent and far more dramatic example occurred in 1951, again to two English women on holiday in France in August. This time it was at the seaside village of Puys, near Dieppe. At about 4am on 4 August the two sisters-in-law were woken by the thunder of gunfire, and for three solid hours they heard going on around them a singularly bloody battle that had been fought on the Dieppe beaches nine years before, during the same hours on 19 August 1942. They heard sounds of dive-bombing and the cries of men. At 5.07am there came waves of particularly loud noise, at exactly the moment when nine years before the landing craft had reached the Puys beach. At 5.40am silence fell, which coincided with the time when the naval bombardment had

stopped. Ten minutes later came more aircraft sounds, which coincided with the appearance of Allied air reinforcements.

With hindsight the Dieppe raid has been seen as an essential rehearsal for the D-Day action two years later, without which D-Day might have gone hopelessly wrong. The raid itself, however, was a catastrophic failure, in which more than 50 per cent of the Canadian and British troops involved were killed or wounded. Did the disaster and the violence and agony of it somehow leave its imprint on the atmosphere of the place where it happened? The two women had read about the battle, but it did not seem credible that they had made the story up, with such accuracy of detail. The Society for Psychical Research came to the conclusion that 'a genuine psychic experience' had occurred.

HARBINGERS OF DEATH

· I·SAW·THE·BANSHEE·FLYING, · · · WILD·IN·THE·WIND·OF·MARCH ·

‡

Most of us can be glad that we do not know exactly when death is going to take us, but there are reports of people warned of their imminent demise by a spectral visitant. It can be an apparition of a human person or an animal, and some families take a certain pride in having their own.

‡

*The Edwardians liked Celtic lore. Left: an art nouveau version of the deathly banshee, from a book illustration of 1910.
Right: the hounds of hell harry the spirit of Tregeagle, the wicked steward of Cornish legend, in this magazine illustration of 1909.*

The Hohenzollern dynasty, rulers successively of Brandenburg, Prussia and united Germany down to the abdication of Kaiser Wilhelm II after World War I, boasted a family ghost. She was a White Lady, seen quite frequently at the royal residences in Berlin and elsewhere in Germany – usually shortly before the death of a member of the family. Dressed in white, she wore a widow's band, and it was suspected that she was the ghost of a 15th-century princess who had been cruelly misused by her Hohenzollern husband.

The Hesse dynasty of Darmstadt in Germany inherited a similar warning apparition, this time a Black Lady in funereal garments and a forbidding black veil, thought to be the Grand Duchess Marianna, wife of the Grand Duke Ferdinand. The Danish royal house is allegedly warned of trouble by the appearance at Gurre, south of Helsingor (the Elsinore of Shakespeare's *Hamlet*), of the spectre of the formidable King Valdemar IV, who ruled Denmark in the 14th century. He died at Gurre in 1375.

Another oddity in Danish royal annals, incidentally, followed the death of Queen Astrid, who was killed in a road accident in 1935. She subsequently appeared at seances held in Copenhagen by the medium Einar Nielsen, or so it was claimed, and many people were convinced they had seen her. A photograph of the supposed 'materialisation' was taken, but unfortunately evidence of this kind is too easily faked to be treated seriously.

The Habsburg dynasty, rulers of the Austro-Hungarian Empire, were traditionally warned of approaching tragedy by a flock of large white birds, wheeling and crying in the sky. Allegedly they were seen before the double suicide of Crown Prince Rudolf and his mistress at Mayerling in 1889. Emperor Franz Josef I is also supposed to have seen them on the day before his wilful and much-loved empress, Elizabeth, was assassinated in Geneva in 1898. Inevitably, the ominous birds were said to have appeared again before the murder of Archduke Franz Ferdinand in Sarajevo in 1914, an event which sparked off World War I.

‡

THE WAILING IN THE NIGHT

‡

Perhaps the most famous of the harbingers of death is the banshee of Ireland, a prized possession of the oldest and best-connected Irish families. She makes a melancholy, wailing cry in the night, lamenting a death in the family shortly before it occurs. She is seen either as a young and beautiful woman in a red petticoat or a green dress beneath a grey cloak, or as an ancient crone. Both are aspects of the great goddesses of pagan, pre-Christian Irish belief, from whom the banshee is probably descended. She is not easily got rid of, either, as there are reports of her wailing outside the former homes of people who have long since emigrated.

An American visiting the Aran Islands in Galway Bay not so many years ago gave a party, with dancing. In the early hours a young guest left, playing his accordion as he walked home. The sound caused alarm and word was sent to an old man who lay dying near by that the awful noise was not his family banshee, but an inexpert musician. Reassured, the old man lived for three weeks more, until the real banshee was heard and he gave up the ghost.

Sir Arthur Conan Doyle's
THE HOUND OF THE BASKERVILLES

WITH Richard GREENE · Basil RATHBONE · Wendy BARRIE

Nigel BRUCE · Lionel ATWILL · John CARRADINE · Barlowe BORLAND
Beryl MERCER · Morton LOWRY · Ralph FORBES

A 20th CENTURY-FOX PICTURE
Darryl F. Zanuck IN CHARGE OF PRODUCTION
DIRECTED BY SIDNEY LANFIELD
ASSOCIATE PRODUCER Gene Markey
SCREEN PLAY BY ERNEST PASCAL

Left: baleful eyes and slavering jaws mark the film-poster hound.
Below: a medieval version of the evil Judas cat at its master's feet.

black dog tried to batter its way into their house while they frantically piled furniture against the door to keep it out. At dawn it went away, leaving behind it no paw-marks in the muddy ground outside.

This happened on a stormy night, significantly perhaps, for in many of the old beliefs a pack of dogs from hell, howling and tearing their way across country, are an embodiment of the storm winds. Their leader is the Wild Huntsman, urging on his phantom pack, and their howling threatens death, madness or misfortune. In Denmark he is the same King Valdemar, in Normandy he is the Devil. In the North of England the pack are the Gabriel Hounds and the huntsman is the Angel of Death. On Dartmoor he is Sir Francis Drake and he drives a hearse. Superstitious beliefs of this kind inspired Sherlock Holmes's Dartmoor adventure in *The Hound of the Baskervilles*.

THE DEMONIC CAT

THE HOUNDS OF HELL

Before the death of every Bishop of Salisbury, tradition has it, mysterious white birds will be seen hovering above Salisbury Plain. Not necessarily omens of death, but harbingers of misfortune are the black dogs, sometimes of gigantic size, believed to prowl about Britain. Peel Castle on the Isle of Man is the lair of one of them, the Moddy Dhu, and to see it is to die. It is equally fatal to see the dog called Shriker in Burnley, Lancashire, which lurks in the parish churchyard, or the other sinister black dogs in Lancashire that prowl the roads leading to graveyards.

Dogs are closely linked with death and the dead in popular belief, perhaps because of a distant memory from man's earliest days of wild dogs devouring corpses. There may also be a connection with the widespread belief that dogs can sense the presence of ghosts and uncanny presences before human beings do.

Phantom dogs are particularly prevalent in East Anglia, where the gigantic Black Shuck is said to have only one eye, which shines in the dark. During World War II an American airman and his wife living at Walberswick in Suffolk had a terrifying experience one night. An enormous

Cats are more sinister even than dogs, because they are nocturnal and so linked with the powers of darkness and the dead – hence the particular evilness of the black cat in popular belief. In Britain and Germany (and the United States) it means bad luck if a black cat crosses your path, and there is an old fear that a cat will sneak into a baby's cradle to kill it by stealing its breath. Cats are linked with the Devil: sacks of live cats were flung on to Guy Fawkes Night bonfires in England; and at Aix-en-Provence in France, on the feast of Corpus Christi every year, a tomcat was wrapped in swaddling clothes and venerated at a special shrine before being burnt.

WITCH COUNTRY

The great witch persecutions in Europe in the 15th, 16th and 17th centuries condemned many thousands of innocent people to agonised deaths. The accusations brought against the suspects and the confessions extorted from them – often under torture – reveal not so much what real witches did, but patterns of ideas and fears lying deep in the European popular mind.

Witches were believed to be worshippers of the Devil, in whose service they had enlisted as part of a gigantic conspiracy to destroy Christianity, undermine all decent values and lure human souls into Satan's kingdom of hell. (The same kind of conspiracy-mongering underlies present-day scares about Satanist child abuse.) They were said to meet for hellish ceremonies at 'sabbaths' or 'synagogues', where they worshipped their Satanic master. He appeared to them sometimes in human form but more often in animal form, especially as a monstrous black goat.

According to the judgement passed on a group of witches sentenced at Avignon in 1582: 'in the common synagogue of witches, sorcerers, heretics, conjurers and devil-worshippers, you did kindle a foul fire and after many rejoicings, dancings, eating and drinking and lewd games in honour of

The double-edged relationship between human beings and the rest of the animal world emerges in stories of witches with the uncanny power of transforming themselves into animals, and of old hags with extremely sinister pets.

your president Beelzebub, the Prince of Devils, in the shape and appearance of a deformed and hideous black goat, you did worship him in deed and word as very God...'

A DOG WITH HORNS

The Devil, the supreme master of disguise, had many other animal shapes. Witches tried at Lyons in the 15th century said he appeared to them as a bull or a cat. Elsewhere he might be a dog, a cow, a horse, a mule, a ram or a sheep, a pig, a fox, a spider or a monkey. Supreme evil lies in ambush behind even the most innocent and trifling appearances, and Satan could be a hare, a bird, a hen, a mouse, a fly. A woman in Guernsey in the 17th century said that when she went to a sabbath, the Devil appeared to her as a dog with horns, standing on his hind legs. He took her hand with his paw and welcomed her. If he was real at all and not a fantasy, he was presumably the human leader of the local coven, dressed up.

In this 19th-century illustration Old Chattox, a Lancashire witch, persuades the grave-digger to give her a nice bit off the corpse. She reckons it will strengthen her spell.

An eerie painting by a 17th-century artist, Cornelis Saftleven, emphasises the intimate connection between the animal world and supernatural evil in the figure of the Satanic goat and the various beasts which attend on him.

One of the powers which the Satanic master conferred on his faithful worshippers was the power to transform themselves into animals. In 1525 a woman from Ituren in the Basque area of Spanish Navarra was tortured into confessing that her group of witches turned themselves into horses and flew through the air. The others accused from the same area all denied it, but the tradition that witches ride on mysterious horses and take the shape of cats, rats and donkeys survived in the Basque areas of the Pyrenees until recent times. They could even turn themselves into herbs or autumn leaves, drifting and rustling in the wind.

WOMAN INTO CAT
✣

The motif goes far back beyond the medieval witch persecutions to ancient, pre-Christian folk beliefs about shamans, magicians and witches able to change shape. So does a tale from the Isle of Skye about a man whose wife was away from home night after night. Suspicious, he secretly followed her and was horrified to see her change herself into a sleek black cat and, with seven other black cats, sail out to sea in a sieve.

Stories were passed down from generation to generation in Europe

about people injuring a cat, a dog or a hare and next day finding the same wound on the body of the local witch. At Strasbourg a man was walking along the street one night when he was fiercely attacked by three huge cats. While fighting them off, he injured them. He was arrested soon afterwards for assaulting three women of the town, but later proved their wounds were those he had inflicted on the cats.

✣

FAMILIAR EVILS
✣

It was also widely believed that witches kept 'familiar spirits' close about them. These were evil spirits in the form of small animals – the household pet gone wrong, as it were. Many a mumbling old crone's harmless

A witch's familiar spirit, from a 16th-century English tract. It figured in the witch trials of 1579.

cat or dog was eyed askance as a demon that she could send to harm people. In 1556, at Hatfield Peverel in Essex, evidence was given that Mother Waterhouse, aged 54, had a white, spotted cat which she fed on bread and milk, and also on her own blood. She called it Satan (which seems incautious) and she could turn it into a toad – as her 18-year-old daughter Joan confirmed.

Joan Flower, one of the Earl of Rutland's servants at Belvoir Castle, was found to have killed the earl's two young sons by sending her black cat, Rutterkin, to them. Arrested, she died on her way to gaol, but her two daughters were duly hanged in 1619.

Silvain Nevillon of Orléans, tried in 1614, said that witches kept toads as familiars and fed them on milk and flour. In general, though, the familiar is a particularly English contribution to the lore of witchcraft, perhaps a twisted reflection of the English fondness for animals.

I Shall Go Into A Hare

Isobel Gowdie of Auldearn in Scotland was a young farmer's wife who, in 1662, to general astonishment, confessed voluntarily and without pressure to being a witch. Among other things, she said that she and her fellow-witches could change themselves into cats or hares and she told how, once when she was in her hare shape, she was chased by dogs and only just escaped. To turn into a hare, she would chant the following rhyme:

> I shall go into a hare,
> With sorrow and sighing and mickel care,
> And I shall go in the Divel's name,
> Aye, till I come home again.

Similar spells would transform her into a cat or a crow. To return to human form yet another spell was needed.

THE WOLF BENEATH THE SKIN

The Wolfman who appears in Hollywood films, sometimes with comical effect, is the entertainment industry's adaptation of an old terror – the human being who changes into a wolf to prey on his own kind. In the year 1603, for instance, in the extreme south-west of France, ripples of fear spread as reports came of young children vanishing without trace. In one case a baby disappeared from its cradle in a cottage. There was talk of wolves, and uneasy whispers of something darker still.

Then a 13-year-old girl from a hamlet near Esperons (since renamed Eugénie-les-Bains) was out minding the cows one day when she was suddenly attacked by a creature like a big dog with reddish fur and sharp teeth. It tore her clothes, but she fended it off with her iron-tipped cattle prod. A boy of 13 or 14 named Jean Grenier was heard boasting that he had attacked her in the form of a wolf and that he had earlier killed and devoured three or four children. He told another, older girl – apparently hoping to gain her favours – that he owned a wolf's pelt and when he put it on he went hunting with other werewolves of his kind. Often they killed dogs and ate them, but he preferred to gnaw the tasty flesh of young boys.

Jean Grenier was arrested and confessed, quite freely it seems, that he was a werewolf and had been given his wolfskin and an ointment to rub on his body by a tall dark man in the woods, the Lord of the Forest, whom he had sworn to serve. He gave full details of the children he had killed and devoured, which agreed with the evidence from the bereaved families. The tall dark man was, inevitably, identified by everyone as the Devil, but Grenier was not sent to the stake. Presumably the court felt that he was insane and could not help himself, and he was shut up in the Franciscan friary at Bordeaux, where he died in 1611. A visitor the year before

Down into the 18th and 19th centuries in substantial areas of Europe people had good reason to fear predatory animals, especially wolves. They also feared the predatory, animal impulses in human nature – the wolf within – and the two fears coalesced in the fantasy figure of the werewolf.

The woman's cross fails to protect her from the monster seemingly intent on devouring her. The sado-masochistic sexuality of the werewolf myth has helped to keep it alive.

described him as lean and gaunt, with deep-set black eyes, long sharp teeth and claw-like hands with long, crooked fingernails. He loved to hear talk of wolves and often went on all fours.

MEAT ON FRIDAY

Another celebrated French werewolf was Gilles Garnier, who came from Lyons and was burned alive at Dole in 1573. His body was burned to ashes, to leave as little trace as possible of him on the earth. A recluse of solitary habit, Garnier wandered in the woods, where allegedly he encountered a ghostly man who taught him how to turn himself into a wolf by smearing an ointment on his body. However this might be, he was convicted of strangling children in the area and feasting on their flesh.

It is significant that in the one case where Garnier was seen attacking a victim and beaten off – the incident which led to his arrest, presumably – he was not in the shape of a wolf, but in ordinary human form. The court reprovingly noted, however, that if not interrupted he would certainly have killed and eaten his victim, even though it was a Friday, when eating meat was forbidden to all good Christians.

THE DEVOURING BEAST

Germany also knew its werewolves. The best-known case is that of Peter Stubb (or Stump), who was executed at Bedburg, near Cologne, in 1590. He was broken on the wheel and his flesh was torn with red-hot pincers before his head was cut off and his body burned to ashes. He was said to have been a werewolf for 25 years before he was caught and to have killed and savagely devoured many men, women and children, as well as numerous farm animals. He was accused of raping some of the women before murdering them, of sexually abusing his sister and his own daughter, on whom he fathered a child, and of killing and eating his own son. He confessed to his crimes after being put to the rack.

The Devil, it was alleged, had given him a magic girdle and when Peter put this belt round him – in the words of the contemporary pamphlet about his atrocities – 'he was straight transformed into the likeness of a greedy devouring Wolf, strong and mighty, with eyes great and large, which in the night sparkled like unto brands of fire, a mouth great and wide, with most sharp and cruel teeth, a huge body and mighty paws: and no sooner should he put off the same girdle, but presently he should appear in his former shape, according to the proportion of a man, as if he had never been changed.' The description of the wolf form closely resembles accounts of the huge phantom dogs of widespread European folk belief.

✣

THE GREY WOLF IN THE NIGHT
✣

Cases of hideous cannibalistic murders are all too well-known in our own time, though they do not involve the killer turning into a wolf or putting on a wolfskin. The 'werewolves' of the past may have been afflicted by what is now a recognised form of insanity in which the patient believes he has become an animal. The magic ointment which is a feature of some of the stories could have contained a hallucinogen that assisted fantasies of being a wild beast.

Fear of the werewolf has lasted down the centuries and the were-beast was not always a man. In 1881 a poor gypsy musician was murdered at a place in Hungary called Toresz. His wife often

sneaked away in the night. Keeping secret watch, he saw her slip out of their hut and then at dawn the door opened and a big grey wolf came in, with a dead lamb in its mouth. Later his wife duly served him a delicious meal of lamb and, as time went by, they ate beef and pork in plenty, with enough left over for the gypsy to sell it in the nearby town. Suspicion mounted, however, as the wolf attacked the flocks and herds, until the villagers seized the gypsy and his wife. The priest sprinkled holy water on them and the wolf-wife shrieked horribly and disappeared. The angry villagers then put the gypsy to death.

Above: a curious picture called Les Lupins *by Maurice Sand shows the werewolves of Normandy, believed to devour corpses in graveyards. Below: sex raises its wolfish head again in* I Was a Teenage Werewolf, *one of many exploitations of the theme by the film industry.*

THE FEAST OF BLOOD

Horror stories about the evil, blood-drinking dead come from many parts of the world, but in Europe the heartland of vampire beliefs is the Balkans and eastern Europe – Hungary, Transylvania, Romania, Greece, Poland and Russia.

In 1732 three army doctors and two other officers signed an official report on a case of suspected vampire activity at the village of Meduegna, near Belgrade in Serbia. A young soldier had returned home after serving at Kostaritsa in Greece in the army. He confided to his sweetheart that while away he had been attacked by a vampire. Soon afterwards he died and was buried in the village graveyard, but then he was seen walking at night and those who had seen him began to feel strangely weak and enervated. Some of them died, too, and panic began to spread through the whole area.

A military party, sent to investigate, went to the churchyard and dug up the young soldier's body. It looked as fresh as if it had died the day before and a thin trickle of blood had run out of its mouth. The officers scattered garlic on it and drove a wooden stake through its heart, at which it let out a piercing, unearthly screech and spouted a jet of bright crimson blood. The shaken party went grimly on to exhume the bodies of four other people, who were believed to have died as a result of the vampire's activities. They drove stakes through them, too, and then burned all five corpses to destroy them as thoroughly as possible.

✛

SATURDAY EXHUMATIONS
✛

It is quite possible that cases of people being buried prematurely, while still alive, and coming round in the grave, may account for some of the stories of coffins being opened to reveal corpses

✛

The human mind is a prolific inventor of monsters in its own image. One of the most sinister and insinuating of them is the vampire – the dead body which emanates from its coffin in the night and prowls the darkness, driven by a desperate need for the blood of the living on which to prolong its hideous existence.

✛

Above: cases of insanity have kept the vampire terror alive, like that of the Hungarian Countess Elizabeth Bathory who was found guilty in 1614 of bathing in the blood of scores of servant girls.

suspiciously fresh and with blood round the mouth or the nails. This was not how they were explained by the Christian authorities, however. They saw the Devil at work, preserving corpses from decay, infusing them with an evil, demonic parody of human life and sending them to attack the living and so recruit more souls into his service.

That the creature's victims become vampires in their turn is one of the most subtly frightening strands in the vampire legend. The stake through the vampire's heart that puts an end to its evil career not only rids the land of it, but gives the poor, tormented thing rest at last.

In 1657 a Jesuit priest named François Richard published an account of his experiences on the Greek island of Santorini (Thíra) in the Aegean. If the local people suspected that a vampire was at work, they would assemble at its grave on a Saturday. That was the one day of the week when they could be sure of finding it there. They would say prayers and dig up the body. If it looked suspiciously fresh and disagreeably plump, the local priest would gather his spiritual resources and formally command the Devil to come out of it. If the exorcism worked, the body would rapidly dwindle and lose its lifelike colour. If it did not, they seized it and burned it to ashes.

The fear of the vampire has never died. As late as 1910, at Sujos in Serbia, the body of an old woman suspected of being one of the undead was disinterred, pierced with a stake and burned. As recently as 1973 in England, in Stoke-on-Trent, the body of a Polish immigrant was discovered. Terrified of vampires, he had choked to death on a clove of garlic, which he had evidently placed in his mouth before settling down to sleep. He had also put bags of salt between his legs and by his head, as an additional precaution against what might come for him in the night.

COUNT DRACULA AT HOME

✣

Like the werewolf, the vampire is no doubt partly based on real cases of murderous insanity, like that of the 'acid bath murderer', John George Haigh, hanged in 1949, who liked to drink a victim's blood. A subtler component of the belief, perhaps, is the observation that in real life some people seem to prey on the nervous energy of others, to drain them of vitality and feed on it in a kind of psychological 'vampirism'. In traditional belief, the vampire draws strength from his victims, not only by sucking their blood but through sex. This aspect of the monster's activities was partly

bowdlerised away in the 19th century, but the erotic element has returned again in 20th-century screen treatments.

The vampire gave the emerging film industry a richly romantic, blood-chilling and sexy theme, which it was delighted to exploit. Perhaps the most chilling vampire film ever made was *Nosferatu*, the silent 'symphony of horror' created by the German director Friedrich Wilhelm Murnau in 1922. Its hideous, gaunt, bald, ageing central character arrives in a town by ship, in a coffin stowed in the hold. As he emanates subtly from the coffin and goes on shore, he is followed by a creeping horde of huge rats, which come to infect the citizens with plague. The situation is saved by a compassionate young girl, who gives herself to the vampire out of pity and so rescues him.

The arrival by sea follows the precedent set in Bram Stoker's *Dracula*, one of the most powerful and successful horror stories ever written. It gave the blameless Yorkshire town of Whitby its creepy renown as the place where Count Dracula arrived by ship. He came from his remote castle in the Carpathians, packed in a coffin filled with his native Transylvanian earth. It was also destined to give many a film company a welcome source of profits. The book came out in 1897 and inspired a succession of vampire chillers which shows no sign of ending.

Above left: the original Dracula? Vampire beliefs lingered for centuries in Romania and Transylvania, and the ancestry of Bram Stoker's Dracula, fiction's most famous vampire, has been traced back to a 15th-century Romanian warlord, Vlad the Impaler, who was renowned for his cruelty. The picture is based on an anonymous contemporary portrait of him. Left: a dramatic still from Dracula Has Risen From The Grave. *The sinister count has been nourished on the vital energies of several generations of film-goers.*

THE TALKING MONGOOSE

The Isle of Man's talking mongoose is one of the weirdest ghostly visitants on record, but it was only one of many strange phenomena investigated by Harry Price, who became the world's most famous investigator of 'things that go bump in the night'.

In 1932 strange noises were reported from the farmhouse of Cashens Gap at Dalby, a little place in the west of the Isle of Man, not far from Peel. No one took much notice until the farmer, Mr James Irving, claimed that he had seen an unexplained shadow in the house and then, looking up through a crack in the ceiling, had spotted little furry feet.

The owner of the feet began talking to him, in English, explaining that its name was Gef and it was a mongoose. The animal, it was proudly announced, could speak several languages, sing hymns and read people's thoughts. Sometimes it rudely threw things at people.

Journalists and psychical researchers hurried to the Isle of Man, the popular press fell on the case with glee and an American showman was reputed to have offered $50,000 to put the talking mongoose on exhibition in the United States. Interest gradually ebbed away, however, and a few years later a new owner of the farmhouse reported having shot a little furry animal in the grounds. If this was a bid to give the whole nonsense its quietus, it succeeded. No one ever heard from Gef again.

EYES IN THE DARK

One of the researchers who went to the Isle of Man was Harry Price, though the mongoose hid as soon as he arrived and did not manifest itself again until he had left. Price was in his fifties at this time. Born in Shrewsbury in 1881, he encountered a poltergeist in a Shropshire village when he was 15 and later worked in his father's paper-making business while developing his interests in amateur conjuring and exposing fake mediums. In Warsaw in 1923, for instance, he exposed a Polish medium named Jean Guzik who used his hands and feet surreptitiously to

William Hope faked the 'spirit' extra in this photograph of Harry Price, in about 1930. Later Price helped to show up Hope as a fraud.

'materialise' frightening animals. These growled and grunted while their eyes shone eerily in the darkness of the seance room. The 'eyes' were actually spots of luminous paint on a woman's stocking with Guzik's hand inside it. Price also helped to puncture the reputation of the 'spirit' photographer, William Hope.

Initially strongly sceptical, Price became convinced that some mediums did have genuine psychic powers, even though they might still cheat if opportunity offered. In 1926 he opened his own laboratory in London for the scientific investigation of psychic phenomena, and he used his gifts for showmanship and publicity to make himself a worldwide reputation as far and away the best-known 'ghost-hunter' of his time.

One of Price's subjects was a famous Austrian medium, Rudi Schneider, who came from Braunau. Handkerchiefs and other small objects moved about in his presence, apparently by themselves. When infra-red rays were set up to sound an alarm if intercepted by the medium's arm or any concealed reaching device, objects moved and the alarm went off although nothing had crossed the rays. There was fierce dispute about Schneider's effects, and they gradually waned before his death in 1957.

THE MOST HAUNTED HOUSE

Price's most celebrated case was his investigation of Borley Rectory, which he made famous as 'the most haunted house in England'. Close to the border of Essex and Suffolk, it was a grim Victorian pile, built for the Reverend Henry Bull in 1863. He was succeeded as rector by his son, Harry Bull, who was there until his death in 1927. By that time, possibly stimulated by the fact that Harry Bull was known to be interested in Spiritualism, stories were being bruited about in the neighbourhood of galloping horses hauling a spectral coach along the road, of headless men and a girl in white, and of a nun who sometimes stalked the rectory and the garden. She was seen on the lawn by the Bull family in broad daylight, and a 'black shape' disquietingly invaded the gardener's cottage in the grounds.

Harry Price duly descended on this promising scene in 1929,

Ghost on the Orient Express

Harry Price travelled widely and once occupied a haunted compartment in the *Orient Express* on its way from Vienna to Ostend. A noise like a gunshot woke him at 2am, but everything seemed quiet. Later he was awakened by what felt like somebody shaking him, but no one was there. At Ostend the attendant admitted that an embezzler had shot himself in that compartment at about 2am on a previous journey, and that other passengers had complained about the disturbance.

Top: Harry Price in judiciously scientific mode in his London laboratory. Above: Borley Rectory, famous as 'the most haunted house in England', photographed in 1929. Inset is part of a message to Marianne Foyster which appeared scrawled on one of the rectory walls, apparently spontaneously.

characteristically accompanied by a *Daily Mirror* journalist, and it was to occupy him for the rest of his life. He unearthed a romantic tale of a 14th-century nun who had been murdered after an illicit love affair with a monk. An elderly clergyman named Foyster presently moved in, with his good-looking young wife, Marianne, who was knocked about, given a black eye and thrown out of bed. Her husband was pelted with stones. Scrawled pencilled messages appeared on the walls, addressed to Marianne and piteously pleading for prayers and sayings of Mass, as if from a soul in torment.

✢

THE BURIED SKULL

✢

Price was in little doubt that Marianne was secretly responsible for much of this, and after the Foysters moved out in 1935 the rectory went comparatively quiet. Price and other researchers spent time in the house, but nothing particularly dramatic happened, until in 1939 the house was gutted in an accidental fire and the stories sprang up again. The locals, including the policeman, claimed to have seen strange figures inside among the flames. Psychical researchers returned to the scene and in 1943 the story of the murdered nun was given support when the skull and jawbone of a woman were found buried in the cellar. In 1944 the remains of the rectory were demolished, but by this time psychic disturbances were being reported from the parish church across the road.

Price died in 1948, of a heart attack, aged 67. His reputation slumped and intemperate attacks were published denouncing his amateurishness as an investigator and suggesting that he had faked some of the Borley phenomena. A review of the Borley material convicted him of being careless, but found no proof of fraud.

TO THE EYE OF FAITH

Visions of supernatural holy beings have profoundly affected the lives, not only of individual visionaries, but of thousands or millions of others. Some have affected the whole course of subsequent history. An example is the occasion in 1204 when a rich young man named Francisco was in the run-down little church of San Damiano in his home town of Assisi in Italy. The figure on the crucifix above the altar spoke to him and told him to 'repair my house, which you see is falling down'. This experience changed the entire direction of St Francis's life and led eventually to the founding of the Franciscan Order, which has played so notable a part in Christian history.

St Dominic, according to a much-loved legend, depressed by his failure to convert the Cathar heretics in the south of France to orthodoxy, was slumped in despair in a cave near Toulouse when the Virgin Mary appeared to him, with a great retinue of maidens. She comforted him and bestowed on him the rosary, which has become so fundamental a part of Christian devotion and symbolism.

Austria's most famous pilgrimage centre is Mariazell, with its much-venerated medieval wooden image of the

✣

Many places in Europe are considered especially holy, and are venerated as sites where Jesus, the Virgin Mary or one of the saints have been seen in visions. The most famous of them attract throngs of pilgrims.

✣

Virgin and Child. A victory over the Turks in 1377 was attributed to the intervention of the Virgin of Mariazell, who became a symbol of the Austro-Hungarian Empire. The empire is long dead, but crowds of pilgrims still attend upon her, while the wonder-working Virgin of St Maria Luggau in the Tyrol is another magnet to the faithful.

✣

THE LADY OF LOURDES

✣

Visions of martyrs were not uncommon in the Middle Ages, and later of the crucified Jesus or the Sacred Heart, while St Lidwine of Schiedam was accustomed to surveying all heaven,

earth and hell, every night for 28 years. In the last 200 years, however, it has been visions of the Virgin Mary which have created the greatest excitement. Much the most famous occurred in France in 1858, at a grotto beside the River Gave at Lourdes. Here Bernadette Soubirous, the pious, asthmatic 14-year-old daughter of an impoverished local family, saw 'a girl' or 'a lady'. She wore a white dress with a blue sash, had forget-me-not blue eyes, and made the sign of the cross before disappearing.

Awed, the girl returned to the same spot and saw the Virgin again and again. Towards the end she was accompanied by thousands of spectators, who saw Bernadette apparently in conversation with someone invisible (only a few claimed to have seen the Queen of Heaven themselves, and they were not taken seriously). Halfway through the series of visions, Bernadette was told to 'drink at the spring and wash in it'. There was no spring, but she found one when she obediently scratched at the floor of the grotto. It has flowed ever since and millions of pilgrims have visited it in hope of healing or spiritual refreshment. Bernadette died in 1879, aged 35, and her body has remained uncorrupted in her coffin.

The Moving Virgins

Not only are religious figures seen in visions, but there are persistent reports of religious statues and images which move, weep or bleed. The most notable recent cases occurred in Ireland. Worshippers flocked eagerly to the church of St Mary at Asdee, County Kerry, in 1985 after word spread that four schoolchildren had seen the statues of the Virgin Mary and Jesus in the church moving and their eyes moving. It was infectious and something like an epidemic followed, with excited claims of moving Virgins coming from more than 40 other places in Ireland. A plaster figure of the Virgin in a roadside shrine at Balinspittle was said to have started moving her hands and swaying to and fro, and thousands who went to look for themselves insisted that they had seen the figure move. The Roman Catholic Church remained cautiously noncommittal and the reports presently died away.

A statue of Our Lady the Mystic Rose at Maasmechelen in Belgium.

IN LIGHT AND ROSES

Earlier, in 1846, in an incident which Bernadette may have known about, a boy and girl of 11 and 14 had seen the Virgin, all glorious in light and roses. It was at the village of La Salette, near Grenoble. In 1888 at Vallensages, near St Etienne, a boy of 13 saw her many times, magnificently apparelled and wearing a golden crown. He once threw holy water at her, to test if she was a demon, and she smiled sweetly at him.

In 1879 at Knock in County Mayo, Ireland, 15 or more people saw the Virgin and a group of saints manifest

Right: Bernadette Soubirous, who saw the Virgin Mary at Lourdes and was afterwards canonised as a saint. Below: a statue of the Virgin Mary, the Queen of Heaven, looks towards the pilgrim church at Lourdes.

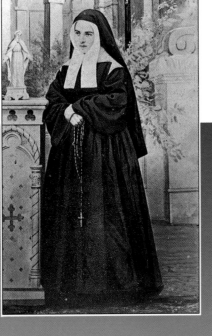

themselves in pelting rain, and miraculous healings were reported. In 1880 four boys aged from nine to 15 saw the Virgin floating in the grounds of Llanthony Abbey in Wales. In 1917, at Fatima in Portugal, three children aged six to nine saw her repeatedly as a beautiful girl, who called herself Our Lady of the Rosary. She told them secrets, which were passed on to the Vatican, and it has been claimed that she predicted the rise of Communism and the outbreak of World War II. People swarmed to the scene, which has become a major pilgrimage centre known as 'the Lourdes of Portugal'.

FAIRY GODMOTHER?

How much reality, and what kind of reality, there is in all this, it is impossible to say. The Christian churches nowadays take a cautious and sceptical attitude, and there is a good story about St Teresa of Avila, who was famous for her dramatic visionary experiences. She appeared long after her death to a Carmelite nun with the message that the great majority of visions are totally untrustworthy.

In the modern cases it is generally children and adolescents who see the vision and mediate it to the grown-ups. Is this because children have a richer fantasy life, tend to be more suggestible than adults and believe even more readily that they have seen what they wanted to see? Poor children, especially, may need a 'fairy godmother' figure.

Or is there a parallel with poltergeist outbreaks? In these, according to some investigators, it is by using the life-energy of a particularly disturbed or unhappy child or adolescent that an entity makes itself apparent in the human world *(see page 26)*.

THE QUEEN OF PEACE

Another case occurred in Spain in the early 1960s, at San Sebastián de Garabandal, where four children saw the Virgin hundreds of times, accompanied by angels, over a period of four years. They fell into trances in which, it was discovered, they could feel no pain.

In 1981, at Medjugorje in what was then Yugoslavia, the Virgin appeared on a hill to six children, whose ages ranged between 11 and 16. They called her 'the Lady' and she told them she was the Queen of Peace. The children saw her many times in subsequent years, and they too went into states of trance in which they were impervious to pain. There were reports of a shining orb seen spinning in the sky. Despite the incredulity and disapproval of the Communist authorities, Medjugorje became a place of pilgrimage and miraculous cures have been claimed.

There was more excitement in Ireland again in 1993, when both the Virgin Mary and Jesus were claimed to have appeared at Inchigeelagh, County Cork.

THE RESTLESS ONES

Poltergeists, for all we know, may have been vexing and troubling human beings for as long as there have been human beings to be vexed. One of the first poltergeist cases of which any record has survived happened at a farm near Bingen, on the Rhine in what is now Germany. Stones were thrown by no visible hand, the walls shook, mysterious fires broke out and a loud voice accused the farmer of sleeping with the daughter of one of his men. Like Mary and the little lamb, everywhere the farmer went, the tiresome poltergeist was sure to follow. Eventually, all his neighbours cold-shouldered him and would not allow him near their houses. The chronicle which records these upsetting events dates them to the 9th century.

Whereas ghosts generally haunt houses or other fixed locations, poltergeists often haunt individual people, like the Bingen farmer. In 1925 in Copenhagen, Harry Price, the famous English ghost-hunter (see page 22), met a man named Iltyd Nicholl. Nicholl complained that for years he had been subjected to repeated aerial bombardment by objects which suddenly materialised out of nowhere and struck him. At that moment, as they were walking side by side, Nicholl was hit on the foot by a careering safety-pin. Price picked it up and it felt warm. Nicholl told Price that once, in a bus, he suddenly found himself clutching a large, hot coffee urn in his arms, while in another bus a gaudy hat-box had appeared as if by magic in his lap, complete with a smart Paris hat inside. He showed Price both the urn and the hat-box.

✢

Poltergeists, or 'noisy spirits', are boisterous. They crash and thump about, make loud noises, and sometimes produce voices, which often tell lies. They also throw things about and they lift and move items of furniture or other objects too heavy for a living person in any normal state to shift. They have been known on the continent of Europe for centuries.

✢

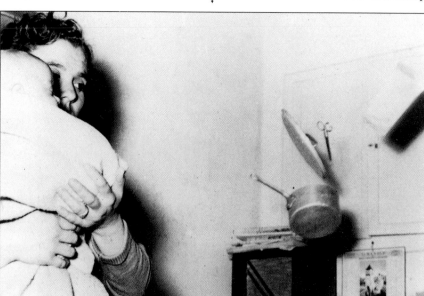

This remarkable photograph was taken in 1955 at a farmhouse at St Jean de Maurienne near the French-Italian border. A saucepan, its lid, a pair of scissors and a telegraph form shot into the air when the only other people in the room, the mother and baby and a man from the village, were too far from the objects to touch them. The photograph was taken by newspapermen while they were investigating poltergeist phenomena in the house and they insisted that the picture was not faked.

✢

THE DEVIL GIRL

✢

In 1926 Price went to Vienna to hunt bigger game – Eleonore Zugun, a 13-year-old Romanian peasant child from Talpa known as 'the Devil Girl' because weird phenomena had started to centre round her when she was about ten. Weals and marks of bites and scratches appeared on her face, hands and body, which she said were inflicted on her by an invisible evil spirit. Her terrified family had sent her to a monastery, from which she had been removed to a flat in Vienna.

At the flat the phenomena continued, accompanied by mysterious rapping noises and unexplained movements of objects. In Price's presence a steel paper-knife, about 10in (25cm) long, shot across the room and hit the door. No one had been nearer than 10ft (3m) to it. Two minutes later Eleonore cried out and Price saw the marks of teeth on her forearm. Then a small mirror sailed through the air, there were more teeth marks, scratches appeared on Eleonore's chest and a large black cloth dog arrived from nowhere.

Price, impressed, arranged for Eleonore to go to London to be tested in his laboratory. He took care to stir up the maximum press interest in 'the girl with a spirit of mischief', and in London there were more inexplicable events. The weals and scratches appeared in the presence of observers. A small metal letter L, from a stock of letters used for the notice board and kept in a locked cupboard on the ground floor, four floors below the laboratory, suddenly appeared in the laboratory itself. A letter C disappeared from the locked cupboard and was found, 11 days later, by one of the observers, Dr Tillyard, an eminent entomologist. It was threaded tightly on the metal rim of his pocket-knife case. Tillyard had used the knife three times earlier that day and the letter had not then been there.

Price was unable to explain incidents like this away and was convinced that the phenomena were genuine. But the Devil Girl lost or abandoned her psychic gifts and returned to Romania, where she tamely became a hairdresser.

✤

LASTING IRRITATION
✤

A curious case occurred in Paris in 1860, in a house in the Rue de Noyers, where a fierce poltergeist broke windows and smashed so many objects that the occupants moved out in alarm. An investigator took a medium to the house, whose spirit guide apparently succeeded in making contact with the poltergeist. In this way the poltergeist was able to explain itself as the ghost of a junk-man who had died 60 years or so before and was still furious that people had mocked him when alive for his heavy drinking. Through the medium he was asked if anyone in the house had helped him to play his tricks and he said yes, he had worked through a maid. Confidence can hardly be placed in information obtained in this way but, so far as it goes, it supports the opinion of

some recent investigators that a poltergeist is an entity of some kind which uses the energy of one of the living people on the scene.

✤

THE BODY ELECTRIC
✤

A young woman named Anne-Marie was thought to be at the storm-centre of remarkable goings-on in a law office in Rosenheim, in Bavaria, in 1967, where light bulbs shattered and the four telephones kept ringing for no reason. The technicians called in discovered numerous phone calls which were not dialled but which registered on their

meters. Among them was a torrent of calls to the speaking clock, which on one particular afternoon, for instance, was called 46 times in 15 minutes. Electricians inspecting the lighting system found weird mayhem going on there as well, including sudden colossal surges of current which yet did not blow out a single fuse. Later the overhead lamps began to swing by themselves, so hard that they crashed into the ceiling and broke the plaster, and paintings on the walls began twirling round and round. The phenomena only occurred during office hours.

The case was investigated by Professor Hans Bender, a well-known psychical researcher, who concluded that the phenomena were all associated with the 19-year-old Anne Marie who, it was discovered, was stressed and hated working for the law firm. The situation grew worse, with office furniture lumbering about, desk drawers opening spontaneously, the girls suffering electric shocks, and Anne-Marie's typing chair rising and sinking under her of its own volition. After she was fired, the outbreaks came to an end.

The implications for the innate powers of the human mind are remarkable. Poor Anne-Marie had trouble at subsequent jobs, and the ominous word 'witch' began to follow her around. She lost her boyfriend, too, when they went bowling together and the electric scoreboard went crazy. However, she later moved away and married, and things settled down.

Above left: normally peaceable domestic objects seem to take on a devilish life of their own in poltergeist attacks, which have plagued people for many centuries past. This dramatic illustration of household equipment flying through the air of its own accord is based on a case that occurred at Guillonville in France in 1849.
Left: Professor Hans Bender, who is seen here at the left, investigated the extraordinary Rosenheim case in 1967. Here, at Mulhouse in France, he is recording a group trying to get in touch with the 'spirit', or the subconscious mind, of the human focus of the poltergeist activity by means of an upturned glass in a circle of letters.

THE GLASTONBURY MYSTERIES

By the early 19th century the once magnificent abbey of Glastonbury in Somerset had fallen into a pitiful state. After it had been closed down in 1539, and the aged abbot dragged ignominiously on a hurdle up to the top of Glastonbury Tor and hanged, the majestic buildings were left to moulder away. They were also ruthlessly pillaged by the locals for building stone. Fortunately, 19th-century owners of the property were more responsible and in 1908 the ruins passed to the Church of England, which appointed a Bristol architect named Frederick Bligh Bond to conduct a thorough archaeological examination of the site.

Bond's excavations over more than ten years were much assisted by a number of long-departed Glastonbury brethren, who were able to communicate with him and tell him exactly where to dig. They were led by a monk called Johannes Bryant, who had died in 1533. 'A simple child of nature', according to Bond, he used to love to go fishing and strolling in the woods (and interestingly, he bears a close resemblance to a real Glastonbury monk of the same period,

The first major archaeological dig at Glastonbury Abbey, early in this century, was guided by the spirits of long-dead monks – or so the archaeologist in charge maintained.

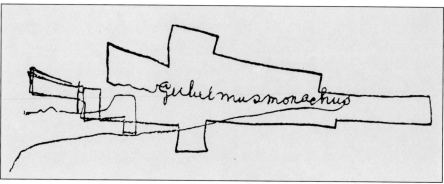

Above: a communication from a long-dead Glastonbury monk, obtained at a seance by Frederick Bligh Bond. Below: Glastonbury Tor with its terraces, perhaps once a maze.

named John Neot). Although Bond's researches were fruitful, his belief in his spiritual mentors was so embarrassing that he was dismissed in 1922.

THE HOLY GRAIL

If there is any spot on English soil which is especially close to the supernatural, it must be Glastonbury. It was almost certainly a Celtic holy place long before the coming of Christianity, and it was here, according to tradition, that St Joseph of Arimathea and 11 companions came from Palestine to found a Christian community among the marshes and build the hallowed 'old church' of Glastonbury. Dedicated to the Virgin Mary, it was the first church ever constructed in the British Isles. Still growing today in the abbey grounds is a descendant of the famous Holy Thorn of Glastonbury, the tree which miraculously sprouted from St Joseph's staff when he thrust it into the ground, and which displays its sacredness by flowering at Christmas time. There is another outside the parish church but the most famous of all, the one on Wearyall Hill, has fallen victim to time and weather.

With him,

ARTHUR IN AVALON

The abbey certainly did claim to possess the bodies of the redoubtable King Arthur and his beautiful queen, Guinevere. Buried in the monks' cemetery, they were discovered in 1191. The remains were moved to a splendid tomb in front of the high altar (and a sign marks the place today). The association with Arthur has given Glastonbury a special magic ever since, and is linked with the place's identification as the Isle of Avalon, the Celtic paradise of apple trees in the West. In popular belief, recorded in the 12th century, the ruler of the otherworld and king of the uncanny fairy folk had a palace on top of Glastonbury Tor – a palace normally invisible to ordinary mortals. And it was to Avalon, as the legends developed, that Arthur was said to have been taken, mortally wounded, after his last battle.

Rising steeply to 500ft (152m) from low-lying ground, the Tor is powerfully evocative. For centuries it stood on a small island among almost impenetrable marshes, and long before the Romans came to Britain a village stood on an artificial platform in the swamp near by. The sides of the Tor are marked by terraces, spiralling round it. These may well be the remains of a ceremonial path, along which religious processions in pre-Christian times made their way to the summit. In effect it was a three-dimensional maze, which had to be negotiated to reach the sacred and awesome place at the centre, the summit. It is perhaps significant that the tower on the top today is left over from a medieval chapel dedicated to St Michael, the vanquisher of demons.

Zodiac on the Ground

The theory that Glastonbury Tor stands at the heart of a colossal zodiac in the surrounding territory was put forward by Mrs K E Maltwood in 1929. Looking down from the air, she maintained, giant astrological symbols of the signs of the zodiac could be seen in the landscape, and could be shown on a map by drawing lines to connect rivers, contours, roads and other natural or ancient man-made features. She believed that in prehistoric times Glastonbury was both a centre of scientific enquiry and a 'temple of the stars', where an advanced knowledge of astronomy was marked out on the ground. She also connected the zodiac signs with the principal characters of the Grail legends. There is no reason to take the theory seriously, but it has added to Glastonbury's powerful aura of mystery and ancient wisdom.

according to the Glastonbury monks, St Joseph brought two small phials containing some of the blood and the sweat of the crucified Christ. In time, however, the story grew up that what he really brought to Britain was something far more awesome – the Holy Grail itself, the communion cup of the Last Supper, the container of the wine which was the Saviour's redeeming blood. The authorities at the abbey never claimed to have the Grail among their formidable collection of relics, which included a thorn from the crown of thorns and some of the earth in which the cross had stood. A popular legend has grown up, however, that the Grail is buried at the foot of the Tor in Chalice Well, whose waters have the reddish tinge of blood.

THE ISLE IS FULL OF NOISES

It was on a summer evening in 1977 that a woman in an ordinary semi-detached house in the North London suburb of Enfield heard a shuffling noise, like someone walking in loose slippers. This was followed by four loud knocks, after which a heavy chest of drawers began to move away from the wall by itself. It was the beginning of an extraordinary and frightening experience for her and her three children which attracted considerable media attention as the case of the Enfield Poltergeist.

As days went by other objects in the house, including substantial pieces of furniture, began to move about by themselves. One of the children was hit by a hairbrush that flung itself through the air and a policewoman who was called in saw a chair rise in the air, move to one side and then return to its place. A curtain wrapped itself lovingly round the neck of one of the girls and tightened, and her mother had a struggle to pull it away. There were unexplained knocking and drumming sounds, drawers opened and shut of their own volition, messages wrote themselves on walls. Two of the children started talking without moving their lips, like ventriloquists, in rough masculine voices, using obscene language and spouting much gibberish. The disturbances stopped in 1979 after more than a year and a half, as suddenly and inexplicably as they had begun.

✣

INTRUDER IN THE HOUSE

✣

People were naturally quick to assume that the whole thing was a put-up job by one or more of the family, perhaps the two girls, but outsiders who had a close view of the events, including police

✣

Many ghost stories can be enjoyed, but dismissed as just that – stories. When crockery and other household objects start to fly through the air by themselves, however, people living in the middle of the disturbances are not in much doubt that something uncanny is happening.

✣

Above: this kitchen was wrecked by a poltergeist in 1985. The 'attack' happened while messages from a man who lived in the 16th century were coming through the computer.

officers and journalists, found it impossible to write them all off as trickery. A widely accepted line of explanation of poltergeist cases (poltergeist comes from the German for 'noisy spirit') is that the disturbances centre around an unhappy and disturbed person under stress – often an adolescent – who makes furniture fly about and other remarkable things happen, by sheer, pent-up mental and emotional force. If true, this means that the human mind can directly influence and alter the behaviour of matter.

The two psychical researchers principally involved in investigating the Enfield Poltergeist, however – Guy Lyon Playfair and Maurice Grosse, who at one point was hit on the head by a cardboard box full of cushions which flew at him from a spot on the floor 8ft (2.4m) away – did not find an explanation in these terms adequate. They were both driven to the more old-fashioned conclusion that some kind of disembodied entity, or 'spirit' (whatever exactly that might mean), was involved. Maurice Grosse has suggested that a poltergeist may be an entity which fastens on a person in the house, through whom it can act on matter.

Although the Enfield business attracted the full glare of media attention, cases of this kind are not particularly rare. In 1981, for instance, a young couple moved out of a house in Sheerness in Kent because they could no longer stand coins flying about the rooms, doors slamming mysteriously, lights unexpectedly turning on and off, sounds of footsteps and gasping noises. A priest exorcised the house, but this proved to have no effect.

Other people's houses can turn out to have more inside them than meets the eye. A family who rented a detached,

Above: the Enfield Poltergeist case attracted lively interest from the tabloid press in 1977 and journalists were often on hand to photograph events. After a while it was thought that all the bizarre goings-on that occurred in the Hodgson household were the work of the mother – Peggy – and her three children John, Margaret and Janet. However, in the end investigators and observers close to the case found it impossible to explain all that happened as trickery. Right: a satirical print of people frightened by the Drummer of Tedworth – dead, of course – who allegedly roamed Salisbury Plain beating his drum noisily the while.

modern house overlooking Brixham harbour in Devon, in 1962, were kept awake at night by sounds of hammering when no hammering was going on and by the noise of armies of mice and birds where none were to be found. In addition, there was something indefinably nasty about the kitchen and neither the husband nor the wife liked being left alone there.

✥

ONWARD, CHRISTIAN SOLDIERS
✥

Colin Wilson, the well-known writer, investigated the curious occurrences in a house in the Yorkshire town of Pontefract. It started in 1966, when it became chillingly cold, pools of water kept forming, a wardrobe went for a walk and a wedding photograph was

smashed and ripped. Later the disturbances became wilder and wilder. A jug of milk removed itself from the refrigerator and poured itself over the head of a previously sceptical witness, pots and pans sailed about and a pair of fur gloves began beckoning in mid-air in front of one of the family. When she rather desperately began singing 'Onward, Christian Soldiers', the gloves helpfully started conducting her.

There was talk of the figure of a 'black monk' being seen. Colin Wilson did not believe in the black monk, but came to the conclusion that some kind of entity was 'latent in the house...waiting for someone to provide the energy it needs to manifest itself'. The energy, he thought, might have come from two puberty-age children in the house.

✥

PLAYING CHILDISH GAMES
✥

Adolescents or children are often involved in poltergeist cases, but not invariably. There were none, for example, involved in the peculiar things going on in the late 1980s in a suburb of Cardiff, in Wales, in a small light-engineering workshop. Small stones, bolts and coins flew through the air and hit people, though not hard enough to hurt them. The missiles were never seen actually being thrown, but only in mid-flight or when they landed.

A special oddity of this case was that when one of the men in the workshop irritably threw a stone into a corner, a stone was promptly thrown back at him. Intrigued, they all started throwing more stones and 'Pete', as they called the poltergeist, retaliated. Sometimes 'he' threw back stones they had specially marked, sometimes other stones. These stones, too, were not seen until they actually landed.

The experiences culminated in the sad sighting of a ghostly figure which seemed to be a schoolboy of about 12, in short trousers and a cap. A rubber ball and a teddy bear, which had been kept in the workshop, disappeared and when odd, repetitive sounds were heard coming from the space above the suspended ceiling in the workshop, two of the men climbed up to have a look. They found the ball and the teddy up there, and it struck them then that the sounds they had heard had been those of someone bouncing a ball.

ANCIENT SORCERIES

Writing in the 2nd century and drawing on his own experience, the Greek writer Pausanias wrote a vivid description of the frightening procedure of consulting the oracle of Trophonius at Lebadeia (modern Levádhia). Trophonius was one of the 'heroes', the powerful dead, and the purpose of consulting the oracle was to find out about the future. After offering preliminary sacrifices, washing in a stream by night and other preparatory rituals, the enquirer went to the oracle, which was on a hillside, sheltered by a grove of trees. There on the ground was a circular floor of white marble and apparently the enquirer went in through a maze, which may have been put there to prevent whatever it was that lived beneath from making its way out into the world of the living.

Climbing down a ladder inside, nervously clutching his propitiatory offering of honey-cakes, the enquirer came to a cleft going further down into the ground. He had to lie on his back, put his feet into the hole and push his knees down hard into it. At this he would be pulled down rapidly into the hole, as if drawn down by a river. Down below, what he wanted to know would be revealed to him – visually or audibly. He

⁘

Some places in Europe have a powerful aura of sanctity and holiness, but there are others whose atmosphere is quite different and whose links are with evil, black magic, the gods of pre-Christian religions and the world of the dead.

⁘

would come back up through the same hole, feet first and paralysed with fear, and the priests would take him to a nearby building to rest and recover. It was commonly believed that anyone who had been through this experience never laughed again.

⁘

THE THRESHOLDS OF THE DEAD

⁘

To go down into that dark cleft on a sunny Greek hillside was to cross the threshold of the land of the dead – the grim, shadowy, terrifying underworld of classical Greek and Roman belief. There were several other entrances, including one on the River Styx in Arcadia, which was believed to flow into the underworld, and another on Cape Tainaron in the south of the Peloponnese.

In Ancient Rome there was a pit at the centre of the city, which was believed to be an entrance to the underworld of the dead. It was blocked by a stone, which on three solemn days each year was raised to allow the spirits of the ancestors access to the city.

In the south of Italy, the sulphurous crater of Lake Averno was believed to be another gateway to the lower world. The medieval Irish equivalent was St Patrick's Purgatory in Lough Derg *(see page 38).*

⁘

DRUID SANCTUARIES

⁘

The Romans were generally tolerant of other people's religions, but when they conquered France and Britain they encountered the Druids, the priests and

Above right: detail from Brueghel's nightmare vision of the classical underworld combined with the Christian hell, with its grotesque demons and tormented sinners. Right: a shaft leads down to a subterranean sanctuary at Ephyra on the River Acheron, where underworld powers were venerated.

sages of the native Celtic tribes. The name Druid is connected with a word meaning 'oak tree' and they carried out their rituals in sacred groves of trees and in forest clearings. The Romans disapproved of the Druid appetite for human sacrifice and did their best to wipe them out. The island of Anglesey, off the north coast of Wales, was an important Druid centre. When the Roman soldiers attacked it across the Menai Strait in AD61 they were alarmed by the threatening spectacle of Druids raising their hands to the sky and screaming curses, while women in black robes with dishevelled hair brandished torches. The soldiers were awed at first, but recovered their nerve and made short work of their opponents.

The prestige of the Druids, their reputation for wisdom and magical power, has accompanied them down history, and places connected with them in popular tradition command a certain awe. The magnificent medieval cathedral of Chartres, famed for its sculpture and its stained glass, stands on the site of a major Celtic sanctuary. Down to the 18th century (until it was destroyed during the French Revolution) an ancient figure of the Virgin Mary, pregnant with the child Jesus, was held in profound veneration there. Said to date from pre-Christian times, it may have originally been an image of a great Celtic mother goddess. Popular belief has also linked the Druids with many of the uncanny prehistoric stone circles and standing stones of western Europe, such as Stonehenge or the Castlerigg stone circle in Cumbria.

✤

THE HIGH PLACES

✤

At some impressive places legends have grown up which blend the forces of supernatural good and evil. One of them is Mont-St-Michel in Normandy, which

Top: the fortified island of Mont-St-Michel, off the coast of Normandy, where the archangel is said to have appeared in the 8th century, is today crowned by its great church.
Above: the Archangel Michael vanquishes the Devil among 'high places' in Raphael's painting, now in the Louvre, in Paris.

owes its name to the great Archangel Michael, commander of the heavenly host. His statue, with its flashing sword, tops the abbey's highest spire. According to hallowed tradition, he appeared to St Aubert and instructed him to build a church here. When Aubert was slow to obey, the archangel stamped his foot on the ground with such force that he opened up the great cleft in the rock that is still to be admired. Another story, however, has it that the cleft is the legacy of a fearsome combat fought between St Michael and the Devil on this spot. This version may reflect the fact that Christianity here replaced the earlier worship of Mithras, the Persian god of light, who was a favourite deity with Roman soldiers. Today, curiously enough, the fierce archangel is the unlikely patron saint of grocers. This is because of his scales, in which it was believed he would weigh the souls of the dead on the Last Day.

The archangel is frequently associated with the vanquishing of the powers of evil in high places, as at his famous shrine on Monte Gargano in Italy, where he was also said to have appeared, and where he also replaced Mithras. It was to Gargano that a party was sent to bring relics of the saint for the church on Mont-St-Michel. 'High places' had an ill ring for Christians because of the denunciations in the Old Testament of the worship of fertility deities in mountain shrines. Widespread medieval belief identified hilltops as places where evil witches gathered in multitudes to worship their master, the Devil.

In Germany, on Walpurgisnacht, or May Eve, they swarmed to the peak of the Brocken in the Harz Mountains. The mountain's ill fame was heightened by the phenomenon known as the Spectre of the Brocken, a towering figure which struck fear into the hearts of those who saw it, until in 1818 it was discovered to be merely a trick of the light.

SHADOWS OF WAR

In the year 1685 at Sedgemoor in the flat country of the Somerset marshes the rebel Duke of Monmouth's army, largely composed of untrained rustics inadequately armed with clubs and pitchforks, was routed with fierce slaughter by King James II's regular troops. The battlefield has been unquiet ever since, with reports of flickering lights seen in the night and the sound of long-dead voices. Soldiers and horsemen loom up suddenly out of a mist and melt into it again. A wailing woman in white mourns her dead lover. The Duke himself has been seen riding in panic from the field. In the 1930s a London pressman, driving across the moor in swirling fog, nearly hit a man on a horse. He called out a greeting to which there came no reply, and just as he realised that the horse's hooves were making no sound on the road, the animal bounded over a bridge and disappeared. When the swirl of fog cleared, there was no sign of horse, rider or bridge.

✦

IN BATTLE ARRAY

✦

The battle of Edgehill in 1642 was the first major engagement of the Civil War in England. Two months or so afterwards, on Christmas Eve, a group of local shepherds said they had suddenly found themselves surrounded by the two armies fighting the battle again, cannons thundering, drums beating and banners fluttering. King

Does the tension and agony of war create ghosts? Battlefields are restless with uneasy spectres, phantom armies fight their battles over again and many strange tales are told of wartime experiences.

This World War I group photograph seems to include a mechanic who had, in fact, been killed by an aircraft propellor two days before the picture was taken. He can be seen peeping round behind the fourth man from the left in the back row (see inset enlargement).

Charles I sent officers to report, who returned to say that they themselves had witnessed the same phenomenon and had recognised among the ghostly combatants Sir Edmund Verney, the royal standard-bearer, who was one of the casualties of the real battle.

At Culloden in Scotland, where the

last hopes of the Stuarts went down to bloody ruin in 1746, there are reports of the armies fighting the bitter struggle again in the sky. At Ujazd in Silesia (now in Poland) in 1785, at the funeral of a local hero, General von Cosel, hundreds of spectators saw soldiers in uniform parading among the clouds. They were assumed to be the casualties of the general's battles who had come to do him honour. In 1888 at Varazdin in Croatia a number of witnesses insisted that they had seen infantry marching in the sky, led by an officer with a flaming sword. The phenomenon lasted for several hours and occurred, apparently, on three successive days.

The Dieppe Raid case of 1951 is a dramatic recent example *(see page 13)*. In the same year, on the anniversary of Waterloo, a man in Belgium claimed to have heard the din of the battle, the roar of cannon, the screams of horses, the clash of steel, shouts and commands – though he said he saw nothing.

In 1956 an astonished workman saw a detachment of Roman legionaries, led by an officer on horseback, march through a cellar beneath the Treasurer's House in York, close to the Minster and the site of the Roman military headquarters 15 centuries before. There were persistent reports of a phantom army at Otterburn in Northumberland, site of a 14th-century battle famous in the ballads of the Border country. In 1960 a woman in a taxi saw it and at the same time the engine died and the meter went crazy. 'The soldiers seemed to close in on us', she said, 'and then fade into thin air.'

Ten years before this, a woman with her dog was walking to her home in the village of Letham in Scotland, at about 2am, when she saw lights flickering ahead. As she went on, she saw figures carrying flaming torches. The one nearest to her was moving among bodies on the ground, which were apparently dead. It would turn a body over, look at its face and then go on to the next one. The woman's dog began to growl, but she reached the village and thought no more of it until the following morning, when it struck home to her how strange the experience had been. It seems that no real people were moving about with torches that night, but she had walked past the site of a battle that had been fought in about 685.

✢

FROM A KILL TO A VIEW

✢

Wartime brings numerous accounts of 'crisis apparitions' – people seen by their loved ones or friends at a distance away, at or soon after the time of their death. Wilfred Owen, the World War I poet, killed in Flanders in 1918, was seen at about the moment of his death by his younger brother, Harold, who was hundreds of miles away in a ship. Smiling, he looked entirely lifelike. In another example, an airman named McConnel left his base at Scampton in Lincolnshire on a routine flight in the morning and that afternoon was seen on the base by a close friend. He was wearing his flying gear, spoke quite normally and said, 'Well, cheerio' before going out of the room and shutting the door behind him. It was only some time later that the friend discovered that McConnel had crashed in fog and been killed at about the time he had been speaking to him.

One of the most remarkable wartime cases centres on a group photograph of the members of a Royal Air Force squadron in World War I. Peeping over the shoulder of one of the men in the back row there appears to be the face of a mechanic who had been killed in an accident on the airfield two days before the photograph was taken. It has been suggested that his 'face' is merely a blemish on the film, but it looks extremely lifelike. Did he dutifully turn up for the photograph because he did not realise he was dead?

Left: phantom cavalry seen in the clouds over Lyons in 1557, from a contemporary account.
Below: the spectral bowmen come to the aid of British troops at Mons, in a drawing published in the Illustrated London News.

The Angels of Mons

Early in World War I, in September 1914, a story called 'The Bowmen' was published in a London newspaper. It described how a British soldier, desperately hard-pressed at the Battle of Mons the month before, had spoken a prayer for help and had been astounded to see a group of phantom bowmen, figures from Agincourt, appear and send flights of shining arrows against the advancing German troops. The Germans fell in hundreds and the British soldier and his comrades found that the bodies of the stricken enemy showed no sign of wounds. The author of this tale, Arthur Machen, had a strong interest in the occult, but always insisted that the story was pure fiction.

So inspiring was it, however, that reports began to come from the front in France of British soldiers who maintained they had seen phantom warriors during the fighting, though they were not bowmen but angels. One officer described how his men had been guarded by spectral horsemen, while others said that angels had put an advancing force of German cavalry to flight. After the war it was discovered, somewhat disconcertingly, that French and German soldiers also claimed to have seen unearthly warriors at Mons, fighting for them.

THE SCREAMING SKULL

In the 17th century one of the Pinney family of Bettiscombe emigrated to the island of Nevis in the West Indies. He made money there and his grandson, John Frederick Pinney, returned home in the 1740s. With him he brought a faithful black slave, and when the slave lay dying promised him that his body would be sent back to Nevis (or, according to another version, to Africa). The promise was broken, however, and the slave was buried in the village churchyard.

Soon the most hideous screams began to sound from the graveyard, terrifying everyone who heard them, until the slave's remains were dug up and the skull was taken back to the house and tucked away in a special niche under the roof. Peace was restored, but every time an attempt was made to take the skull away from the manor house, the frightful screams burst out once more and the attempt was abandoned. One of the family once threw it into a pond, but a formidable clap of thunder followed by the most frightful screams saw it hastily fished out and restored to its accustomed place. Another time it was buried in the garden, but it dug its way back to the surface with its teeth in three days.

✣

A PLACE FOR EVERYTHING...

✣

There's another strong-willed skull in the Somerset village of Chilton Cantelo, where a man named Theophilus Broome left a will requiring his head to be separated from the rest of his carcass and kept in his home at Higher Farm. When he died in 1670, his wish was duly honoured, but when later tenants of the house tried to get rid of it, they were deterred by 'horrid noises, portentive of sad displeasure' (according to an account of 1797). When the sexton went to dig a grave for the skull, his spade suddenly

✣

The peace of the Dorset countryside at Bettiscombe is sometimes rent by the atrocious screams of the skull walled up in the manor house, or so hallowed tradition has it. There are other disquieting skulls about, and pleasant inns are stalked by ghosts.

✣

broke in two, and he desisted. The skull is still in the house. At one time some workmen used it to drink beer out of, which it seemed not to mind.

In 1930 a skull of formidable powers was stolen from Wardley Hall in Lancashire, but it apparently made the lives of the thieves such a nightmare that they repentantly sneaked it back. The skull was restored to its place at the head of the staircase, where it had long reposed, because any attempt to remove it and give it a decent burial had provoked the most terrifying thunderstorm, hovering immediately above the house. According to legend it is the head of Father Ambrose Barlow, a Roman Catholic priest of the district. He was caught and executed in the 1640s and his severed head was stuck on a spike until rescued and smuggled in to Wardley Hall.

Belief in the magic power of the head goes back to Celtic head-hunting and underlies the legend of Bettiscombe's screaming skull.

Last Post

The Grenadier is a pleasant pub in Old Barracks Yard in London's Knightsbridge area. It was formerly called the Guardsman and the Guards officers from the nearby barracks used to play cards there for high stakes. A young officer was caught cheating, it is said. He was severely beaten and then either fell or was pushed down into the cellar, where he died of his injuries. The episode was hushed up, but there have since been many sightings of a mysterious figure or an inexplicable shadow. An unpleasant 'atmosphere' makes itself felt in September, the month when the young officer died. Lights in the pub turn on and off by themselves, so do taps; there are uncanny knockings and objects are moved when no one has touched them. And dogs display a distinct reluctance to go into the cellar.

‡

A FIDDLE IN THE BAR

‡

Many inns add a ghost to their more conventional attractions, like the George and Dragon at West Wycombe, where a past landlord cannot bring himself to leave and can still be heard occasionally, playing his fiddle. The famous Jamaica Inn on Bodmin Moor is amply equipped with spectres and the Red Lion at Wirksworth plays host to a headless coachman, while guests in bed at the Lord Crewe Arms in Blanchland complain of a strange, unexplained weight on their feet. Ghosts haunt the Skirrid Inn at Llanfihangel Crucorney, claimed to be the oldest pub in Wales: many men were hanged there and a beam inside still bears the marks of the rope.

At the Bull, an old coaching inn in

Top: St Ambrose Barlow, the martyred priest of Wardley Hall.
Above: Father Barlow's skull is kept in a glass reliquary in the house.

Wargrave, a woman who died in childbirth in the house is heard piteously calling for her child, cold chills occur, a man in a long black coat and hat drifts silently through the bar and a woman occasionally goes through one of the bedroom doors without opening it. The customers seem stoically unperturbed by these manifestations.

Remaining unperturbed is not always easy. A man who ran a restaurant in the former White Lion on Ashbourne Road in Derby was knocked about and bruised several times by a spectral assailant, who shoved him against the walls of the former brewhouse. There was 'a definite thickness in the air', he said, and his dog would howl horribly. So there may be more to a drink or a meal out than meets the eye.

CELTIC TWILIGHT

Long-cherished folk beliefs have survived in better shape in Ireland than anywhere else in the British Isles, especially in the Gaeltacht – the Erse-speaking areas of the west and north-west, in Connemara and Donegal. W B Yeats and other Irish writers drew creative inspiration from these rich traditions, among them the tradition of the fairy folk. They live in the hills and in the barrows and mounds which are the tombs of Ireland's prehistoric dead, like those in the Valley of the Boyne, where Knowth and Newgrange raise their massive bulk. Tieveragh Hill among the beautiful glens of Antrim is one of the fairies' strongholds, and misty Slieve Gullion in the Mountains of Mourne is another, while deep in the waters of Lough Neagh are the glimmering walls and columns of fairy palaces.

Any concept of fairies as the little, gauzy-winged, petal-hopping sprites of Victorian fancy is far wide of the mark. These are not sugarily idealised children, but formidable and unchancy beings. They were in Ireland long before the first humans arrived there. The fairy host rides to battle as swift as the wind, while the fairy mist confuses the unwary traveller and the enchanting sound of fairy music can lead him a terrible dance.

‡

BANISHING THE SNAKES

‡

When Christianity reached Ireland, the tendrils of legend swiftly clung to St Patrick and the other early missionaries. Croagh Patrick in County Mayo, for

The magic and poetry of the Celts lies behind the traditional lore of the lands on the fringe of Europe – Ireland, Scotland, Wales, Cornwall and Brittany – which are lapped by the western sea.

‡

Green and lovely, the Eildon Hills in the Scots Border country are associated with fairyland. Thomas the Rhymer fell asleep by a hawthorn tree there and the beautiful Queen of Elfland ravished him away.

instance, was identified as the place where St Patrick banished all the snakes from the Emerald Isle. It has become a centre of pilgrimage, but it was dwarfed in fame for centuries by St Patrick's Purgatory. Here on an island in Lough Derg, in Donegal, was a cave or a pit or possibly a man-made underground passage which was believed to be an entrance to the realm of the dead, and was regarded with profound awe.

In later ages many of Ireland's prehistoric monuments were thought to be the creations of the Druids.

Astonishingly, the graceful round towers of early Irish monasteries were also attributed to these pagan sages.

‡

THE HORNS OF ELFLAND

‡

Scottish tradition shared the Irish respect for the fairy folk. It was on the shapely Eildon Hills in the Border country that Thomas the Rhymer met the lovely, laughing Queen of Elfland, dressed in fairy green, and she took him away with her for seven years to her realm beyond the edge of the land of the living. According to popular belief, in the pele towers of the Lowlands, where the memory of dark deeds lingered, there also lurked the sinister Redcaps, waiting to redye their headgear in the fresh blood of unsuspecting passing travellers.

The old traditions have lasted longer, however, in the remote Highlands and Islands. If you see a horse feeding quietly beside a loch in the Highlands or lingering at a ford across a stream, beware. It may not be a real horse, but a kelpie, and if you are unwise enough to climb on its back, it will plunge you into deep water and drown you. Tales are told of one in Glen Keltney, near Schiehallion, and of many others. In both Ireland and Scotland seals were widely believed to be a fairy race and there were stories of seal women luring humans to their doom. So powerful were these beliefs that in the Orkneys down into this century boatmen would refuse to rescue someone from drowning because to do so would risk cheating the water spirits of their prey.

Top: the fairies of traditional lore were wild and compelling dancers, and there was a belief that a mortal drawn into their circle would not escape again. In this 19th-century illustration a man is being pulled back by a friend to stop him entering a fairy ring.
Above left: Celtic folk myths were much loved in the 19th century, but they were also sometimes laughed at, as in George Cruikshank's 1865 depiction of the Giant Bolster covering six miles at one stride in Cornwall.
Above right: Fingal's Cave on the island of Staffa was said to be the home of a giant of Irish tradition who built the Giant's Causeway.

‡

HAGS AND GIANTS

‡

In Wales, industrialisation and the influence of the Nonconformist chapels killed off much of the old lore. Some leading Welsh families had their own harbinger of death, like the Irish banshee *(see page 14)*. This was the gwrach-y-rhibyn, or hag of the dribble, a grim crone with a high-pitched voice who foretold an approaching death. The De Clares of Caerphilly Castle boasted one, as did the Stradlings of St Donats, while another still haunts the ruins of Pennard Castle on the Gower Peninsula.

The piskeys of Cornwall have degenerated into repellently arch little

adjuncts to the tourist trade (like the ill-used leprechauns of Ireland). So far this fate has been escaped by the knockers, the spirits who made mysterious rapping sounds deep in the shafts of the tin mines. They worked there themselves and were usually sympathetic to humans, but they hated the sign of the cross so Cornish miners took great care not to cross themselves while underground.

Cornwall is pre-eminently a country of giants, and of dangerously uncanny standing stones which come to life and lurch down to streams to drink. A giant named Cormelian made St Michael's Mount by piling up huge rocks. Another giant and his wife built the huge walls of the hillfort of Treryn Dinas on its southern headland, with the famous rocking stone called the Logan Rock, where witches are believed to gather. Many of the boulders that lie about on the Cornish moors were thrown there by giants hurling missiles at each other or playing a riotous form of mega-hockey.

Among the mermaids of Cornwall is the one carved in Zennor church, with her comb and mirror. She fell in love with a young man of the village and lured him away to his doom.

‡

THE LORD OF DEATH

‡

Brittany has many affinities with Cornwall, and here again are stories of the standing stones going to quench their thirst in streams, while the evil fairy of the Ile du Loch used to turn her human lovers into fish to stock her fishpond. The Breton writer Chateaubriand lived as a child in the gloomy castle of Combourg, where he slept in a turret room which was called the Cat's Tower because a former lord of the castle returned there every night in feline form.

The world of death was believed to overlap with the world of the living at certain points, and on the west coast the ghosts of drowned seamen clustered at Pointe du Raz. Held in profound awe was Ankou, the personification of death. He was seen as a man in a wide-brimmed hat, carrying a scythe. If encountered on country roads, riding in a creaking cart, he was an omen of death. But in Brittany, as elsewhere, the old traditions themselves are dying out.

STONES OF MYSTERY

By medieval times, knowledge of the prehistoric people who built such great religious sanctuaries as Stonehenge and Avebury in England, Callanish in the Hebrides and Carnac in Brittany had long been lost. It was clear that these mysterious constructions dated from pre-Christian times, however, and they were attributed to powerful supernatural forces, wicked pagans and beings of dubious repute, such as the Devil or giants or the Druids.

The huge standing stones at Boroughbridge in Yorkshire, for instance, are called the Devil's Arrows. There is a story that Satan launched them irritably at early Christians in the vicinity in Roman days. In Cornwall the stone circle called the Merry Maidens has two sinister-looking outlying standing stones called the Pipers and another called the Fiddler. In legend the maidens and their musicians were all turned to stone as a punishment for dancing on a Sunday.

The idea of the stones as a dance, caught and literally petrified, appears again at Stonehenge, which was called the Giants' Dance in legend, and was said to have been built long ago by giants in Ireland. The great wizard Merlin, King Arthur's resident sorcerer and counsellor, moved it from Ireland to Salisbury Plain by magic art (assisted by the Devil, some said). The massive stones were locally believed to have healing power, and popular tradition still connects them with the Druids (an idea brought to life by modern Druids, greeting the dawn at Stonehenge on Midsummer Day).

At Avebury the hulking stones make

✣

Standing silent in their inscrutable patterns in the sunshine or looming up out of a morning mist, there is something profoundly uncanny about the megalithic monuments of western Europe, which have become the focus of fascinating new theories in this century.

✣

another impressive spectacle and a superstition has been recorded in the village that it is extremely unlucky to live in a house built of Avebury stone. Anyone who does attracts the unwelcome attention of an appallingly chilling presence known simply as 'the Haunt'. The enigmatic man-made mound of Silbury Hill near by was said to have been created when the Devil emptied a sack of earth he was carrying there.

At Carnac some 3000 stones stand in complex alignments, with stone circles and tombs. Legend explains them as a great host of pagans who were pursuing St Cornely with evil intent when he turned them all to stone.

✣

WORD OF POWER

✣

It has long been recognised that Stonehenge is orientated to the midsummer sunrise, and many archaeologists now accept that these vast monuments were not only temples of prehistoric deities, but also astronomical observatories, used for predicting events in the sky and fixing the calendar. They were designed by priest-magicians, who had a remarkably advanced grasp of astronomy, mathematics and geometry.

Some writers have attributed still greater powers to the

According to classical writers, the Druids presided over human holocausts in which victims, penned inside a wicker colossus, were burned alive. Popular tradition connected the Druids with stone circles.

prehistoric priests, as masters of subtle electro-magnetic energy currents in the earth, susceptible to psychical control by human beings. It has even been suggested that the priests built the stone circles simply by speaking a word of command.

✝

LINES OF FORCE

✝

Sir Norman Lockyer, a distinguished astronomer at the turn of the 19th and 20th centuries, suggested that Stonehenge and other megalithic sites in Britain (as well as Egyptian and classical temples) had been orientated to the sun and the stars. He also pointed out some interesting alignments between Stonehenge and other ancient sites, earthworks and religious centres. For example, a straight line can be drawn on

Stonehenge was built and rebuilt many times, reaching its final form some 3500 years ago. Aligned to the sunrise at midsummer, it was probably a giant stone calendar as well as a temple, served by astronomer-priests.

the map which connects Stonehenge with Old Sarum, Salisbury Cathedral and Clearbury Ring, while Old Sarum, Stonehenge and Grovely Castle form an equilateral triangle. Lockyer suggested that these alignments might well not be merely coincidental.

Independently, apparently, an elderly photographer named Alfred Watkins, looking casually at a map one day in 1921, suddenly had a vision of a network of straight lines running across the countryside and joining together natural features of the landscape, prehistoric sites, churches and other

landmarks. He called these lines 'leys' (pronounced to rhyme with maze) and believed they were prehistoric tracks and that some of them were aligned to the sun and the stars.

The idea of the ley lines as prehistoric tracks is no longer taken seriously, and the lines are now regarded – by believers, at least – as channels of force, created aeons ago as the earth slowly cooled. They are also channels of spiritual and psychic energy. Places where several of these lines meet, like Stonehenge or the Arbor Low stone circle in Derbyshire or Cley Hill, near Warminster in Wiltshire – which is a famous magnet for UFOs – are like power stations, where massive quantities of energy are concentrated.

Enthusiastic ley-hunters have discovered numerous apparently significant alignments, such as the isosceles triangle which connects the White Horse of Uffington with two other white horses (of far later date) at Pewsey and Cherhill in Wiltshire. The case for ley lines has been marred by too many far-fetched claims, but there is evidence that the builders of the megalithic temples did sometimes align them with natural features of the surrounding landscape, for purposes not yet understood.

A Yorkshire ley line. Seen from Pecket Well, the distant obelisk on Studley Pike is exactly aligned with Heptonstall church tower.
Inset is the cover of Alfred Watkins's manual on ley hunting, which came out in 1927.

THE HOUSE OF FACES

⁜

Fear of ghosts goes far back to the earliest days of the human race, but one of the strangest hauntings on record in Europe occurred in a remote Spanish village in the 1970s.

⁜

In August 1971 a Spanish farmer's wife in the village of Bélmez, near Cordoba in Andalusia, was disturbed by a strange mark on her kitchen floor which gradually turned into a face. It seemed to have an anguished expression and she did not like it. Nor did her husband, and their son removed it, but a second face formed. The local authorities came, cut the affected area from the stone floor and repaired the damage, but another face appeared on the new bit of floor. It was joined by yet another face and, as the months passed, by several more. Crosses formed on the floor as well, and disturbing sounds were heard in the house, including the voice of a child. At the end of the year some of the faces vanished and were replaced by others. By this time word had spread and police were needed to control the crowds at the house.

The house, it was discovered, stood on the site of an old cemetery, in which five murder victims of the 17th century were said to have been buried. Human remains were found in excavations under the house and others close to it. Investigators took over the haunted kitchen and covered the floor with foil, but more faces formed beneath the foil. The family used another room for cooking, but there were reports of faces appearing in the new kitchen, too.

It was suggested that possibly the farmer's wife was somehow mentally able to imprint the faces on the stone of the floor, and one investigator said that the faces seemed to respond to her state of health: when she was not feeling well, the faces lost colour in sympathy. In the end, the outbreak died away as inexplicably as it had begun and the mystery has remained unsolved.

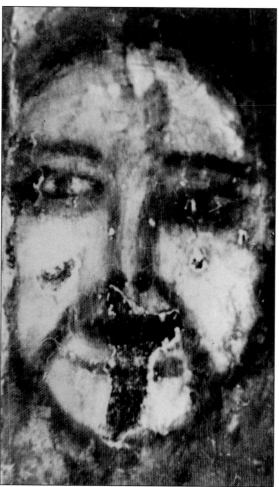

One of the sad and haunting faces that appeared, apparently of their own volition, on the concrete floor of Mrs Maria Gómez Pereira's kitchen at Bélmez de la Moraleda in Spain. This one manifested itself late in August 1971 and its photograph was taken in the September.

⁜

FOR THE BIRDS

⁜

Mysterious voices are quite often reported. In 1959 a man in Stockholm was playing an innocent recording of birdsong back on his tape-recorder when he was astonished to hear voices on it which seemed to be trying to convey messages from the dead. Over the next few years dozens of voices apparently manifested themselves in a scratchy, intermittent way on his tapes when they had no business to be there, and his own voice was sometimes completely drowned out. The intrusive voices included that of Adolf Hitler, and another investigator claimed to have heard an entire Nuremberg rally in full swing.

⁜

THE FATAL CAR

⁜

There are stories of other pieces of equipment which seem to take on a life of their own, sometimes malignant. Among them is the colourful tale of the six-seater open touring car, painted bright red, in which the Archduke Franz Ferdinand made the fatal mistake of riding through Sarajevo one June day in 1914. After the war the car was refurbished for a high Yugoslavian official, who had so many accidents in it that he gave it to a friend. Six months later a subsequent owner was killed when it overturned on him. Another owner decided to break the hoodoo by painting the car bright blue. Displeased, perhaps, it careered into a head-on smash which killed him and four passengers. Repaired, it was nervously palmed off on a museum in Vienna, where both the car and the museum were completely destroyed by a bomb in World War II.

Above: Hitler at Nuremberg in 1938. It seems that the sound of his voice has never entirely died away.
Below: moments before the fateful assassination at Sarajevo in 1914, the doomed Archduke Franz Ferdinand and his wife approach the jinxed car through ranks of saluting officers and important officials.

CAUGHT IN THE BATH

Some ghosts appear where you might expect them. The widow of Chancellor Biener haunts the ruined fortress of Rattenburg in the Austrian Tyrol, where her husband was unjustly executed in 1651. The sombre castle at Lockenhaus is roamed by the unquiet spectre of a vampirish female who disported herself sadistically with the village girls.

Other ghosts are entirely unexpected. In 1950 a party of diplomats in Norway were out skiing near Oslo when three of them were challenged by an elderly lady, dressed in old-fashioned clothes and speaking with a Scots accent. She then vanished, and on enquiry they found that 40 years before the nearby house had been owned by a farmer with a Scots wife.

Similarly unexpected was the young woman who walked in on an American officer in 1945 when he was enjoying a bath at Wildenstein Castle in Germany. He got out of the bath and went to push her out of his way, but his hand went right through her and she disappeared.

During World War I there was a jinxed German submarine which was involved in several accidents. One of them killed the second officer, who was afterwards seen haunting the boat on several occasions. In the end, in 1918, the boat blew up in a mysterious explosion and took her entire crew to the bottom of the sea.

NORTH AND CENTRAL ✦ AMERICA ✦

In the 1960s an American entrepreneur bought London Bridge, not the old medieval bridge famed in nursery rhyme and story, but a later replacement, dating from the 1820s. It was dismantled and shipped stone by stone to Lake Havasu City in Arizona, where it was reassembled alongside an English village and a pub. After the official opening in 1971 it soon transpired that the packing cases in which the bridge had travelled to the Arizona desert had contained ghosts as well. Spectres in Victorian costume were seen strolling across the span, oblivious to their new surroundings, and sightseers crossing

On All Souls' Day the people of Mexico purchase 'Bread of the Dead' and repair to the graves of their departed loved ones for a picnic.

The first incomers to settle the Americas were the ancestors of today's American Indians, who came in from Asia across the Bering Strait. When white invaders intruded on them, from the late 15th century onwards, the indigenous peoples had rich and complicated beliefs about supernatural spirits. Their shamans, or 'medicine men', had techniques of exploring the spirit world which made them favourite 'guides' for the new Spiritualist movement, which began in the United States in the 19th century.

Mexico, Central America and the southern areas of today's United States

the bridge were bumped into by invisible entities going the other way.

These stories may have been more publicity puffs than anything else, but they illustrate the fact that the teeming ghosts and spirits of the Old World travelled to the New with the more solidly human immigrants. The august White House itself was not immune to the process and is the home of the ghost of Abraham Lincoln.

Above left: an idealised view of a Voodoo ceremony by 20th-century artist Gerard Valcin. The central tree in a sanctuary often plays a key role in the proceedings.
Above right: a shaman, or 'medicine man', belonging to the North American Hidatsa tribe. In this painting by Karl Bodmer he is dressed in the striking costume necessary for the performance of the Dog Dance.

were conquered by the Spaniards. Hot on the heels of the ruthless conquistadors came the Roman Catholic missionaries, to convert the Indian population to Christianity wholesale. The result was a distinctive form of Christianity, richly imbued with indigenous beliefs.

In the West Indies and the American South thousands of black slaves were imported from West Africa, where they

1 West Point
2 New York City
3 Rochester
4 Pittsfield
5 Hyndsville

were sold by their own kings and chiefs to be shipped across the Atlantic in abominable conditions. They took their own mental furniture with them – it was all they were allowed to take – and it blended with the Christianity they were taught on the plantations to create Voodoo, obeah and conjure magic in another powerful blend of Christian and non-Christian elements.

Canada and the northern part of the

United States were first settled by French and British incomers, who were followed in the 19th century by vast numbers of immigrants from Ireland, Italy, Germany and Scandinavia, eastern Europe and Russia. All these new arrivals brought their own mental baggage with them and it included old religious and folk beliefs and superstitions. The poltergeist, the evil spirit, the witch and the wistful ghost all

sailed to the land of opportunity, where they made themselves at home.

Today, new variations on ancient themes include the hitchhiker who haunts America's lonely roads, accepts lifts (chatting happily the while) then vanishes into thin air. Another is the appearance of alarming intruders from the far reaches of space. They invade the human world in Unidentified Flying Objects, accompanied by men in black.

FROM SALEM TO NEW ORLEANS

✤

The Puritan divines who ruled New England in the 17th century were in no doubt of the reality of the Devil and his animosity to their godly theocracy. With their flock, they had brought with them from the old country a readiness to see the supernatural at work. In 1647 a richly laden cargo ship sailed from the harbour of New Haven, Connecticut, and vanished. Six months later her phantom was seen in the sky at the mouth of the harbour, where she sailed against the wind for half an hour. Many people beheld what the clergy called 'this great work of God', before the ghostly vessel disappeared into a cloud. The real ship was never seen again.

Quite different in kind were the operations of the witches, the Devil's human fifth column, who had sneaked on to the ships bound for America. They were suspected to be behind the outbreak of poltergeist activity in Portsmouth, New Hampshire, in 1682. Stones kept flying about inside the house of a man named George Walton and the kitchen spit was mysteriously propelled up the chimney. Influential Puritan clergymen, like Cotton Mather, believed in witchcraft and Mather wrote, 'A witch is not to be endured in heaven or earth.'

Everywhere the settlers went in North America, belief in the supernatural went too. Americans of white, black and Mexican descent feared the Devil and the sinister, insinuating machinations of witches.

✤

Above: an old woman being arrested on suspicion of witchcraft, by American illustrator Howard Pyle. Right: extract from a witch-hunting tract printed in Boston in 1693 by the influential New England minister Cotton Mather.

THE HYSTERIA IN SALEM

✤

A dozen or so suspects were sniffed out and hanged for witchcraft in Connecticut before the major panic at Salem Village, Massachusetts, in 1692, which occurred when witch-hunting in Europe had passed its peak. It apparently started with a slave from Barbados called Tituba who told blood-curdling stories of supernatural evil to some of the village's young girls and teenagers. The girls began to behave peculiarly and presently threw hysterical fits. It was at once assumed that they were bewitched and, under pressure from the alarmed adults, they began to name the witches. More and more suspects were arrested, tried and

THE VOODOO DANCE.

A scene from the Salem witch trials, as recreated by Howard Pyle. The women are claiming to see a flock of yellow birds around one of the accused.

An illustration of 1886 by E W Kemble in the Century Magazine *showed blacks in New Orleans dancing and singing in a Voodoo-style ceremony.*

found guilty, on no evidence beyond the ravings of the girls.

A reaction quickly set in, with a feeling that the accused had been condemned on inadequate evidence. Four years after the trials the original jurors signed a confession of error, solemnly stating that they had been misled by the Devil.

✢

HEX CAT FARM
✢

The Salem case was the only major outbreak of witch-hunting in North America, but far from being confined to New England, fear of witches affected every area where immigrants settled. To this day, the spanking barns of the old-fashioned Amish people in Pennsylvania bear the traditional symbols against hexerai (witchcraft).

The case of the Hex Cat Farm, near Pottsville, in 1911 caused a national sensation. The farmer and his daughter, who kept house for him, were warned by a powwow woman, versed in matters of magic, that a supernatural black cat was going to be sent against them by a mysterious enemy from the nearby settlement of Orwigsburg. The daughter armed herself with a revolver in anticipation and when a black cat duly appeared, she fired. To her horror, it swelled up before her eyes to a huge size and stalked disdainfully away.

A string of disasters followed, as every

cow on the farm died one after another, the crops withered and finally the farmer himself took sick and died. His daughter, convinced that all this was due to an evil spell, publicly denounced her married sister from Orwigsburg as the witch responsible. A powwow man pronounced that the hex cat could only be killed with a golden bullet, so the family jewellery was melted down to make one and the cat – or a cat – was shot and nailed to the barn. The spell was broken, everyone agreed, but no buyer could be found for the farm.

✢

A SUSPICION OF OWLS
✢

Traditions in southern areas of the United States have been influenced by Mexican folk beliefs. Owls, for instance, were regarded with a dubious eye by Texans of Mexican descent, for though many owls might be perfectly innocent, the birds could be witches, in disguise.

In 1908, near Harlingen, a group of men were working in the fields one day when a stranger joined them who was afflicted by a mysterious disease which caused him to vomit blood on Thursdays and Fridays, and only those days. It was clear that he had been bewitched. To cure him, 12 knots were ceremoniously tied in a horsehair rope, and when the last knot was tied, two large owls fell out of a nearby mesquite tree and were beaten to death with a

stick. Those present thought they heard voices at this point. After this, all the stranger's clothes were burned on a bonfire, and he was cured.

✢

HOODOO CITY
✢

Among the African slaves imported into the American South were specialists in the supernatural, or 'medicine men'. On the plantations the 'medicine man' developed into the 'conjure doctor', 'trick doctor' or 'hoodooer'. He had an important role as a priest-magician who cast spells, made potions and knew the world of spirits.

Some Africans converted to Christianity by their white masters rejected the conjure doctor as a creature of the Devil, but others maintained that it was God who gave the magician his power. In 1822 Denmark Vesey, a black Methodist leader in Charleston, South Carolina, planned a slave rebellion. The rhetoric came from the Old Testament, but at his elbow was a conjure doctor known as Gullah Jack.

The cosmopolitan city of New Orleans was a great centre of conjure magic. Its famous 19th-century 'Voodoo queen', Marie Laveau, lorded it from her house in the French Quarter, selling love potions and charms and powerful magic against her customers' enemies. In the 1930s New Orleans was called 'the hoodoo capital of the United States'. This aspect of the city's colourful history can be investigated today in the Historic Voodoo Museum and there are still 'Voodoo priestesses' who offer supernatural assistance.

AMITYVILLE
AND OTHER HORRORS

An unusual case reached the Manhattan Supreme Court in 1990. A Wall Street bond-trader had put down a deposit on an 18-room Victorian house in Nyack, New York, a suburb of New York City. He subsequently found out that the house was haunted by three ghosts, all from the pre-Revolutionary War era. They were a young naval officer, a young woman and an elderly man. At this he demanded his money back, but the vendor refused to return his deposit.

The vendor, a Mrs Helen Ackley, said there was nothing wrong with the ghosts, which were 'gracious, thoughtful, only occasionally frightening, and thoroughly entertaining', and she only wished she could take them with her when she moved. 'I feel they are very good friends', she said. 'It's very comforting to have them around when you are by yourself.' When her children had been young, the ghosts had thoughtfully brought them presents and would also wake them up of a morning by shaking their beds.

The court held for the vendor, but on a subsequent appeal the Supreme Court of New York State ruled the other way, stating that the house was clearly haunted and the buyer should have been informed of this material (or immaterial) fact. The judges clearly enjoyed the case, and one of the grounds for their decision was that the vendor could not deliver vacant possession of the house because the ghosts counted as residents.

⁜

THE EVIL IN THE HOUSE
⁜

The plaintiff in this lawsuit at one stage mentioned America's most famous postwar haunted-house case – the sensationally named Amityville Horror. Whether the 'horror' was real or not, it certainly made large quantities of real money for some of those associated with it. The tale began in 1975, when a

⁜

The theme of 'the old dark house', the eerie Victorian Gothic mansion with its ample domestic staff of malevolent spooks, chilling atmospheres and supernatural terrors, has come vividly to life in some American towns.

⁜

couple named George and Kathleen Lutz bought a house in the pleasant middle-class settlement of Amityville on Long Island, New York State. They got it cheap and moved into it with their three children. Amityville turned out, however, to be a remarkably unsuitable name for their new environment. They stayed in the house only four weeks, during which they were subjected to the most nightmarish assault by unseen powers.

First there were peculiar noises in the night. Then the heavy front door was wrenched off its hinges by some unknown but formidable force. Windows started opening and closing of their own accord and one night George woke up to see Kathleen floating in the air above the bed. He hauled her down, switched the light on and was horrified to find himself looking at a hideous, drooling and dishevelled crone. It took hours for her to return gradually to her normal appearance (and it apparently did not occur to him to call a doctor). Another night they both saw red eyes glowing outside the house in the night and found the prints of cloven hooves in the snow. Eventually, as green slime began exuding from the walls, the family gathered their belongings and left.

The reason the Lutzes had been able to buy the Amityville house cheap was that, shortly before, it had been the site of a particularly unpleasant multiple murder. A young man had slaughtered his entire family – father, mother and

four brothers and sisters. He claimed that supernatural 'voices' had ordered him to commit the crime (though the police believed it was the family insurance money that actually inspired him).

A best-selling book, *The Amityville Horror*, came out in 1978 and was made into a film, with Rod Steiger in the role of a priest who had tried to exorcise the house, in vain. There were reports of uncanny accidents on the film set, though it was not set in the actual house, and it was said that when the manuscript of the book was delivered to the editor, his car promptly caught fire. On the other hand, the next family to live in the Amityville house experienced nothing untoward whatever, and a good deal of cold water has been thrown on the whole story.

⁜

SOMETHING NASTY IN THE BEDROOM
⁜

Another case of a nightmare house, apparently bent on injuring or even killing its occupants, broke surface in the Detroit press in 1962. The house belonged to a car worker on night shift, who slept during the day in a tiny back bedroom. He began to experience appalling dreams, from which he woke up in terror, screaming aloud. In one dream he went to the small cupboard in the room, opened the door and found a mutilated corpse inside. The dreams ceased when he moved to the main bedroom. His grandmother, who came for a visit and spent one night in the back room, refused to sleep in it again. Then a friend came to stay, went to bed unsuspectingly in the room and saw a woman with long hair, standing with her back to him and looking into the kitchen. There was something desperately frightening about the figure and he ran from the room in panic. A dreadful wailing sound came from the room and there was a terrible smell.

The car worker decided to sort the

whole thing out and went to the apparently haunted room to lie down and see what would happen. What happened was that he heard a noise, turned over and found himself looking straight into the most horrible face he had ever seen in his life. The mouth was making a hissing noise and there was an appalling, fetid stench. He ran out in terror and the next morning he moved

The Amityville house is an example of a peculiarly unsettling nightmare – the warm, cosy home that turns into something hideously threatening, evil and malignant.

his family out of the house.

There was no report of any traumatic event in the house's past history. This story carries to an extreme something

many people have experienced – an unpleasant 'atmosphere' which makes a house or a particular room uncomfortable to be in. Houses of this kind tend to change hands often, but there is frequently nothing in the known history of the place that can be linked with the phenomenon. The experience is reported too frequently for it to be dismissed as mere imagination.

PRESIDENTS AND GHOSTS

Of all the great Presidents of the United States, Abraham Lincoln enjoys perhaps the securest hold on the respect and affection of posterity, and as in addition he was cut off before his time by assassination, it may not be surprising that his is the ghost most often seen haunting the White House in Washington.

Mrs Lincoln was a believer in Spiritualism. Mr Lincoln himself took a lively interest in the spirit world and attended several seances. At one of them he and his bodyguard were sitting on a piano when the instrument, with them aboard it, suddenly rose in the air by itself. Another time, a 'spirit' speaking through the medium urged earnestly on him the importance of abolishing slavery. Not long before his death he had a dream in which a dead body was lying in state in the East Room, its face covered. In the dream he asked who it was, and was told, 'The President. He was killed by an assassin.'

✢

STILL IN OFFICE

✢

After his death in 1865, President Lincoln seems to have taken up a prolonged residence in the White House and it is said that his ghost has been seen there during every administration since his time. During President Benjamin Harrison's term of office, between 1889 and 1893, one of the attendants is said to have gone to a seance to beg President Lincoln's ghost

✢

President Andrew Jackson of the United States encountered a celebrated and singularly unpleasant ghost in Tennessee, and President Lincoln's ghost has had a longer tenure of the White House than any duly elected occupant.

✢

to stop haunting him, because it frightened him and distracted him from his duties. This appeal was successful, apparently. President Theodore Roosevelt, speaking of Lincoln – 'shambling, homely, with his sad, strong, deeply furrowed face' – said that he saw him in various rooms and halls. Mrs Grace Coolidge, wife of the 30th President, saw Lincoln 'dressed in black with a stole draped over his shoulders to ward off the draughts and chills'.

In 1934 one of the White House staff saw Lincoln sitting on the bed in the Rose Room. After a moment or two he vanished. When Queen Wilhelmina of the Netherlands stayed at the White House, she was given the Rose Room. She heard a knock at the door, opened it and found herself staring at the great man. She fainted. When she told President Roosevelt what had happened, he said that hers was only the latest of many similar reports. Sir Winston Churchill did not like sleeping in the room and moved across the hall to another one. A White House aide saw the ghost several times during World War II and afterwards President Eisenhower said he had sensed Lincoln's presence in the White House more than once.

Above: Lincoln was assassinated at Ford's Theatre in Washington. The fact that he met an untimely end helped fuel belief that his ghost haunted the White House.
Left: President Lincoln in 1865, the year of his death.

THE BELL WITCH

Years before all this, Andrew Jackson, who was President from 1829 to 1837 and considered a notably hard-headed, no-nonsense character – nicknamed 'Old Hickory' for his toughness – was driving a wagon and horses along the road to a plantation in Robertson County, Tennessee. It was owned by a close friend of his named John Bell. The wagon suddenly stopped and stayed as if rooted to the spot, while the horses strained to move it forward. Jackson exclaimed aloud that it must be a witch, and a voice spoke in the air, saying 'let the wagon move'. At this, Jackson said, the wagon rolled on again.

John Bell's plantation, where Jackson was staying, was notorious for the activities of a murderous poltergeist known as the Bell Witch. For four years, between 1817 and 1821, this disagreeable entity made knocking noises inside the house and out, plus noises like dogs fighting. It pulled the bedclothes off the eight Bell children, smacked them, pinched them and pulled their hair. The family and their servants were pelted by stones and bits of wood, and though two of the Bell boys were caught throwing pieces of wood on one occasion, they were apparently imitating the poltergeist and it was not thought possible for them to have faked all the phenomena. The disturbances appear to have centred round 12-year-old Betsy Bell and when she went to stay with a neighbour, the poltergeist went with her. She also began vomiting up pins and needles.

Andrew Jackson, nicknamed 'Old Hickory', was not a man easily frightened – quite the contrary – but he was taken aback by his encounter with the murderous Bell family poltergeist, or 'witch', which created havoc on a Tennessee plantation in the early 19th century.

A WHISPERING VOICE

The Bells tried to coax the spirit to speak. They heard faint noises and whistles, and after a time a creaky voice began to whisper, 'I am a spirit who was once very happy, but has been disturbed and made unhappy'. Other voices were heard, too, as John Bell was persecuted and fiercely struck by invisible hands.

As word of the disturbances spread, numerous visitors came to see things for themselves and many of them attracted the attentions of the spirit. One man, for instance, was in bed when it tried to pull the bedclothes off him.

Eventually the spirit proclaimed: 'I am nothing more than old Kate Bell's witch and I'm determined to torment Jack Bell as long as he lives'. Which it did, for in 1820 the unfortunate John Bell died, by poison mysteriously placed in his bottle of medicine. Whether it was suicide or not has never been established. Soon afterwards something like a cannonball rolled out of the fireplace and announced, 'I'm going and will be gone for seven years'. It kept its promise and did not return until 1828, when the disturbances were much weaker and lasted only two weeks.

Was there an independent entity in the house which fed on the energy of Betsy Bell? Or did she unconsciously cause the phenomena, powered by unhappiness and hatred of her father? Or was the whole thing a cover for the murder of John Bell? Anyone who knew at the time wasn't saying, and certainly nobody knows now.

The Ghost Train

Abraham Lincoln was carried by a special train on his last journey, from Washington DC to the Oak Ridge cemetery at his home town of Springfield, Illinois, where he was to be buried. As the funeral train crossed the country, thousands of people gathered by the track to see it pass and the train stopped for eight minutes at each station on the route to allow the local citizens to pay their respects to the murdered president. A legend grew up that every year a phantom of the train, draped in its funereal black, made the same solemn journey. If it was a moonlight night, the clouds gathered to cover the moon, and all along the route as the train passed silently by the clocks stopped – for exactly eight minutes.

THE DIVINE RIDERS

Though long associated in white minds with black magic, Voodoo is the religion of the masses in Haiti and one of its principal concerns is to protect its devotees against sorcery and witchcraft. It also brings its worshippers into direct contact with their deities in ceremonies of frenzied drumming and dancing. These work up to a pitch at which one or more of the devotees goes into trance and becomes possessed by one of the gods. Rooted to the floor and unable to move, the worshipper is invisibly 'mounted' by the god and then gradually begins to dance, eat, drink and behave in the way traditionally associated with the god, as if the deity had invaded his (or her) body and mind.

There are Voodoo temples in the slums of Port au Prince, the capital, but the religion's natural home is in the villages of the island. It is a mixture of African and Christian ingredients, and many Voodoo worshippers also attend Roman Catholic services without any feeling of incongruity. When slaves were brought over from West Africa to the West Indies and were taught Christianity, it was natural for them to identify the great spiritual beings of this new faith with the deities of their own African heritage. Jesus was identified with the god Oxala, and when the slaves

✢

Devotees of the Voodoo religion in Haiti describe themselves as being 'mounted by the divine horsemen' when they go into trance during the rituals and become the vehicles of the gods.

✢

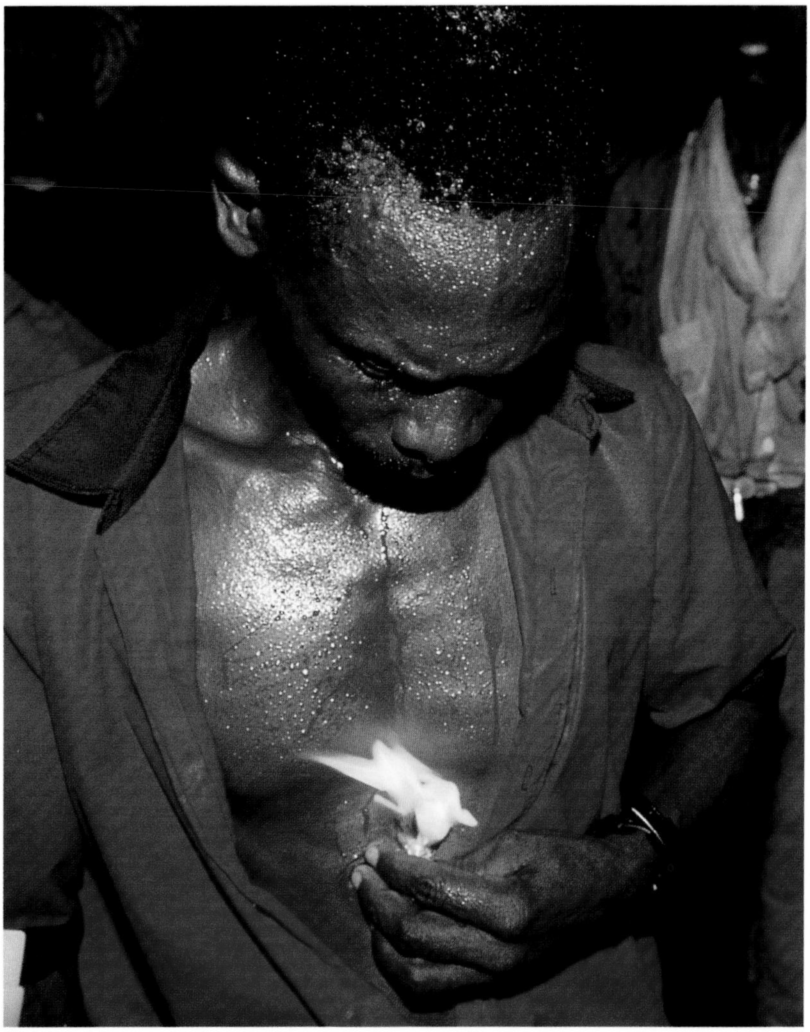

Voodoo is Haiti's popular religion, created by slaves from Africa. This 'Voodoo' fire-eater is part of a ceremony commemorating the abolition of slavery.

were shown images of Jesus, it was Oxala they saw, while in St John the Baptist they recognised their own storm-god Shango – apparently because the weather around St John's feast day is often stormy.

✢

'REMOVE THE BARRIER FOR ME'

✢

The Voodoo gods and spirits, the loa, are divided into different 'nations', according to the area of Africa from which they originally hailed – Rada from Dahomey, Wangol from Angola, and so on. There are also the Petro loa, who seem to have been taken over from the original Indian population of Haiti.

Before any of them can take possession of a worshipper, permission must be obtained from the god Legba, who was originally the interpreter and go-between among the gods of Dahomey. The central post or tree in the sanctuary is sacred to him. When he shows himself, he is a shuffling old man, shabbily dressed and supporting his tottering steps on a crutch. Because he guards the gate between the realms of gods and men, he is identified with St Peter, who in Christian tradition holds the keys of heaven and hell.

Voodoo ceremonies invariably

commence with an invocation to Legba:

Atibon-Legba, remove the barrier for me...
Papa Legba, remove the barrier
So I may pass through.
When I come back I will salute the loa.
Voodoo Legba, remove the barrier for me
So that I may come back.
When I come back, I will thank the loa.

Worshippers 'ridden' by the god Ogu put on old military uniforms or tie red rags round their heads, and talk in rough, soldierly fashion with much obscenity, demanding rum and a woman. The blacksmith of the gods in West Africa, he is the Voodoo god of war. Zaka, the god of farming, is a much more peaceful character, a typical Haitian peasant in a straw hat, carrying his machete in his hand – though beneath his placid exterior there lurks an explosive temper. A devotee possessed by Zaka talks in a caricature of a rustic accent.

Above: Voodoo Dance In The Forest *by Jean-Pierre, one of the 20th-century artists who have hailed the religion as an expression of the spirit of the African population.*
Below: two figures from a Voodoo ceremony in Port au Prince.

✣

GODDESS OF LOVE

✣

Strangely, the Virgin Mary was identified with Erzulie, the beautiful and distinctly unvirginal goddess of love. When Erzulie possesses a worshipper, the latter is taken to the goddess's corner of the sanctuary, where smart dresses are spread out, with a comb and make-up, and perhaps some jewellery. 'She' (it may be a man) titivates herself and dresses in her finery, flirts sexily with the other worshippers and demands sweet biscuits and champagne. She speaks in exaggeratedly high-pitched tones and if she is denied anything she wants, she bursts into tears.

A worshipper ridden by Damballah, the snake god, may meanwhile be writhing on the ground like a snake or curling up among the rafters of

the temple. He is identified with St Patrick because of the tradition that the saint had power over all snakes, which he banished from Ireland.

Associated with cemeteries are the Guede, the death spirits, who dress like undertakers in black frock-coats and top-hats. Their chief is the sinister Baron Samedi, the lord of the underworld and master of magic. He is represented in the sanctuaries by a wooden cross, topped by a black bowler hat and with a black coat or waistcoat draped round it. Baron Samedi is lascivious and greedy, and likely to steal offerings put out for the other loa. Lewd songs are sung in his honour in the cemeteries in Haiti on All Souls' Day, the great feast of the dead.

THE LIVING DEAD

✢

The American journalist William Seabrook, who loved a good story and was not above making one up, gave a vivid account of seeing 'the walking dead' on a visit to a farm on La Gonave, an island off the mainland of Haiti. Three labourers were working in a cotton field, chopping at the ground with machetes. Expressionless, they were bent silently over their work. When one of them straightened up, Seabrook got a sickening shock. 'The eyes were the worst. It was not my imagination. They were in truth like the eyes of a dead man, not blind, but staring, unfocused, unseeing. The whole face, for that matter, was inhuman. It was vacant, as if there was nothing behind it, and drained of expression.' Seabrook decided that the labourers must be unfortunate mental defectives, forced to toil on the land, but Haitian friends told him otherwise.

Like vampires, the zombie has been a boon to the horror film industry ever since the film *White Zombie*, starring Bela Lugosi, came out in 1932 (three years after Seabrook's book). In Haiti, however, zombies are taken perfectly seriously. Under the Duvalier regime, which was overthrown in 1986, the sinister Tonton Macoutes – the Duvaliers' ruthless private army – were popularly believed to number zombies in their ranks, a belief which they

Film still from I Walked With A Zombie, *which adapted the story of Jane Eyre to a Haitian setting.*
Opposite: a poster advertising the film.

The zombies of the chilling Haitian legend are dead human beings, disinterred from their graves and restored to a semblance of life by a sorcerer. They have no souls and are said often to be employed as unpaid labour to drudge in the fields.

✢

encouraged. 'Papa Doc' Duvalier was feared for his magical powers and after his death, it is said, his widow put a curse on an American army officer who wrote a book about the late dictator. The American made the mistake of visiting St Barthélemy, an island near Haiti, but never left it. He dropped dead.

✢

THE CAPTIVE CORPSE

✢

Many stories are told about zombies, such as the one about a girl from a prosperous family who died and was buried, and four years later was found working as a drudge in a shop. Her neck was bent, because she had been buried in a coffin that was too small for her, and there was a mark on her foot where a candle by the bier had fallen and burned her body. A Roman Catholic priest told the anthropologist Francis Huxley that he had seen a zombie, in a village, gnawing at the rope with which his hands were tied. Someone brought him a drink of salt water, which restored his ability to speak. He told his name and his aunt was sent for, who recognised him at once. She said he had died four years before. Two days later the zombie collapsed, and was reburied.

It has also been known for a Voodoo priest to gain substantial prestige by faking the creation of an obedient zombie. In one case, the priest solemnly dug a fresh corpse out of its grave and brought it impressively back to sluggish life, but one of those present noticed an unobtrusive pipe sticking out of the grave – through which the 'corpse', the priest's accomplice, had been able to breathe. The Voodoo religion provides a ritual which protects the believer's soul against

Above: this woman, photographed alive and well in Haiti in 1937, was alleged to have died and been buried in 1907, 30 years before.

capture as a zombie after death. In addition, to guard against being made a zombie, corpses are sometimes buried face down with earth stuffed into the mouth to fill it, or with the lips sewn together. A knife may be placed by the dead hand for use as a weapon if necessary, or the dead body may even be strangled or shot through the head.

✛

SLAVE LABOUR
✛

If a zombie is given salt water, or salted food, it is released from its bondage and will march to its grave and try to dig its way back in. William Seabrook was told that in 1918 the huge factory of the Haitian-American Sugar Company at Port au Prince was in urgent need of labour and offered a bonus to attract employees. One day a black headman from Colombier arrived at the head of a group of nine shuffling men, glassy-eyed and apparently in a daze. He registered them as labourers, explaining that they were poor ignorant men from the mountains. They were put to work in the cane fields and every week the headman collected their wages.

His wife began to feel sorry for the poor zombies and when her husband was away she took them into town and bought them some biscuits. She did not realise that the baker had put salt in the biscuits, and as soon as the nine zombies tasted them they knew they were dead

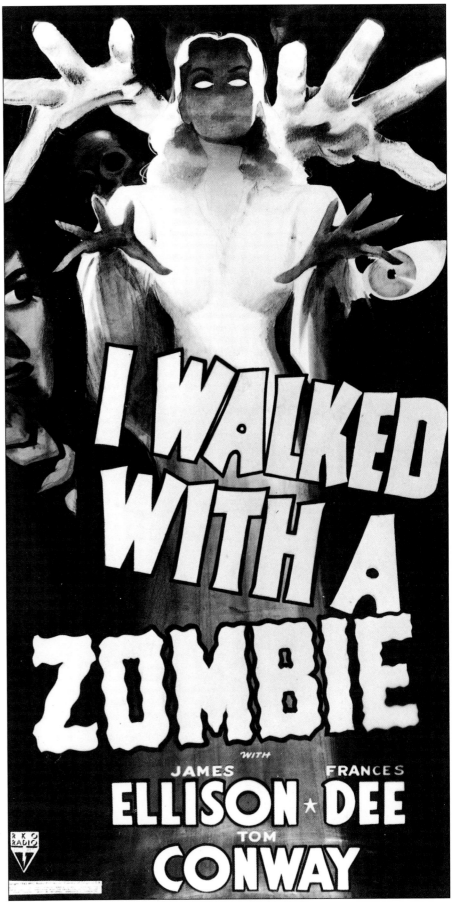

and walked grimly back to the cemetery from which they had come. There they clawed up the earth over their graves and lay still beside them until their relatives came and returned the piteous things to their resting places.

CARIBBEAN ENCHANTMENTS

Voodoo is most closely identified with Haiti, but a similar mingling of African and Christian beliefs occurred among the slave and slave-descended populations of the other islands of the West Indies as well. The Santeria cult in Cuba, which resembles Voodoo, was taken to the United States by Cuban exiles in the 1950s and 1960s, and has caused alarm with its ritual sacrifices of animals.

William Sargant, a distinguished British psychiatrist and authority on brainwashing, attended a ceremony in Port of Spain, the capital of Trinidad, in the 1960s. After the sacrifice of a goat to the African god Ogoun, who was also identified as the Archangel Michael, there was drumming and dancing. Presently women worshippers were possessed by the Virgin Mary, St Joseph, St Francis and other saints, who were also linked with deities believed to have travelled over from Africa to 'ride' them.

Sargant spoke to the women after they had returned to normal. 'These people's faith in the reality of their saints was absolute because they had personally experienced them', he said in his book, *The Mind Possessed*. He went on to comment on 'the difference between their intense personal experience of possession and our forms of Christian service, in which few now have any real sense that God or Christ or the saints are near or in them'.

✣

Possession cults in the Caribbean blend African religion with Christianity, and African magic has survived in an ostensibly Christian environment, while ghost stories similarly mix European traditions with native sorcery.

✣

Fishing boats are drawn up on an idyllic beach on Martinique in the Windward Islands. Like people everywhere in the world who make their living from the unchancy sea, the fishermen hand down many traditional superstitions and observances, which here blend Christian and African beliefs. A side benefit is that they often also discourage overfishing.

Dr Sargant also attended a meeting of the Pocomania cult in Jamaica. This was nearer to a Christian service of the 'Holy Roller' kind, with vigorous singing of hymns, gospel reading and preaching, and 'tromping' – rhythmic overbreathing which helped to induce trance and possession.

✣

OBEAH AND THE DEVIL

✣

In 1760 a law was passed in Jamaica against the practitioners of 'the wicked art of Negroes, going under the Appellation of Obeah Men and Women pretending to have communication with the Devil and other evil spirits...' Their magic was said to involve blood, feathers, grave dirt, rum, eggshells, broken bottles and other dubious materials. They also evidently provided protection against hostile duppies (spirits), witchcraft and the malice of enemies and supplied healing charms and love potions. One of their traditional skills was to kill a man by shadow-catching, which meant trapping his shadow and incarcerating it in a miniature coffin. They were called 'four-eye' or 'do-good', among numerous nicknames.

Like the conjure doctors of the American South, the obeah practitioners were originally the black community's

specialists in the supernatural, and like them they took an important role in slave rebellions. None of the great West Indian plantations of former days could manage without one, and although incessantly condemned by the authorities, the churches and schools, they were respected, resorted to and feared – and still are. Many traditional West Indian beliefs and superstitions have been taken to North America and Britain by emigrants in this century.

The belief that the obeah man gains his power and skills – 'the science' – from the Devil, stated in the Jamaican legislation of 1760, has also survived. The Devil is customarily and significantly pictured in the West Indies as a white man, riding a horse and dragging a chain behind him. There is a separate Sea Devil, too, the powerful and capricious lord of the ocean. The fishermen of St Lucia, in the Windward Islands, consider it essential to employ the right quantity of obeah to catch a good haul of fish without catching so many as to offend the Sea Devil – a good example of an effective supernatural sanction against overfishing. It is also generally believed in the Windward Islands that a fishing boat, or indeed any boat, needs a supernatural guardian to watch over it which must be the spirit of a dead person – preferably a dead child.

Top: the great house at Rosehall, in Jamaica, which was at the heart of a flourishing sugar plantation in the 18th century, has a ghost story that interweaves a conventional European theme with the local spice of obeah. Above: this carnival in St Lucia similarly joins and celebrates traditions with both European and African roots.

✢

THE WITCH OF ROSEHALL
✢

West Indian ghost stories sometimes combine conventional European themes with the distinctive local flavour of obeah. One of them centres on the now abandoned estate of Rosehall at Montego Bay in Jamaica, which belonged in the 1790s to a leading sugar-planter named John Palmer. Late in life, he took a young second wife named Annie, who had already outlived three husbands and was rumoured to have sinister links with a local obeah man. Sexually voracious and sadistic, Annie turned what had been a happy, well-run plantation into a hell, where slaves were tortured to death for her pleasure.

Eventually the Rosehall slaves could bear no more. They rebelled and killed her, and left her corpse to rot under a tree. This meant that her spirit could never rest, and after John Palmer's death the estate was abandoned. Those brave enough to go near it reported hearing terrible screams and cries coming from the empty house. When the caretaker was found dead in the cellar, it was believed that the vicious ghost of Annie Palmer had propelled him down the stone steps to his death. Even now, Rosehall is not considered a comfortable place to pass at night.

✢

THE MOVING COFFINS
✢

Another celebrated West Indian story involves the Chase family, prosperous planters of Christ Church in Barbados. In 1808 they acquired a fine stone tomb, built into the cliffs above Oisin's Bay, which contained one coffin. This belonged to a lady of the previous family, a Mrs Goddard. Over the following years, each time the Chases unsealed the tomb to bury their dead there, it was found that the heavy lead coffins previously placed in the mausoleum had been lifted and flung about. This was despite the fact that the tomb was rigorously sealed each time, and remained unopened. Nobody could work out how it could have been done, but the only coffin which remained undisturbed throughout was that of Mrs Goddard. In the end the Chase dead were taken away to be reinterred elsewhere, and the triumphant Mrs Goddard was left to her solitary reign.

CANADA UNCANNY

Generally speaking, hotels are not keen to have ghosts on the premises. They disturb the guests and are bad for business, and they don't pay their bills. If they insist on hanging around, however, there may not be much to be done except keep quiet about them. So it seems to have been with a hotel somewhere in Southern Alberta, where a 14-year-old girl was staying with her parents one summer weekend. Because she was a diabetic and had to give herself an injection every morning, an 8am wake-up call was organised. Sure enough, the phone in her room rang as arranged and a pleasant female voice told her it was eight o'clock. She presently went along to her parents' room, but they were distinctly unenthusiastic about being dragged from their slumbers at five in the morning.

Later, when the family complained to the staff, it turned out that there had been nobody on duty at 5am to make the call, and there never was anyone on so early. The desk clerk suddenly realised which room the girl had occupied and cheerfully explained that the wake-up call must have come from the ghost of a previous clerk, who had died in the hotel some

‡

Canada can claim its fair share of hauntings, poltergeist outbreaks and uncanny happenings, ranging from the comparatively casual and minor to the positively terrifying, and including a ghost that rang a hotel guest on the telephone.

‡

The house in Amherst involved in strange phenomena in 1878.

The Philip Experiment

A remarkable experiment was carried out in Toronto in the 1970s by a group led by a seasoned psychical researcher, A R G Owen. The group invented a non-existent ghost and then attempted to communicate with him. They called him Philip and made up a life-story for him as an English nobleman of the 17th century, who had killed himself after the execution of his mistress as a witch. They then held seances round a table, and after a time, as expectation built up, they heard raps on the table. Using the conventional 'one rap for yes and two raps for no' method, they questioned 'Philip' and got answers. Presently, the table began to behave in a weird way. 'Philip' somehow seemed to have become incarnate in the table and it jumped up and down, and sometimes chased after people. On television in Toronto in 1974, the table walked up three steps on to the platform and answered questions by rapping. The group, in effect, had successfully created a ghost.

years before but had never entirely quit duty. Many guests in the same room before had reported similar experiences.

‡

'MINE TO KILL'

‡

A wake-up call from a ghost, if unusual, is in a different league from the famous Amherst Mystery, one of the weirdest poltergeist cases on record. It happened in the small town of Amherst, Nova Scotia, in 1878, in a perfectly ordinary two-storey, timber-framed house. Living in the house was a 19-year-old girl named Esther Cox, who shortly before had suffered a traumatic experience when the man she was walking out with tried to rape her at gunpoint.

Strange noises were heard in the house and one night Esther screamed because she thought a mouse had got into her bed, but there was nothing to be seen. Soon things accelerated, and the whole family were horrified to see Esther swell in size before their gaze, while her eyes bulged, her hair stood on end and she shrieked that she was dying. A terrible hammer blow of noise like a thunderclap sounded through the house. After a while Esther's body returned to normal.

Much more was in store. The peculiar swelling up of Esther's body kept happening again, bedclothes were torn off the beds and pillows hurled about, there were loud knocking and scratching noises, and to the family's horror a message wrote itself on the wall: 'Esther Cox, you are mine to kill' in letters a foot high.

The phenomena, which were observed by the local doctor, clergymen and other reputable witnesses, continued. It was abundantly clear that the outbreak centred on Esther. When she left the house, the disturbances ceased, and when she returned, so did they. When a local restaurateur kindly took her in for a time, the poltergeist began throwing the furniture in his restaurant about. In the hope of making a profit out of it all, Esther was put on show. She sat on the stage, but nothing happened.

In the end Esther was turned out of the house altogether. She left Amherst and the disturbances stopped. No one knows much about what happened to her afterwards, except that she was later accused of burning down a barn. Unlike the equally celebrated Bell Witch case (*see page 51*), at Amherst the apparent centre of the manifestations was also their victim. If Esther Cox was responsible for what happened, it was herself she hurt. It has been suggested that this was a case of a genuine psychic invasion by a force from outside.

Below: the Papineau family house, between Montreal and Ottawa. During World War I, Talbot Papineau was away serving in the army in France, when his mother saw him, in uniform, from the window and heard him say 'I'm all right, mother'. In fact, at or close to that moment in 1917 he was killed in combat, at Passchendaele, and all his mother ever received was his twisted cigarette case. Bottom: Talbot Papineau in uniform.

‡

GRANDFATHER'S CLOCK

‡

Other Canadian cases which have attracted fascinated attention include a jinxed house in Montreal which for a century had far more than its share of murders, suicides and arson attacks before it finally burned down in 1906; the 'fire spook' which kept trying to burn down a farmhouse in the Caledonia Hills in Nova Scotia in 1922; the 'witch balls', or flying missiles, that persistently pelted a family on a farm at Baldoon in Ontario in 1829; and the disquieting experiences of a babysitter in a smart apartment in London, Ontario. In this instance the family poodle howled at something invisible, the air grew heavy and foul-smelling and the chandelier in the hall started to spin round by itself.

There is a charming little story from Winnipeg about a grandfather clock which stopped when its 72-year-old owner died. No one could find anything wrong with it, but no one could get it to go either. It was supposed by long tradition to be inherited by the oldest male in the family, but there were no sons, and at this time no grandsons. The widow kept the clock, which still refused to work, until one day she came home to find it ticking loudly. It had started by itself while she was out. A few moments later the phone rang with a message that the widow's first grandson had been born in hospital 15 minutes before.

MARVELS AND MADONNAS

It rained in Mexico City for a week before 12 December 1976, the feast day of the Virgin of Guadalupe, when the most venerated image in all Latin America was to be reverently transferred to her new shrine. It had been built for her because the multitude of pilgrims had become too great for her old one. The day dawned grey and gloomy, but just at the moment when La Senora de Guadalupe set out from her old home, the sun came out. None of her devotees was in the least surprised.

The shrine, now in Mexico City's

✢

The missionaries who went to Mexico and Central America in the wake of the Spanish conquistadores strove mightily to convert the conquered Indians to Christianity. What occurred, however, was not the intended take-over, but an amalgamation of Christian and Indian beliefs.

✢

instance, the image of St Francis of Assisi in the parish church attracts throngs of pilgrims drawn by its reputation for healing. Another famous healing image, in the church of Nuestra Senora de la Salud in Patzcuaro, in central Mexico, is a figure of the Virgin made of a corn cob in 1546.

Pilgrims venerate the charred and blistered wooden image of the Cristo de las Ambillas (Christ of the Blisters) in the cathedral at Merida in Yucatan. According to local legend, it was carved from a tree at Ichmul which had been struck by lightning and burned all night, but was not consumed. When the Ichmul church burned down, the

northern suburbs, is at the place where in 1531 the Virgin Mary appeared to an Aztec Indian who had been converted to Christianity. She was radiant in beauty, her garments shining like the sun, and the whole landscape was lit by her presence. With the aid of a miraculous shower of roses and an image of herself magically imprinted on the Indian's cloak, she succeeded in persuading the Spanish bishop to build her a church on the hill. That the hill had previously been sacred to the Aztec mother goddess, that the Mother of God had appeared to an Indian, not a Spaniard, and that she was dark-skinned, made a profound impression on the conquered people. Numerous

Blazingly colourful carnival costumes in Mexico celebrate the country's rich mixture of European and indigenous traditions.

miracles of healing were reported from the shrine, pilgrims flocked there and the Virgin of Guadalupe became the figurehead of Mexican nationalism and the successful movement for independence from Spain.

✢

THE BLISTERED CHRIST

✢

Guadalupe is only the most famous of many miraculous shrines in Mexico. At Real de Catorce in the north-east, for

figure miraculously survived and was moved to the cathedral. At Queretaro the Convent of the Holy Cross stands on the spot where St James appeared in a vision to awe the local Indians into surrendering to the conquistadores and a tree sprouted miraculously from a pious friar's staff.

In Nicaragua, when the authorities ordered the Black Christ of the mining town of Santa Lucia to be removed to Tegucigalpa, the image simply sulked. It grew steadily heavier until its bearers could move it no further. They decided to take it back home again, and it grew lighter every step of the way.

‡

THE HONOURED GODS

‡

Before the Spanish Conquest, the Indian peoples knew many gods and spirits. When Christianity overtook them, they did not stop revering them, but gave them the names of Christian figures and saints, and honoured them at ostensibly Christian festivals. They also continued to rely on their shamans, or 'prayer men', who understood the spirit world and could use magic to heal or harm.

Among the mountains of the southern Mexican state of Oaxaca, the Mixes Indians do not allow outsiders to attend their religious ceremonies, and rely on their shamans rather than western-style doctors. The tremendous Guelaguetza festival at Oaxaca every July goes back originally to celebrations in honour of the pre-Hispanic maize gods. The Tarahumara Indians of the west coast go readily to church, but also honour their ancestral deities of the sun and the moon. They too cherish their shamans and ancient rituals involving the sacred cactus and the hallucinogenic peyote derived from it.

At Chichicastenango in the highlands of Guatemala the Indians bring cobs of maize, the sacred plant of their native tradition, to the two churches of San Tomas and Calvario as offerings to Christian saints. They also worship a black image of a Maya god on a hilltop outside the town.

‡

HIGH FLIERS

‡

The state of Veracruz in eastern Mexico is famous for the spectacular ritual of the voladores, in blazingly colourful costumes. They climb to the top of a pole 65ft (20m) high, tie a rope to one ankle and then jump off and dangle upside down as their ropes

Riotously exotic costumes and head-dresses at a Roman Catholic ceremony in Mexico indicate the blend of Christianity with older, more deeply rooted ways and beliefs.

unwind and they descend to the ground.

The performance is packed with pre-Hispanic calendar symbolism. According to one interpretation, the men represent the sun and the four seasons of the year, and the four fliers circle the pole 13 times each on the way down, making 52 revolutions altogether, which is the number of weeks in the year and also a crucial number in the pre-Hispanic ritual calendar.

‡

THE SPEAKING CROSS

‡

Religion is inextricably entangled with politics in this area and miracles can be used for political purposes. The cross was a powerful religious symbol in Central America long before Christianity arrived. The Maya people connected it with the sacred maize plant, which they depicted as a human being with arms stretched out, to form a cross. They absorbed the figure of Christ on the cross into this tradition. On the Yucatan Peninsula green crosses are planted in the fields for fertility magic, and in the Mass the communion wafer is made of maize flour.

In 1850 a speaking cross began delivering oracles in the Maya language to its followers at a well in the remote district of Quintana Roo. It warned them against dealings with the whites and under its inspiration they raided European plantations. When a well-known local ventriloquist died, the cross seemed to lose its appetite for speaking and took to sending written messages. Nevertheless, the Maya have believed in it ever since.

In Nicaragua in 1981 the image of the Virgin in the church at Cuapa began to sweat – and later cry. Cynics maintained that every night the figure was dipped in water and put in a freezer, so that in the heat of the day it would exude water. Whatever the explanation, the reports fortified the confidence of the faithful.

THE DEVIL TO PAY

The number of Satanists at large in North America at any given moment is tiny – far smaller than either the media or fundamentalist Christians like to believe – but every now and again a case surfaces which stirs up ancient fears. In April 1989 headlines blazed across America after Mexican police discovered the murdered victims of a supposed 'Satanic cult of drug smugglers'. The 15 mangled bodies found on a ranch near Matamoros had been dismembered in gruesome rituals of human sacrifice and their brains had been cooked in a cauldron. The suspected head of the organisation was a Cuban immigrant and it was believed that the cult was related either to Santeria, the Cuban variety of Voodoo, or to a Devil-worshipping sect called Santismo. It was said that their 'Voodoo rites' were meant to protect the drugs gang from arrest and make them immune to police bullets. That the leader was not immune to all bullets was drastically demonstrated a month later, when he was machine-gunned to death in his flat in Mexico City by one of his own henchmen as the police closed in.

Later that year another sensation erupted with the conviction in Los Angeles of a vicious 29-year-old drifter from El Paso, Texas, named

The worship of the Devil, or Satanism, always bulks much larger in the popular imagination than reality remotely justifies, but there are occasional dramatic cases which nourish the fantasy.

Richard Ramirez, on multiple charges of murder and rape. He claimed to be a worshipper of the Devil and shouted 'Hail Satan' at the news cameras. 'Lucifer lives in all of us', he proclaimed in court. 'You maggots make me sick.'

Ramirez was a deranged loner and there was no suggestion that he belonged to a sect or group of any kind, but by the following year a deputy sheriff in Chicago was solemnly informing the media that 50,000 human sacrifices a year occurred in the United States – but no one had ever been convicted for such a crime. How he arrived at his absurd statistic the media failed to state. When the Boston Red Sox baseball team, said to have been jinxed ever since the owner sold the mighty Babe Ruth way back in 1920, erected a 'Voodoo shrine' in its clubhouse in the hope of changing the team's luck, amusement was muted.

Fear of the Devil can have comic consequences, even so. In 1993 at Vinton, Louisiana, a car which hit a tree was found to have 20 people in it, without a stitch of clothing between them. They were not having an orgy or trying to break a record. They were respectable Pentecostalists from Texas who had decided to travel together in this way, packed in like naked sardines, to outwit the Devil, who they feared had intended to accompany them.

Left: gruesome objects found on the ranch. Below: a typical headline.

Horror at Satan's Ranch

From GEORGE GORDON in New York

PLEADING for mercy, 23-year-old Sergio Martinez stood in a rain-sodden grave as he was forced to dig up the body of a man he helped to murder.

With sweat pouring down his face he slowly uncovered the 13th victim of the drug-smuggling Satanic cult...

SUSPECT DIGS UP VICTIM No. 13

the run with her boyfriend Adolfo de Jesus Constanzo who headed the drug ring and orchestrated the slaughter. He was known as the Godfather and she...

✣

TAKING POSSESSION

✣

Religions like Voodoo are no more dedicated to evil powers than Christianity is. What links them with the Devil in popular imagination and media fantasy is the phenomenon of 'possession'. The dramatic and eerie taking over of a person by what appears to be an alien non-human intelligence frightened those who witnessed it for centuries in Christian Europe, where everything strange and inexplicable tended to be attributed to Satan.

There was a whole succession of 'demonic possession' outbreaks in nunneries, when holy women dedicated to Christ went into frenzies in which they behaved in a most unsaintly manner. They howled obscenities and abuse, writhed lasciviously on the floor and twisted their limbs into extraordinary postures, claimed to be witches and to have practised cannibalism. Once this started, more and more nuns in a convent tended to be infected. When gruff voices spoke through their mouths, claiming to be demons, they were taken at their own valuation and everyone around crossed themselves urgently and sent for the exorcists. The theme has inevitably attracted the film industry and a minor epidemic of 'possession' films accompanied the post-war age of permissiveness.

Prostrate nuns in a scene from Mother Joan of the Angels, *one of a rash of post-war films about demonic possession.*

✣

'OUR AIM WAS TO GET YOU'

✣

Nowadays, when belief in the Devil is out of intellectual fashion, outbreaks of this kind are put down to contagious hysteria or other mental disturbance. Nevertheless, there are some modern examples where this explanation is contradicted by medical evidence.

In 1928 a 40-year-old woman known as Mary was exorcised repeatedly for more than three weeks at a community of Poor Clares at Earling, Iowa. She heard voices which put obscene and sacrilegious suggestions to her, she understood foreign languages which she had never been taught and she vomited up large quantities of repulsive matter. Her body swelled in size and she assumed demonic personalities which spoke through her. A series of medical examinations, however, failed to find anything wrong with her and she was declared to be mentally normal.

The 'demons' which spoke through Mary gave their names, which included Beelzebub and Judas. For some reason they particularly hated Father Joseph Steiger, a priest who assisted at the exorcisms. They followed him to his home (while Mary was confined in the convent) and made nasty gnawing noises and rappings on his walls. One day he was driving towards a bridge when a black cloud seemed to gather about him which made it impossible for him to see. He hit the bridge, wrecked the car and was badly shaken. When he returned to the convent, one of the demonic voices said through Mary, 'What about your new auto...smashed to smithereens...Our aim was to get you...' Eventually the exorcists triumphed and the demons were driven screaming from Mary's body, but she had to be exorcised again some years afterwards.

The Exorcist

William Blatty's celebrated bestseller, *The Exorcist*, was loosely – very loosely – based on a real-life case of 'demonic possession' in a Lutheran household at Georgetown, in the suburbs of Washington DC, in 1949. The victim was a 13-year-old boy, and poltergeist phenomena began to occur in the house after he had been fooling about with a ouija board. There were strange knocks and raps, and then mysterious footsteps sounded in his room. The family feared that the ghost of a relative who had recently died was responsible. Objects began to move about and the 'spirit' took to accompanying the boy to school and moving the desks. Taken to hospital for tests, he and his mattress both floated up into the air. The medical and psychological tests, however, showed no abnormalities.

When clergymen were called in, full-scale possession phenomena erupted. The boy had frightening seizures, he spoke in 'a gravelly, raucous voice' which poured out obscenities, he exhibited almost superhuman strength, his body swelled up and he spoke in Latin, which he had never learned. There were normal intervals between the attacks and eventually he went into a spasm and a mysterious explosion was heard. At that moment he was cured.

Scene from The Exorcist III, *part of a long-running, profitable saga.*

PATHS OF TRANCE AND VISION

The Indian peoples of what became Canada and the United States shared their world with numerous gods and spirits. These ranged from deities who were personifications of the great forces of nature – sky father and earth mother, sun and moon, wind and rain – to spirits inherent in animals and plants, guardian spirits and the souls of the dead. Religious rituals were required to establish friendly relations with these supernatural beings. There were specialists in the sacred, shamans or medicine men, who went into trances to make contact with the spirit world and who were sometimes possessed by the spirits. They also cured disease, predicted the future and warded off the hostile magic of enemies.

Beliefs varied with the different life-styles of Indian nations. The Algonquins of the north-east, who allied themselves with the French settlers in Canada, lived principally by agriculture. The fertility of the ground was a primary theme with them and their shamans conducted ceremonies on the sacred dancing grounds. The Ojibway, south of the Great Lakes, believed in a supreme being, the Great Manitou, who made the earth, and shook it in earthquakes, and who also made the human race. Longfellow's 'Hiawatha' was based on their traditions.

The Indians of the Great Plains – the Sioux, the Cheyenne, the Comanche and others – were the 'redskins' round whom such a rich Western mythology has gathered. It was in the 18th century that they acquired horses, the descendants of steeds brought to America originally by the Spaniards. They became formidable buffalo hunters and their religious rituals were directed primarily to ensure success in hunting and war. Each young

Visions and trances played a crucial role in the spirituality of the North American Indians, and in their resistance to the destruction of their ways of life by the white invaders of their land.

Top: one of the special 'ghost dance' shirts which were erroneously believed to be proof against the white man's bullets.
Above: Karl Bodmer's painting of the buffalo dance of the Mandan Indians.

warrior fasted until his personal guardian spirit revealed itself to him in a vision – usually in the form of an animal – and their greatest religious ritual, the

Sun Dance, was another route to the seeing of visions, through self-torture and the agonising rending of the warrior's flesh as he hung from a pole on skewers thrust into his body.

THE GHOST DANCE

With the coming of the white man and the missionary, many Indians were converted in whole or in part to Christianity, but some tried to blend it with their own traditions. In 1799, for instance, the Good Message movement was founded by a Seneca Indian named Handsome Lake after seeing visions. It combined Quaker principles with the traditions of the Iroquois people of the north-eastern United States, and commended the Bible as a good monotheistic spiritual guide, but it had no place for Jesus. It is still alive.

Other Indian visionaries would have no truck with white men's religion. After the Union Pacific railroad was completed, in about 1870, a shaman of the Paiute on the Nevada-California border saw a vision of a mighty train that would bring back all their dead ancestors. This would be followed by the destruction of the whites. One of his pupils became the prophet of the Ghost Dance movement which spread across the Rocky Mountains to the Great Plains, where it was taken up by the Arapaho, the Cheyenne and the Sioux under their veteran leader Sitting Bull. It involved a distinctive, shuffling dance by men, women and children. The steps had come to the prophet in a vision. It was performed for several nights at a time and was accompanied by singing. The dancers wore their full ceremonial dress, with paint and feathers, and during the dance some of them would go into trance to communicate with the dead ancestors.

The movement promised the reappearance of the ancestors. The whites would be driven away, the prairies would be black with the buffalo herds once again and the old way of life would be restored. Its adherents wore 'ghost shirts', which were believed to make the wearers immune to the white man's bullets. They did not, as was demonstrated when some 300 Sioux were mowed down by the rapid-firing Hotchkiss guns of the Seventh Cavalry at Wounded Knee Creek in 1890. The movement died away, but it had created a consciousness of Indian identity, across tribal barriers, which was its legacy to the peyote cults of the following century.

⁙

A SPIRITUAL KALEIDOSCOPE
⁙

The peyote religion spread slowly through the Indian reservations from the south, and had travelled all the way up into Canada among the Crow and the Blackfoot by World War II. It is thought to have been introduced originally from Mexico by the Apache, and the Comanche and the Kiowa took it up early on.

Peyote is a cactus native to Texas and northern Mexico which, when chewed, induces hallucinations often involving elaborate designs and vivid colours that change and re-form as if in a kaleidoscope. Through it the Indian escapes from the ordinary, everyday, depressing world of hopelessness to enter a richer spiritual plane of visions and dreams, and peyote is regarded as a healer and a potential saviour of the Indian people.

Rituals and practices vary considerably from one group to another. Women may or not be admitted, blacks usually are, whites usually are not. Ritual songs are sung to the beat of a drum. Some peyote leaders regard the religion as the Indian alternative to Christianity, but others have tried to blend the two. The Native American Church was founded in Oklahoma in 1918, specifically to foster belief in 'the Christian religion with the practice of the Peyote sacrament'. The Bible is set on an altar at services, invocations are addressed to the Trinity and the taking of peyote is treated as the equivalent of the Eucharist.

Spiritual Dimensions

Indian religious artefacts which the non-Indian outsider can admire today include the sand paintings of the Navajo people of Arizona and New Mexico. The paintings are symbolic pictures which illustrate Navajo mythology and are used in healing by a 'singer', who cures a patient after a 'hand trembler' has diagnosed the disease. Tourists in the south-west can also see, and buy, the Kachina dolls which are made by the Hopi and Zuni Indians, whose dancers impersonate spirits called Kachinas. The dolls are made for the young, to help them learn to identify the various spirits, and among their ranks is a frightening black one which punishes naughty children.

Right: an example of a Kachina doll, made by the Hopi Indians to teach the young about spirits.
Below: in this Navajo sand painting the cross is related to the four directions of spiritual space.

IS THERE ANYONE THERE?

The modern Spiritualist movement was born in 1848 in a little wooden house at Hyndsville in a backwoods area of New York State, where the Fox family began to hear disturbing rapping sounds at night. Two of the daughters, 14-year-old Margaretta and 12-year-old Kate, discovered that the rappings would respond to knocking noises, and worked out a code that enabled whatever was doing the rapping to answer questions. The 'spirit', which the girls nicknamed Mr Splitfoot, claimed to be the ghost of a man who had been murdered in the cottage.

When Mrs Fox took the girls to Rochester, the rappings went with them, and conveyed messages from dead relatives and friends of those present, for as word spread, many visitors came. One of them tried an interesting experiment. He took some small shells, closed his hand and put it out of sight, and asked for as many raps as there were shells in his hand. He got a correct answer. In case his own mind might be influencing the result, he tried again, this time picking up a handful without knowing how many he had taken, and again got a correct answer. Other sceptics were impressed, too, and if the Fox girls were somehow faking the raps (and no convincing explanation of how they did it has yet been produced), it still looks as if they may have had genuine psychic powers or were at the heart of an authentic poltergeist experience.

PALE HANDS I LOVE

Visitors witnessed other peculiar phenomena besides the thunderous rappings, which could be heard several rooms away. The table would tilt and move as they sat round it, a transparent hand was seen and chilly fingers touched

Almost everyone has played at communicating with the beyond by means of an upturned glass and a ring of letters, or sat round a table in dim light holding hands to await messages from spirits. It all goes back to a small house in upstate New York 150 years ago.

The three Fox sisters – Margaretta, Kate and Leah – are seen here wearing severely respectable apparel and expressions of virtuous solemnity. However, their uninhibited performances caused a sensation in the United States which spread to Europe and made communication with the dead all the rage.

people's faces or toyed with their hair. It was infectious. Other households in Rochester reported similar phenomena and when Kate Fox went to stay in Auburn, the same thing began happening there.

The time was ripe, and the Fox family's experiences caused an explosion of interest. The press trumpeted the case and the Fox girls and their older sister, Leah, became professional mediums. The legendary showman P T Barnum soon put them on stage, vulgarising communication with the dead into a music hall act.

HEAVENLY BAND

An epidemic of mysterious rappings, table tiltings and paranormal phenomena spread rapidly across the country as a host of mediums suddenly appeared out of the woodwork and a craze for seances and communicating with spirits gripped America.

At a farm owned by Jonathan Koons and his family in Dover, Ohio, spirits which apparently had nothing better to do in the afterlife played musical instruments, sang and addressed the assembled company through speaking trumpets. Elsewhere at seances objects appeared out of nowhere or moved about by themselves, spirits scribbled on slates, mysterious scents and lights materialised and melodious twangs issued from guitars strummed by no visible hand.

In 1860 a lifesize visible spirit – 'a veiled and luminous female figure' – materialised at one of the Fox Sisters' performances. It was the first of an army, for rival mediums were not to be outdone and visible spirits made of 'ectoplasm' – which all too frequently turned out to be cheesecloth or chewed-up newspaper – promenaded wispily about under the eyes of credulous audiences.

The Fox girls themselves led increasingly unhappy lives and sank into alcoholism. They hired a hall to confess that the whole thing had been a put-up job, but then quickly retracted the confession. Meantime, however, small groups of believers were forming. From these the first Spiritualist societies and churches developed. Many Spiritualists believed that they were demonstrating the truth of Christianity, some that they were the vanguard of a new religion, while opponents identified the movement as the work of the Devil and the 'spirits' as malevolent demons.

The movement also inspired the formation of the first organised psychical research societies. The Society for Psychical Research was founded in England in 1882 and the American Society for Psychical Research three years later.

✣

THE MEDIUM AND THE MESSAGE

✣

Spiritualism received a powerful boost in 1917 with the conversion of Sir Arthur Conan Doyle, author of the Sherlock Holmes stories, and the carnage of World War I substantially increased the numbers of the bereaved who longed to hear from their lamented dead. For all the fraud and fakery, and the cheating and exploitation of the bereaved and the gullible by charlatans, psychical research seems to have demonstrated that some mediums possessed genuine paranormal abilities – and that some mediums who would cheat when they could get away with it would produce genuine phenomena

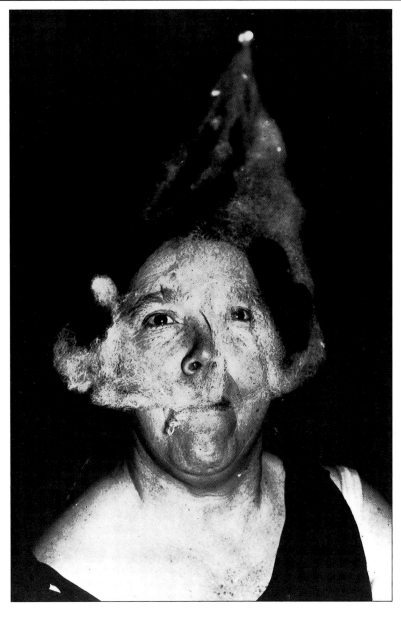

Ectoplasm extrudes from the mouth of a medium named Mary Marshall at a seance in Winnipeg, Canada, in the 1920s. Many fake mediums convincingly mastered this trick.

when they could not. This did not necessarily mean that genuine mediums were in communication with the dead. Their results could be put down to clairvoyance or to telepathy from the sitters, without the need to believe in an afterlife.

Some mediums go into trance, some into an abstracted, once-removed frame of mind. A voice may speak through the medium's mouth, claiming to be her 'control' or 'guide', which passes on messages from the dead to the sitters. In the early days, the guides were often small children or Red Indians (as they were called then). American Indian

shamans were specialists in communicating with the spirit world and the influence of Longfellow's much admired 'Hiawatha' was strong. Those who do not believe in survival of death explain the control as a secondary personality of the medium, split off from the medium's everyday consciousness.

Although the spirits with whom contact is made at most seances are, or purport to be, dead people of no special interest to anyone except the bereaved, mediums have claimed contact with far bigger game – from William Shakespeare to St Paul, Swedenborg to Edgar Allen Poe and Benjamin Franklin to the Archangel Gabriel. Unfortunately, these great beings seem to have little of interest left to communicate to an expectant world. Their exhortations to humanity and their accounts of conditions on 'the other side', though worthy, have seldom amounted to more than vaguely uplifting mush.

The same is true of the products of 'channelling', a phenomenon of recent years in America. The channeller is a person who transmits to humanity messages from someone deceased – an angel or other spiritual entity – by speaking them, writing them down or dictating them into a tape recorder. It is the same function carried out by the shaman, the prophet, the oracle and the medium in times past. A peak of absurdity was scaled in 1992 when a channeller in San Anselmo, California, advertised her service as a pipeline of communication for the profound intimations of the Barbie doll, the 'archetypal feminine essence who embodies the stereotypical wisdom of the 1960s and 70s'. Or perhaps, with luck, it was a joke.

COAST TO COAST

The craze for seances and communicating with the beyond which gripped America from the late 1840s brought with it the uncomfortable discovery – which many people have made for themselves since – that tampering with unseen forces can have unforeseen consequences. A minister in Stratford, Connecticut, for example, a Mr Phelps, was keen to make contact with the spirit world and held a seance in his house in 1850. It turned out to have been altogether too successful, in an unintended way, for soon afterwards he and his family returned from church to find that something odd had been going on at home. Someone or something with a sense of humour had moved the furniture about and made a number of life-size dummy figures out of pillows and cushions. This happened several times more.

Loud inexplicable noises began to sound through the Phelps' house, too, and other objects started moving about of their own accord. Harry Phelps, aged 12, was pelted by flying stones and his sister, Anna, aged 16, was also attacked, while things spontaneously caught fire and objects were smashed. Observers at the time connected the disturbances with the two children and when their mother took them away from the house, the outbreak ended.

✣

'WHERE DO I BELONG?'

✣

If the two living children were consciously or unconsciously responsible for the troubles in the Phelps' household, the ghost of a dead child was blamed for another outbreak in New England, more than 100 years later, in the 1980s. The case was investigated by W G Roll of the Psychical Research Foundation, and involved sightings of a boy, apparently aged about eight or nine, who was dressed in a white shirt, pants and shoes. The mother of the family once watched him walking in the hall for two hours,

✣

A ghost-to-ghost panorama of spectral experiences and encounters stretches across the United States from the Atlantic shore to the Pacific strand, and from New England to the Wild West.

✣

Wanted 'dead or alive' at the age of 18, according to the poster. Billy the Kid's troubled ghost might well have been as unpleasant and chillingly disturbing to meet as he himself was dangerous to encounter in life.

and found nothing frightening about the experience. Another time, she heard him saying sadly, 'Where do all the lonely people go?' and 'Where do I belong?'

Next her husband saw the boy, who told him that a lie had been told and the truth ought to be known. On another occasion he saw the figure apparently trying to pick up the rug in the hall. He picked it up himself and found underneath a small medallion. The ghostly boy allegedly said at one point, in relation to the lie which had been told, that his brother had blamed him when something in the house had gone missing.

The family's best guess as to the boy's identity was that he might be an uncle who had died aged eight 50 years or so before. Every time they mentioned his name over the telephone, the line went dead. There were some poltergeist phenomena in the house, too, but after an exorcism had been held, the disturbances ended.

✣

LAST POST

✣

Even the iron discipline of the United States military academy at West Point cannot deter a soldierly and determined spectre. In 1972 a cadet there saw a

REWARD
($5,000.00)
Reward for the capture, dead or alive, of one Wm. Wright, better known as
"BILLY THE KID"
Age, 18. Height, 5 feet, 3 inches. Weight, 125 lbs. Light hair, blue eyes and even features. He is the leader of the worst band of desperadoes the Territory has ever had to deal with. The above reward will be paid for his capture or positive proof of his death.
JIM DALTON, Sheriff
DEAD OR ALIVE!
"BILLY THE KID"

figure in 19th-century uniform, with a shako and a musket, emerging from a wall in a barracks block. No one was inclined to believe him, but the next night he and his room-mate both saw the ghost, which was afterwards observed by several more cadets. They found the soldier's picture in a print in the academy's gallery.

It is Fort Monroe in Virginia, however, the longest manned military post in the country, which boasts the most distinguished roll-call of phantoms. They include Jefferson Davis, President of the Confederacy, who was imprisoned there in 1865, and the two great adversaries of the Civil War, Robert E Lee and Ulysses S Grant. Virginia claims

keep stamps and small items in. It had been given to her by an aunt of hers, who seemed not unhappy to be rid of it. Presently she saw a strange shadow in the house, and then the ghost of a man. For some reason she associated it with the pottery cottage. Her daughter solved the haunting by taking everything out of the cottage. The ghost appeared no more, having apparently moved into its miniature and now vacant quarters.

The Wild West, too, has thrown up its share of ghost stories. The shade of Wyatt Earp haunts Tombstone, Arizona, where the redoubtable lawman won the famous gunfight at the OK Corral. The old Oregon Trail is haunted still by the dolorous spectres of men, women and

‡

TRUTH FROM THE GRAVE

‡

Over on the Pacific coast a sad story from Portland, Oregon, before World War I, concerns a family whose son was away on officer training for the US Marine Corps at Annapolis in Maryland. A letter arrived from him, which was perfectly cheerful and routine, but his mother, holding it, became convinced that something was terribly wrong. The next day word came from Annapolis that he had committed suicide, but his ghost appeared, trying earnestly to tell her that he had not killed himself but had been beaten up and shot. She saw the ghost several more

the largest and most eminent collection of ghosts of any of the states, headed by Presidents Washington and Jefferson.

The city of Philadelphia's name means 'Brotherly Love', which is appropriate to the story of a woman who looked in her bedroom wardrobe mirror and, instead of seeing the reflection of the room, saw American soldiers fighting in World War I, and her own brother killed. The official news of his death did not arrive until two months later.

GOING WEST

‡

In Las Vegas in 1982 a woman brought a little pottery cottage home from a trip to England and used it to

Above left: like many snuffed out prematurely, Wild Bill Hickok is reported to linger in the world. Above: ruts still mark the Oregon Trail. Ghosts, too, it is said.

children who went west, literally, and were killed by marauding Indians; and in Death Valley, California, the gold prospectors who died there in 1849 and gave the place its ominous name are still sometimes seen. The moustaches of Wild Bill Hickok have been seen in Deadwood, South Dakota, where he was killed in 1876 and lies buried. Jesse James has been spotted in Lawrence, Kansas, and Billy the Kid has never entirely abandoned Fort Sumner in New Mexico, where he was killed in 1881.

times, still trying to tell her what had happened and searching anxiously for the shoulder knot on his uniform, which he said he could not find.

The ghost continued to haunt the Oregon house even after the son had been buried, and eventually the family insisted on an exhumation. An independent examination of the body proved that the young man could not conceivably have shot himself, as claimed, and also, incidentally, noted that the shoulder knot from his uniform was missing. Who caused his death was never settled, but after the fact that he had not killed himself had been proved, the ghost faded away, as if the young man was satisfied that the stain on his honour had been wiped clean.

CALIFORNIA CHILLERS

If there is an ordinary town in California, it must be Bakersfield, 100 miles (160km) or so from Los Angeles, and if there is an ordinary section of Bakersfield, it is the prosperous, middle-class retirement community called Kern City. A widow named Frances Freeborn, however, moved into a house there late in 1981 and found something altogether out of the ordinary lurking inside, something which eventually drove her out of the house in panic in the middle of the night in her nightclothes.

The house had scarcely been occupied since the death of the previous owner, five years before, whose things were still in it. It needed clearing out, repair and redecoration. Mrs Freeborn went to work with a will, but became aware of a resistance, a curious pressure which seemed to be trying to prevent her altering the place. For instance, a small vanity bench which had belonged to the previous owner kept being mysteriously moved from the place where she put it. There were inexplicable noises, too, doors kept opening by themselves, drawers were pulled out and the lights started to act up. Her dog began to react oddly, too, as if someone unseen had called her.

✦

PICTURE, PICTURE ON THE WALL

✦

Then Mrs Freeborn started to hang up her pictures, including one of three women dressed in smart pre-Civil War costumes. She hung this picture up five times in five different places, and each time it was taken down overnight. Each time she found it propped against the wall below the nail, which was still in place, so it had not fallen off the wall. Presently she got a feeling that something forceful was directing her to hang the picture in the second bedroom, next to the light switch, though this was

✦

With its sunshine and its palm trees, its miles of gleaming Pacific beaches and its baking deserts inland, California might not seem to have enough shadows to hide ghosts and entities from other realms. Such an impression would be entirely mistaken.

✦

much too low on the wall for her and not a position she liked. She hung it there, and there it stayed.

It was afterwards discovered that this was exactly the spot where the previous owner had hung a very similar picture, and that the previous owner had been much shorter than Mrs Freeborn, just under 5ft (1.5m) tall, so she preferred her pictures lower on the wall. The previous owner, a Mrs Meg Lyons (not her real name), was a vibrant, vivacious, dominating person, who had absolutely loved the house, and had hoped that her own daughter would occupy it after her.

One day Mrs Freeborn came back to the house with wallpaper to redecorate the main bedroom, which had been Meg's. Late that night, in the bedroom, windows suddenly slammed open and shut, and the closet doors began to open and close, while the dog stood looking from one closet to the other, yapping excitedly. Terrified, she took the dog out into the hallway and sensed something there – 'a zone of pressure', she said, 'a mass out in the hall, as if something ominous and ugly was concentrated there'. Shouting 'Get out of my way' at the top of her voice, she charged along the hall. She says that she brushed past two invisible 'entities', while a third, in front of her, shrank back. She ran out of the house, still carrying the dog, into her car and away into the night.

The case was carefully investigated, and caused considerable dispute. It could be classified as a poltergeist outbreak, but the stock explanation would be that the phenomena were all caused, unconsciously, by Mrs Freeborn herself, and this is not easy to accept. Is she likely to have moved into a house and then created terrifying phenomena inside to prevent herself getting it to her liking? Is Meg's ghost a less improbable answer, and who were the other two entities?

✦

PARTY PIECES

✦

Not all Californian entities are as frightening as this. Los Angeles is famous for the movies and for its huge, lush cemeteries, stocked with solemnity and birdsong (on tape). If the cemeteries have ghosts, they keep them extremely quiet, but the movie world produces an occasional example. Glenn Ford and his wife reported friendly haunting effects from their garden, where some party from Hollywood's golden days seemed to be screening itself over again, with nothing to be seen, but the sounds of laughter and the chink of glasses sounding pleasantly on the night air.

On the other hand, Sir C Aubrey Smith, the veteran British character actor who introduced cricket to Hollywood (Boris Karloff was a stalwart of the team), once light-heartedly joined in a table-turning experiment at the house of friends, only to find himself isolated with an aggressive table which moved by itself and pinned him into a corner of the room.

✦

TAKE GOOD CARE

✦

A story of a crisis apparition, with an extra something in the tail, comes from San Diego, where a man was in his office with his partner when he heard his father's voice say, 'Well, I guess that's it, son. Kiss Katie for me, and you take good care now. Goodbye.' Startled, he turned round to see his father in the room, wearing old trousers and a checked shirt and holding a garden trowel in one hand and a bunch of marigolds in the other. Katie was the old man's much-loved grandchild. When he realised that his partner could not see anyone there, he rushed home and found his father lying dead in the garden, dressed exactly as he had seen him in the office and holding the trowel and the bunch of flowers. The extra ingredient is that later, when a second grandchild was born and the family were gathered at the hospital bed, the son said he wished his father had lived to see the day. 'But Daddy', his daughter Katie said, 'Grandpa's here, standing beside Mommy. Can't you see him?'

Also from San Diego comes another apparent case of alterations to a house stirring up something spectral, which occurred in the 1960s when the old Whaley House –

built for the Whaley family in the 1850s, and later a theatre and a court house – was turned into a historical museum and restored to its original grandeur. Ghosts in old-fashioned costume were seen and there were many reports of invisible presences, mysterious footsteps, blasts of cold air, wafts of perfume and cigar smoke. The organ in one room was heard playing, when there was no one there and the cover on the instrument was still shut. A man who sat down to play the piano felt invisible hands pressing down on his on the keyboard. At one point a whole group of men in frock coats were seen having a meeting in the study. It was as if the ghosts were trying to do their bit to bring the house's history to life.

Glenn Ford and his wife. The actor reported sounds of what seemed like a ghostly party in his garden in Los Angeles, with glasses clinking and a faint tang of the perfume Rudolph Valentino wore.

THE ALL-AMERICAN POLTERGEIST

If a bull is at its most merrily destructive in a china shop, the happiest and most fulfilling place for a poltergeist to find itself must surely be a warehouse full of breakable glasses, plates and ashtrays. This particular poltergeist's paradise was a wholesale novelty store in Miami, Florida, where wholesale mayhem broke out in 1967. The 'spirit' had a marvellous time smashing the stock day after day and it apparently spent one night throwing baseballs about, with deleterious effect. The owner called the police and a patrolman, going in to take a look, was hit in the back by an object. More police arrived. No one was hiding in the place and items kept falling off the shelves by themselves and breaking, until a police sergeant drew his gun and announced that he would shoot the next thing that moved. At which point so many things began moving that he holstered his gun, bewildered. Objects would fall and break noisily on the floor, but they were seldom actually seen moving.

Neither the police, nor a conjurer or the parapsychologists called in could find any normal explanation of the breakages, but it began to seem clear that it all had something to do with one of the employees, a 19-year-old clerk named Julio, a Cuban refugee, because so many of the items which fell were within a few feet of him. Psychological

✢

A whole succession of fascinating poltergeist outbreaks in the United States and Canada have involved the smashing of crockery and glassware, and sometimes vicious stone-throwing, apparently not caused by any normal agency.

✢

tests suggested that he had powerful feelings of hostility to authority figures, which centred on the owner of the business, but which he could not express outwardly. Taken to Duke University in North Carolina for parapsychology testing, he did not score well on psychokinetic (mind over matter) tests, but one of the dice-throwing machines kept malfunctioning when he was working with it, and while he was under observation a vase which was a clear 16ft (5m) away from him fell and smashed on the floor.

✢

CASTING THE FIRST STONE

✢

Smashing cups, plates and glasses is a common feature of poltergeist cases, and another is stone-throwing. A case at a house outside Tucson, Arizona, in 1983 was investigated by D Scott Rogo, a well-known expert on poltergeist infestations. The family in the house were father, mother and three children aged 15 to 20. The stone-throwing had

A still from Steven Spielberg's 1982 film, Poltergeist. *It centres around a small girl who unconsciously stimulated sinister impulses from the nearby graveyard. Supernatural evil was laced with fear and stirred into a witches' brew of nightmare.*

Something Nasty in the Woodshed

Poltergeists often seem more mischievous than downright evil. A weird and somewhat comical case in point was reported in 1889 on a Quebec farm in Canada, where crockery broke and fires started spontaneously. Suspicion centred on an 11-year-old adopted child of the household, named Dinah. Taken to the woodshed by Dinah, a visitor named Woodcock heard both sides of a conversation between her and an invisible entity, which delivered volleys of obscenities, announced that it was the Devil and vowed to break Woodcock's neck. With commendable calm, he managed to pacify it and as by now a small crowd of interested spectators had gathered in the woodshed, the entity obligingly put on a spectacular display for them all; 17 witnesses signed a statement that they had seen stones fly, fires break out and a mouth organ play by itself. Dinah and two other children said they could actually see the spirit. The entity, much encouraged and now a completely reformed character, began to sing beautifully and finally rose into the air 'like an angel' and vanished piously from view.

been going on for about ten weeks, usually starting in the late afternoon and continuing for two or three hours. Some stones landed on the roof, but most of them hit the front of the house or cars parked in front of it.

The family was convinced that a prowler was throwing the stones, but hard as they tried, they could never see or catch the culprit. Nor could the investigating police, whose cars were struck and dented. The family were so often painfully hit by the stones that they never went outside without a hard hat and they had large wooden shields for extra protection. When they shouted angrily at the supposed culprit, it always provoked an even fiercer volley of stones. When a local television station came filming, the stones flew thick and fast, and particularly targeted the sheriff and his car.

The outbreak stopped as suddenly as it had begun. Investigators noted that the stones flew at the house from outside when all the family were inside, but that there was little or no stone-

In San Jose, the oldest town in the state of California, the building known today as the Winchester Mystery House is a strange Victorian pile constructed from 1884 by Sarah L Winchester. Told by a medium that she would not die as long as she kept building, she went on adding towers and staircases, some of which led nowhere, until her death in 1922. She had a seance room inside and spirits are said to have helped her.

throwing when the whole family was away. It seemed clear that paranormal activity was involved.

✢

AERIAL BOMBARDMENT
✢

Other puzzling stone-throwing episodes include one in 1962 at Big Bear City, California, where instead of being hurled with vicious force, stones were seen 'floating' gently down from the sky on to the roof of a bungalow for four months, never hurting anyone and

feeling warm if they were picked up. Neither the police nor anyone else ever discovered where the stones came from. It began after a family with five children moved into the bungalow, but continued when different tenants replaced them.

Two years earlier, a used-car lot at Lynwood in Los Angeles was mysteriously pelted by stones, nuts and bolts, which came from all directions except the east, followed abnormal and unpredictable flight paths at great speed and mostly arrived horizontally. They hit the office and the garage, and were sometimes seen following people, including the investigating police. One flew in through the back door of the office and straight out through the front door. One of the employees, who had only recently been hired and who seemed 'disturbed', was arrested. When he was taken away the bombardment stopped, but the police readily admitted that he had been under surveillance when many of the stones were flying and could not have thrown them without being seen.

JEEPERS CREEPERS

Scratching and wounding people is a particularly threatening and unpleasant speciality of some poltergeists. An outbreak in Indianapolis in 1962 was investigated by W G Roll, the head of the Psychical Research Foundation, based at Duke University in Durham, North Carolina. In the house were a grandmother, who was a German immigrant, a mother and her 13-year-old daughter. Not only did objects move about by themselves and get broken, but the mother, and more often the grandmother, were bitten and scratched by some mysterious agency. Several times when Roll was present, the grandmother cried out and showed fresh punctures on her arm, her chest and elsewhere, which in some cases were bleeding. Investigation ruled out attacks by insects or any animal, nor could any skin condition be blamed.

The woundings stopped and were replaced by knockings, which were always close to the grandmother. At one point, when Roll was holding her to make sure she could not knock on the wall, the sounds were heard. Roll could see the mother and could see into the grand-daughter's room, and he was quite sure that the noises could not have been made by anyone in any normal way.

Poltergeist outbreaks are usually put down to one person, often a child or adolescent, but in this case Roll did not believe that the 13-year-old was responsible. He saw signs of intense strain between the two older women and suggested that both of them had generated the outbreak through their mutual tension.

Other commentators have pointed out the interesting way in which, not infrequently, a poltergeist will change its methods – in this case from biting to knocking – as if an intelligence was at work, with a considered strategy. This may not be easy to reconcile with the theory that someone in the house or on the scene is causing the disturbances unconsciously by psychokinesis (mind acting directly on matter).

The 'poltergeist personality' – the type of person who tends to be found at the centre of an outbreak – has long been recognised, but some cases suggest that there can be such a thing as a whole 'poltergeist family', which collectively creates a poltergeist.

THE FAMILY POLTERGEIST

Another case which seemed not to centre on one member of the family, but to involve the whole household, was investigated by D Scott Rogo in a suburb of Los Angeles in 1978-79. In the three-bedroom apartment lived four people: a man, his wife and the wife's 16-year-old daughter by a previous marriage, with her recently born illegitimate child. They had begun to notice a 'presence' in the hallway two years earlier, then they started to hear mysterious footsteps and at night they heard cutlery jangling and chairs moving in the kitchen. The disturbances tended to peak when the daughter was in the apartment, but they also happened when she was away. The neighbour downstairs heard some of the noises, too. The next development was that a box of cereal threw itself off the kitchen counter when there was no one near it. Other objects began to move about, as well. The disturbances stopped when the man and wife decided to separate, and parted company.

Psychological tests on the members of the family showed a similar pattern. They all possessed traits which have been found to be characteristic of the single agent usually identified at the centre of a poltergeist eruption – unhappiness, insecurity, recourse to an unrealistic fantasy life and fierce aggressiveness, directed against other people. Rogo suggested that as well as the typical 'poltergeist personality', it may be necessary to recognise the 'poltergeist family', whose collective tensions generate the poltergeist phenomena.

TERROR IN THE BASEMENT

It is possible that some hauntings, too, may be generated by the psychological state of the human beings in the case, and the boundary line between a haunting and poltergeist activity is not always clear. In 1970 Brad Steiger, a prolific author on the paranormal, accompanied a medium to a house in Lincoln, Nebraska, where something terrifying was going on in the basement. The two people in the house, a nervous woman and her teenage daughter, who was in an obviously disturbed state of mind, had stopped going down there at all, they were so scared. They had seen the ghost of a man there, thin-faced and shaggy haired, bearded and unshaven, and they had also seemed to see blood running down the wall.

They believed the man was the one who, years before, had murdered his wife in the house by shooting her in the head. He had been seen in a mirror in the house, and the appearance of a disturbing shadow had also been reported. The teenage girl felt that someone often peeped in at her through windows. There were loud unexplained knocking noises in the rooms, too. The medium sensed the presence of several entities in the house, but it is permissible to wonder whether the woman and her daughter had unconsciously called them into being.

FIRE, BURN!

Another exceptionally alarming type of poltergeist is the fire-raising variety. One caused a succession of fires in a house in Glace Bay, Nova Scotia. Every effort was made to find a rational

explanation of them – including faulty wiring and arson – but in vain. At one point, when arson was suspected and a police officer was on watch in the house, the policeman and several of the neighbours saw a section of wallboard begin to smoke and watched as a red glow spread from its centre, before snuffing the flames out. The cause of the fires was never found and they stopped as suddenly and unexpectedly as they had begun.

At Talladega, Alabama, in 1959, 22 fires broke out in a house during a period of a few days – 17 of them in one day alone. The fire experts could find no explanation. The family moved out, and five fires immediately started in the house they moved to. While police were on the scene a quilt hanging on a tree in the back yard caught alight. An officer

pulled it down and then tried to set light to it himself with matches. The material smouldered, but would not catch fire. After the police had gone, a loaf of bread caught fire.

The unfortunate family had to move twice more, despite consulting a local witch who gave them a spell against what she called a 'Voodoo hex' that had been put on them. Then, as so often, all the unpleasant activities suddenly stopped. The family's nine-year-old boy was arrested and confessed, under heavy pressure, to having started all the fires with matches, but neither the court nor the local fire marshal believed him. It has been suggested that the person at the centre of an outbreak like this somehow emits tiny quantities of the body's own electrical energy which act as sparks to start fires.

Fear of poltergeists and spirits in general is often sharpened by unpleasant experiences with a ouija ('yes, yes' in French and German) board or with a glass at the centre of a circle of letters. The device being used here is a planchette, or moving pencil on rollers. Leaving aside cheating, messages which come through from the mysterious 'beyond' are often alarmingly violent or obscene. There are also cases where messages are obtained which convey information not available to the conscious minds of the participants, and which turns out to be accurate. The general tendency is to trace both kinds of message to the unconscious mind and to human powers of extra-sensory perception, rather than to a discarnate entity of any kind.

ALIEN INTRUDERS

T he first reports of 'flying saucers' in American skies date from soon after World War II. The term itself was coined after a businessman named Kenneth Arnold was flying his own plane near Mount Rainier in Washington State one summer afternoon in 1947 when he observed nine disc-shaped, metallic-looking objects proceeding through the air in two files at a speed then attained only by rockets. They appeared to be completely round and moved in an undulating flight path. He said they looked like 'saucers when skipped over water', and the age of the flying saucer, which was to capture the imagination of the world, began from that moment.

A year earlier, however, a saucer had been seen, the first of many, or so he claimed, by a self-styled expert on Oriental religions and temporary short-order cook named George Adamski, a Polish immigrant living in California. In a book published in 1953 called *Flying Saucers Have Landed*, he also maintained that in 1952, near Desert Center in California, he had been the first human being to meet a visitor from a flying saucer, which turned out to have come from Venus. Apparently the Venusian male was about 5.5ft (1.7m) tall, tanned, blond and long-haired, wore a glossy brown uniform with no fasteners or pockets, and appeared to be in his twenties. He struck Adamski as profoundly beautiful, wise and loving. Communicating telepathically and by signs, he told Adamski that he and his people were alarmed by the development and testing of nuclear weapons on earth.

✢

The belief that the gods live in the sky is immensely ancient and widespread, and past centuries have produced many reports of supernatural beings from the sky intruding into life on earth. The dawn of the Space Age gave the idea a whole new lease of life.

✢

Space visitors on the screen: from The Day The Earth Stood Still.

✢

ALIEN HOMILIES
✢

Adamski gained substantial short-order notoriety and he later claimed to have made many other alien contacts – he was always bumping into humanoids from Mars, Jupiter and Saturn in Los Angeles bars (which may not entirely surprise those familiar with the bars of that city). Few students of Unidentified Flying Objects, as the American airforce started calling them in 1953, have ever been able to take him seriously.

However, his dramatic revelations set off a wave of other claims to have encountered beings from outer space. Some of them were of a benevolent, if intellectually sadly undistinguished kind, and others quite the reverse.

The aliens, as time went by, tended to come from further and further away in space and from increasingly weird locations. Tall, fair-haired beings who seized a woman from her car in Norwalk, Connecticut, in 1973 told her they came from the galaxy of Guentatori-Elfi. The visitors frequently lectured the earthlings about the dangers of nuclear war, materialism and human moral degeneracy. They displayed much the same fondness for vaguely uplifting sentiments about peace and love as the beings contacted by early Spiritualist mediums and the later 'channellers'. Cults grew up round some of them, too, and they ranged from Jesus to lovely Aura Rhanes, described as 'tops in shapeliness and beauty', who came from the planet Clarion, which is hidden behind the moon.

✢

ALIEN EUGENICS?

✢

One of the more impressive experiences was reported by a police patrolman from Socorro, New Mexico, in 1964. He saw two figures in white near a large spherical object, which took off with a roar and a jet of blue flame. He found four deep impressions in the ground where it had stood and the marks of a ladder, which he had seen leading from a door in its side.

Far more sensational was the encounter claimed by a married couple, Betty and Barney Hill, who were driving through the White Mountains in New Hampshire in 1961 when they saw a big, puzzling pancake-shaped object with windows descend from the sky near Indian Head. They forgot what happened next, but they seemed to have lost two hours of time and they began to suffer from intensely disturbing dreams.

Under hypnosis by a Boston psychiatrist (who believed they were fantasising) the Hills later recalled being taken on board, undressed and medically examined by the crew. They described the aliens as about 5ft (1.5m) tall, hairless with greyish skin, pear-shaped heads, domed foreheads and slanting cat-like eyes. The aliens, who came from a star named Zeta Reticulii, had been fascinated by Mr Hill's false teeth and they seemed to have taken a sperm sample from him. This revelation sparked off theories about extra-terrestrials conducting human breeding programmes. This in turn inspired the theory that an earlier programme of the kind might have been responsible for the appearance on earth of *Homo sapiens*, a far more advanced type of human being than the previous Neanderthals.

The Hills' story, written up in a successful book and later filmed, set a pattern. Since then, many more experiences with beings from space have been 'revealed' under hypnosis. People under hypnosis are intensely suggestible and will respond to the tiniest hint or indication given them wittingly or unwittingly by the hypnotist. The fact that evidence obtained in this way is totally unverifiable has not prevented it being trumpeted by people anxious to believe in encounters with space beings. Nor has it deterred hypnotists who believe in space beings from inducing improbable 'memories' of encounters.

Above: stories in pulp magazines of weird visitors from space, as in 'Thrilling Wonder Stories' of 1940, helped to inspire encounter tales.
Below left: an artist's impression of one of the aliens who abducted Betty and Barney Hill.
Below: a flying saucer in the desert?

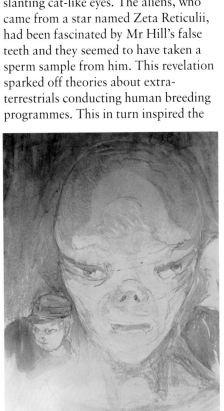

SINISTER VISITORS

One alien encounter which did not require hypnosis to bring it into consciousness occurred near Snowflake, Arizona, in 1975, when a group of men were clearing brush in a forest and suddenly a UFO appeared, hovering above the ground a few yards away. A 22-year-old forester named Travis Walton was hit by a beam of blue light from the craft and knocked unconscious. The others panicked and ran, and when they regained their nerve and went back a few minutes later, there was no sign of him or the UFO. The matter was immediately reported to the police, who mounted an unavailing search and said afterwards that they had no doubt the men were genuinely terrified.

After five days the men insisted on taking lie-detector tests because rumours were going round accusing them of murdering Travis Walton. Five of them passed the test, but the sixth was too nervous for it to be considered valid. That night Travis Walton returned. His memory of what had happened was patchy, but he said he had been taken away in the spaceship and examined by beings who were 5ft (1.5m) tall, hairless, with emaciated bodies, greyish skin and domed foreheads. They had huge eyes, with small noses, mouths and ears. There were others who looked just like human beings. He said the aliens had finally dumped him some miles from the forest.

UFOs and their alien crews may come from outer space, or from the inner space of the human mind. Stories about them, and the eager reactions they arouse, provide textbook examples of the age-old human appetite for evil otherworldly figures.

A still from The Exorcist *suggests the sinister figure of 'the man in black' juxtaposed with an image of the all-pervading bureaucracy associated with him – the 'no parking' sign.*

ALIENS WITHIN

Travis Walton also passed the lie-detector's scrutiny. His description of the aliens, which he said looked like overdeveloped foetuses, resembles those given by many others who claim to have been abducted (though there are plenty of quite different descriptions). Does the foetus-like description stem from a confused traumatic memory of one's own birth experience, as has been suggested, or is there perhaps at the back of it an idea that the human race has gone astray, has developed wrongly from its original potential? This would fit in with the moral and reproving emphasis of the communications reported from so many alien visitors.

No convincing evidence has yet turned up for a single case of a human being encountering an alien from outer space. There is clearly a symbiotic relationship between the stories and science fiction, which had beings from the stars visiting earth long before UFOs were heard of. All the same, the stories throw a fascinating light on the human psyche and the strangely persistent need for otherworldly visitors.

THE MEN IN BLACK

A recurrent motif in some of the stories is the appearance of 'the men in black'. There are many variations of detail, but they are all sinister figures who arrive on the scene after an abduction is over. Very often they arrive so soon afterwards that they can hardly have heard of the abduction by any

The Nephites

Not all otherworldly visitors are sinister. The predecessors of today's aliens from outer space include the three Nephites of Mormon tradition, who come to intervene in human life. According to the Book of Mormon, the Nephites were descended from Jews who emigrated to the New World six centuries before the time of Christ. Visiting them in America, Christ gave three of them a special dispensation to remain alive until the Second Coming. Meantime, they are permitted to show themselves to individual human beings when they think fit. Christopher Columbus encountered them and there are many stories in popular Mormon tradition of the Nephites appearing to help one of the faithful in time of need. In this century the tales have started to blend in with the motif of the vanishing hitchhiker *(see page 81)*.

An example is a story from Ogden, Utah, about two Mormon ladies who saw an elderly man in an old-fashioned tailcoat, with a grey beard, hitching a lift along the road. As he looked kindly and seemed tired, they stopped and picked him up. They drove on and he told them that a time of famine and pestilence was approaching and that they should take care to store food (as the Mormon authorities were officially recommending at this time). When he fell silent and they turned to the back seat, he had mysteriously vanished from the car and they never saw him again.

them. Or perhaps they are zombie-like human beings who are controlled by the alien intelligences. They talk the stiff, inhuman English of the bureaucracy (in the manner of so many real bureaucrats who talk and write English as if it was a foreign language). Their physical movements are often awkward, too, as if they were not used to human bodies.

The men in black – there are usually two or three of them – call on a person who has been abducted, or who has been close to an abduction, to tell them to keep quiet about it. They are polite, but menacing. They may show official identity cards and give their names, but any attempt to track them down afterwards runs into a blank wall.

Behind the men in black is the widespread belief that governments are generally hostile to UFO reports, and want to hush them up, and more generally the awareness that governments are intensely secretive. The men in black satisfy prevalent paranoia. The stories are also, surely, a reaction to the power of the bureaucracy in everyone's lives in the West, and they sometimes provide an escape hatch for people who have fantasised a UFO experience, have become uncomfortable and now want no more to be said about it. The men in black are a remarkable contemporary example of the human fear of, and need for, sinister supernatural figures.

normal means. They have not seen news of it on television, heard of it on the radio, read about it in the press or been told about it by the neighbours. No, the men in black know all about it because they are in league with the aliens, though they often pretend to be secret agents of the government. They look like parodies of government agents, dressed in neat black suits, with immaculate white shirts, quiet ties, dark socks and polished black shoes. They often wear hats.

They may be aliens themselves, disguised as human officials but with something foreign and alarming about

Above: sinister visitants are psychologically needed. This unidentified flying object, resembling nothing so much as a huge black hat, was photographed at Passaic in New Jersey, USA, in 1952. Right: Jeff Morrow in the grip of a weird mutant in a 1955 film. Entitled This Island Earth, *it was one of dozens of the genre.*

LAND OF WONDERS

'If you believe that old country mansions are haunted, why not a jumbo jet?' The remark comes from John Fuller, whose 1978 book, *The Ghost of Flight 401*, told the story of an extraordinary series of spectral appearances on commercial flights. It began in 1972 when an Eastern Airlines jumbo jet, Flight 401, coming in to land at Miami, crashed among the tangled swamps of the Florida Everglades. There was heavy loss of life and among those killed were the captain, Bob Loft, and the flight engineer, Don Repo.

Pretty soon, crews and passengers on other Eastern Airlines flights began to see the ghostly figures of Loft and Repo aboard. In one incident a vice-president of the airline went aboard a Miami-bound plane at John F Kennedy Airport in New York, got talking to a uniformed Eastern Airlines captain and realised to his astonishment that it was Bob Loft. In another, a voice over the intercom told passengers to stop smoking and fasten their seat-belts; none of the crew had made the announcement, and the PA system was not turned on. Another time, a stewardess and an engineer saw Repo, who warned them of fire. Sure enough, a fire did start in one of that plane's engines,

An age of materialism, it may be, but all sorts of marvels are reported from America's technologically advanced society – from haunted aeroplanes to jinxed bridges, deathly automobiles and phantom hitchhikers.

though not until months afterwards. The ghosts were perfectly friendly and in many cases the two dead men seemed to be trying to make sure that no harm came to the flight. It all stopped after an exorcism was held on the plane that had been most affected.

TRANSPORT TALES

After four shipping accidents had taken more than 50 lives in five months at the Sunshine Skyway Bridge at Tampa Bay, Florida, in 1980, word began to spread that the bridge was under a curse. It was rumoured that one of the construction workers had fallen into the wet cement when the bridge was built, 25 years before, and had been built into the structure. He was now taking a delayed revenge.

No curse is said to attach to the ghost train which has been seen several times in Pittsfield, Massachusetts,

Above left: the Sunshine Skyway Bridge in Florida could hardly enjoy a more cheerful, light-drenched name, but so many accidents occurred here it was rumoured to be under a curse.
Left: terror in a diabolical car: a still from Christine.

hauled by a steam engine and heading towards Boston, when no real train was on the track. Reports have come from truck drivers crossing the prairies at night in Dakota and Nebraska, of catching glimpses in their headlights of spectral wagon trains or pony express riders left over from pioneer days.

✢

PHANTOMS OF THE ROADSIDE
✢

Much more frequently told, however, is the story of the vanishing hitchhiker. This is one of a class of tales, nowadays known as 'urban legends', which do the rounds and are fully believed by most of those who pass them on. In this particular one, which is as old as the automobile itself, someone is driving along – often on a deserted highway or at night – and sees a person standing at the side of the road signalling for a lift. The driver gives the hitchhiker a ride, and he or she seems perfectly normal and friendly, but then suddenly vanishes and proves to have been a ghost.

In an example heard in Toronto, Canada, in 1973, a father and his daughter gladly gave a girl a lift a few miles to her home, but when they got there, she had unaccountably vanished from the back seat. They knocked at the house and the people who lived there said their daughter had disappeared years ago and was last seen hitchhiking on that very road. Today, as it happened, was her birthday.

In a variant told in Chicago in 1941, a cab driver picked up a nun downtown and took her to her convent. They chatted pleasantly on the way, but when he drew up at the convent, there was no one in the back of the cab. Alarmed, he rang the convent doorbell and explained what had happened. Inside he saw a photograph of his fare, and was told she had been dead for ten years. In a San Francisco episode of 1942 the cab-driver realises that his passenger was the Virgin Mary herself.

A version from Berkeley, California, 1935 vintage, is about a man driving along who gave a lift to a girl one rainy night. As they were chatting, they nearly crashed into another car – and would have hit it if the girl had not pulled on the emergency brake. When the man recovered from the shock and looked towards his passenger, there was no sign of her. Afterwards he discovered that a

A lonely Californian highway, ripe for a phantom hitchhiker.

girl had been killed in a car crash at that same spot a year before.

✢

THE DEATH CAR
✢

A wealth of folk legend is a by-product of America's love-affair with the car. Among the oft-repeated stories are variants of the one about the girl and her boyfriend who are out in the car one dark night when they hear on the radio that a dangerous escaped maniac is at large. Then they run out of petrol, and he gets out to walk to a gas station, telling her to stay inside the car with the doors locked, and on no account to open the door unless she hears his signal of three knocks on the window. Time goes by and she gets more and more frightened, until she hears knocks on the window, but the knocks don't stop at three. They go on and on, until she discovers that the sound is made by her boyfriend's shoes as his hanged body swings from a tree above the car.

Another favourite story tells of a second-hand automobile which is going unbelievably cheap. It turns out that the reason for this is that a previous owner either committed suicide or was murdered in it, and the corpse remained undiscovered for a week or more. Since then no one has been able to get 'the smell of death' out of the car. This legend has been traced back to Mecosta, Michigan, where in 1938 a man committed suicide in a 1929 Model-A Ford and the body was not discovered for three months. This genuine incident seems to have been the origin of the whole 'death car' legend, now passed eagerly on nationwide.

SOUTH ✦ AMERICA ✦

The biggest New Year's Eve party in the world explodes on the famous Copacabana and Ipanema beaches in Rio de Janeiro on 31 December every year, as hundreds of thousands of Brazilians, clothed in white like the sea foam, gather to the throbbing of the drums to dance and strew white flowers and light candles. At the stroke of midnight they surge into the sea and throw offerings on the waves. The party and the offerings are in honour of Iemanja, the African sea-goddess, who is identified with the Virgin Mary in the cults which are the Brazilian equivalents of the Voodoo religion of Haiti.

A gigantic statue of the Redeeming Christ towers above Rio, while a colossal figure of the Virgin Mary looks out protectively over Santiago, the capital of Chile, and another over Quito, the capital of Ecuador, but the South American 'supernatural' heritage is far more complex than these images suggest. The Christian traditions of the European conquerors and immigrants have mingled with those of the conquered Indians and those of the African blacks who were shipped across the Atlantic as slaves, to create a rich and savoury stew of beliefs and rites. An added ingredient, especially in Brazil, is 19th-century Spiritualism, imported from France.

The two largest and most important

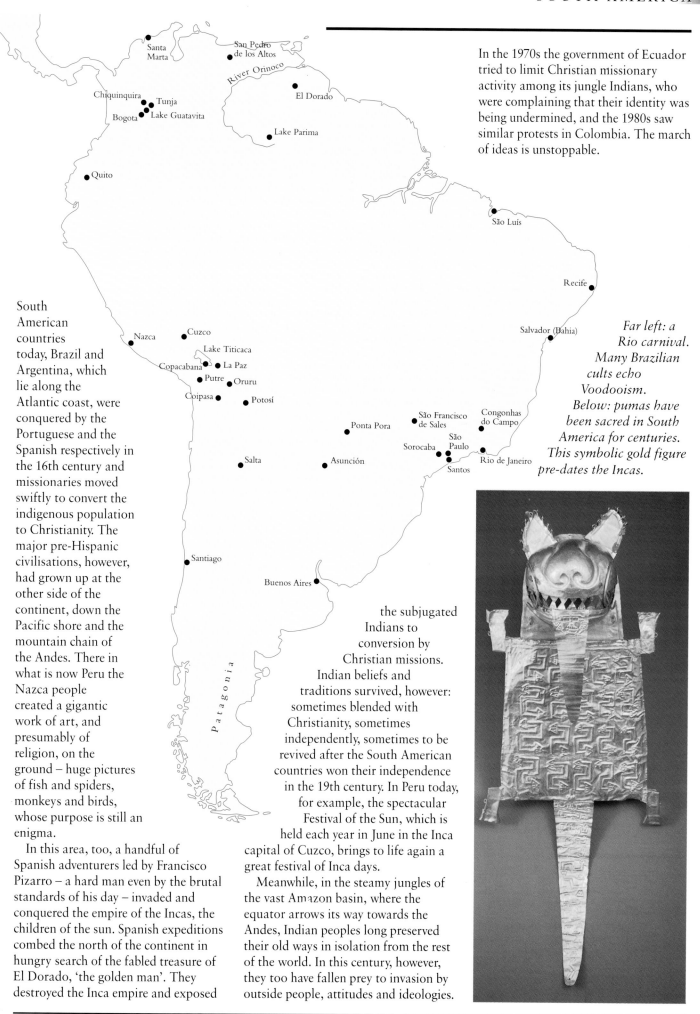

In the 1970s the government of Ecuador tried to limit Christian missionary activity among its jungle Indians, who were complaining that their identity was being undermined, and the 1980s saw similar protests in Colombia. The march of ideas is unstoppable.

Far left: a Rio carnival. Many Brazilian cults echo Voodooism. Below: pumas have been sacred in South America for centuries. This symbolic gold figure pre-dates the Incas.

South American countries today, Brazil and Argentina, which lie along the Atlantic coast, were conquered by the Portuguese and the Spanish respectively in the 16th century and missionaries moved swiftly to convert the indigenous population to Christianity. The major pre-Hispanic civilisations, however, had grown up at the other side of the continent, down the Pacific shore and the mountain chain of the Andes. There in what is now Peru the Nazca people created a gigantic work of art, and presumably of religion, on the ground – huge pictures of fish and spiders, monkeys and birds, whose purpose is still an enigma.

In this area, too, a handful of Spanish adventurers led by Francisco Pizarro – a hard man even by the brutal standards of his day – invaded and conquered the empire of the Incas, the children of the sun. Spanish expeditions combed the north of the continent in hungry search of the fabled treasure of El Dorado, 'the golden man'. They destroyed the Inca empire and exposed the subjugated Indians to conversion by Christian missions. Indian beliefs and traditions survived, however: sometimes blended with Christianity, sometimes independently, sometimes to be revived after the South American countries won their independence in the 19th century. In Peru today, for example, the spectacular Festival of the Sun, which is held each year in June in the Inca capital of Cuzco, brings to life again a great festival of Inca days.

Meanwhile, in the steamy jungles of the vast Amazon basin, where the equator arrows its way towards the Andes, Indian peoples long preserved their old ways in isolation from the rest of the world. In this century, however, they too have fallen prey to invasion by outside people, attitudes and ideologies.

THE SURGERY OF THE DEAD

Devotees of the Umbanda religion (*see page 87*) may find themselves possessed, not only by one of the deities of the cult, but by the dead. Alma Guillermoprieto's friend Celina, for instance, who was the human mouthpiece of the god Omolu (*see page 89*), was also regularly taken over in her home by a spirit named Seu Malandrino. She was then startlingly transformed into a tough, swaggering, masculine character, who wore a white shirt and trousers, and a white boater hat, drank quantities of beer, chain-smoked cigarettes and swore copiously. He was experienced in magic and for a fee sold remedies and spells to people suffering from sickness or the hostility of an enemy.

Seu Malandrino was an egun, the spirit of someone who has died and can move between the different planes of human beings and the gods. In life he had been the wastrel son of a rich family in Bahia and had been killed in a knife fight. Because he had caused his parents such sorrow, he had been sent back to the human world to repair the harm he had done. Alma Guillermoprieto liked Celina, but she did not like Seu Malandrino with his nasty little eyes.

According to widespread Brazilian belief, the dead intervene in the human world in many capacities, from prescribing healing potions to performing successful surgical operations without anaesthetics.

THE BOOK OF THE SPIRITS

Belief in possession by the dead in the Afro-Brazilian cults was influenced by the 19th-century Spiritualist movement, which came to Brazil from France under the name of Spiritism. The craze for seances and table tilting which started in the United States in the late 1840s (*see page 66*) spread swiftly to Europe and was in full swing in France in the 1850s. In 1857 *The Book of the Spirits* was published, under the pseudonym of Allan Kardek, which concealed the identity of Hippolyte Rivail, previously the author of numerous blameless school textbooks. Kardek later wrote *The Book of Mediums* and *The Gospels According to Spiritism*, among other books. He believed he had been a Druid named Allan Kardek in a previous life and said that all his writings on Spiritism had been dictated to him from the other world. He was a Christian and he believed that communications from the dead

proved the folly of scepticism and materialism.

Kardek's teachings had only a brief vogue in France, but much greater impact in the Philippines and also in Brazil, where they were forwarded in the 1920s by a white Brazilian Catholic named Zelio de Moraes, who believed himself possessed by the spirits of dead Indians. Spiritist temples and healing centres were opened, at which souls wandering confused after death were helped to find rest and healers directed curative influences at patients' auras through the laying on of hands.

A DEAD HAND ON THE KNIFE

The most startling development, however, in both the Philippines and Brazil, has been 'psychic surgery', in which operations are carried out without anaesthetics by untrained healers who are supposedly under the control of deceased surgeons. The best-known of these healers, a Brazilian nicknamed Jose Arigo (real name Jose Pedro De Freitas), carried out hundreds of successful surgical operations of this kind in the 1950s and 1960s, using unsterilised kitchen knives, nail scissors and other homely implements, without anaesthetics and without causing pain. He worked under the direction of a dead German army surgeon, 'Dr Fritz', who was killed in World War I.

Arigo seems to have been in a trance during the operations. While they were going on he spoke with a German accent, and once, when he was shown a film of himself merrily butchering away with the knives and scissors, he fainted. He had a surgery in his native town of Congon Las do Campo, where he dealt with hundreds of patients and would accept no fee. He was observed on one typical occasion casually using nail scissors to cut a cataract out of a woman's eye, without antiseptic or

Medical commission for psychic surgery?
DOCTOR WHO HAS HAD SPIRIT OPERATION PROPOSES ON-SPOT PROBE IN BRAZIL

anaesthetic. He wiped the scissors on his shirt and then plunged them straight into the patient's cornea. She felt no pain or alarm at any point, and the treatment was completely successful.

It is easy enough to diagnose Arigo as a case of split personality, but this hardly accounts for his extraordinary surgical feats. He himself apparently simply believed that he was taken over by the German surgeon, with the permission and approval of God, to heal the sick. He was arrested and jailed in 1965 for practising without a licence, but hundreds of grateful patients sang his praises. Arigo was killed in a car crash in 1971.

✣

SLEIGHT OF HAND

✣

There is no evidence that Jose Arigo's feats were anything but genuine, and some other psychic surgeons practising in Brazil and Paraguay may well be entirely sincere, but there is no doubt that fakes and swindlers have moved in on the act. What generally happens is that the 'surgeon' arms himself first with a lump of bloody meat from an animal, which he keeps concealed in his hand. By skilfully moving his fingers on the patient's skin, he creates a convincing impression of having thrust his hand deep into the patient's body. Then he 'withdraws' his hand, triumphantly clutching the chunk of meat as if he had wrenched it from deep inside the patient.

A few smears of blood on the patient's skin are then wiped away, and to the astonishment of all present, no sign of an incision can be seen on the patient's flesh. The 'surgeon's' shills in the crowd lead the enthusiastic applause and the supposedly diseased lump of meat is taken away for 'ritual destruction' – which makes quite sure that it cannot be removed to a laboratory for proper examination.

Far left: Jose Arigo, the most famous of Brazil's psychic surgeons, pictured in a report by Psychic News *in 1966. Right: a sequence of photographs shows stages of an operation being performed by another psychic surgeon. In this case he is removing a malignant growth.*

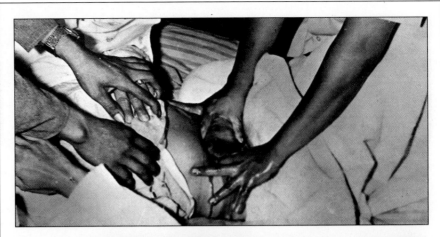

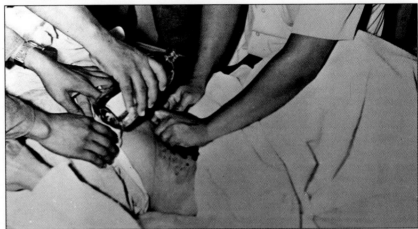

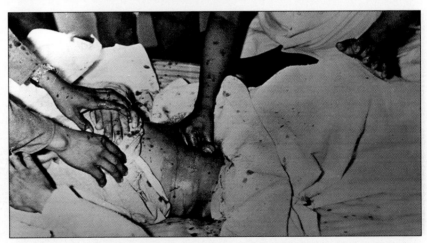

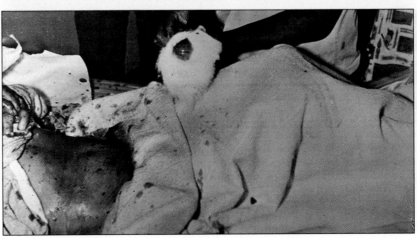

GODS OUT OF AFRICA

In 1992 a footballer was suspended from the Brazilian first division team of Bahia on suspicion of employing sorcery to harm the side's chances by enlisting against it a supernatural entity called Exu-Trancarua. The suspension followed a number of 'inexplicable' errors in the Bahia team's performances and equally 'inexplicable' injuries to key players. The run of disasters culminated in a crucial relegation match when the trusty Bahia goal-keeper, evidently bewitched, passed the ball straight to an opposing forward, who scored the goal that decided the game against Bahia.

The province of Bahia, with its capital at Salvador da Bahia on the coast, on the Bay of Saints north of Rio de Janeiro, is in the north-east of Brazil,

✣

South America's largest country is equal to Europe in size and is overwhelmingly Roman Catholic, but Brazilian Christianity has been powerfully influenced by black gods from Africa.

✣

Above: Brazil is famous for the lavish costumes and wild abandon of its carnivals, with the rival 'schools' of samba dancers parading in their finery. This one is in Pimentel. The carnivals have been strongly influenced by the legacy of the African slaves.

the area to which Africans in their hundreds of thousands were shipped to work as slaves on the sugar plantations. No one knows how many of them were ripped from their homes and lives to endure the horrors of the slave ships that crossed the Atlantic, but the lowest estimate puts the figure at three million and the true figure may have been as high as 15 million. It was the great goddess Iemanja (*see page 88*), they believed, who brought safely over the sea those of them who survived.

✣

THE MELTING POT

✣

The slaves came principally from West Africa, from Nigeria, Angola and the Congo, but some were transported to

Brazil from as far away as the Sudan and Mozambique in eastern Africa. The Yoruba people from Nigeria had a particularly powerful influence. With them the slaves brought their religious beliefs, their deities and their priest-magicians and healers. In Bahia the blacks mingled with the local Tupi Indians and amalgamated some of the Indian gods and spirits, including those of the Jaguar and the Alligator, with their own.

Some of the Africans were Muslims, which introduced Islamic ingredients into the mix. They were forcibly converted to Roman Catholic Christianity by their Portuguese owners and identified the great spiritual beings of this new faith with their own reliable and well-understood deities. Iemanja, the queen of the sea, was the same as the Virgin Mary and acquired the candles of the Virgin in her role as Our Lady of the Lamps. Jesus was the god Oxala, the warlike god Ogun was St George, the hero who slew the dragon, while Xango was St John the Baptist.

Oxossi, a god of hunting, is seen under the guise of St Sebastian, pierced with arrows; the goddess Isana is St Barbara; the mischievous child godlings called Ibeji are St Cosmas and St Damian, and so on. In Brazilian shops selling religious supplies, along with matronly images of the Virgin, are strings of plastic beads in the colours of the African deities – blue and white for Iemanja, red for Isana, blue and green for Oxossi – as well as herbs and magic potions.

✣

AN AFRO-LATIN BEAT
✣

In Bahia the religion was called Candomble. The plantation owners put a ban on African cults, but they generally tolerated night-time sessions of drumming, dancing and singing in the slave quarters, not realising that these were not merely for relaxation and entertainment after the day's work was done, but were part of the worship of the slaves' own deities. From these sessions there developed a distinctive Afro-Brazilian style of music, which produced a characteristic dance, the samba.

The dance was long banned by the authorities because of its wild and

Below: candles outside a Rio church of the Virgin Mary also honour Iemanja, African goddess of the sea. Middle: a ceremony in Rio. The Candomble cult moved to the capital from the slave area in the north-east. Bottom: an offering to the sea-goddess waits for the waves on Rio's famed Copacabana beach.

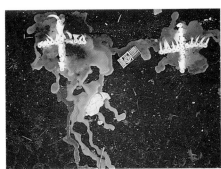

patently non-Christian character, but all attempts to suppress it were in vain and today the 'schools' or associations of samba dancers take the lead in the tremendous Brazilian carnivals which draw tourists from all over the world. Thousands of dancers in spectacular costumes make the most famous one of all – in Rio, on the days leading up to

Shrove Tuesday – a byword for excitement, but Salvador and São Paulo pride themselves on almost equally glittering fiestas and there are others in many Brazilian towns.

✣

OFFERINGS TO THE GODS
✣

Salvador, which was the capital of Brazil until 1763, is said to have a church for each day of the year, but it has ten times as many terreiros, or Candomble temples. In the dying days of slavery, in the 1870s, blacks from Bahia began moving south to Rio and the first temples there were founded. In Rio the religion was called Macumba. A widespread form of it today, all over Brazil, has been influenced by 19th-century Spiritualism and is called Umbanda. No longer a cult of the poor, Umbanda today crosses all social and religious barriers in Brazil and many of its faithful adherents go to church services as well as terreiros. A death in a Catholic family may be followed by a ceremony which involves not only Mass celebrated in a Catholic church, but also the sacrifice of animals to the Umbanda gods and to the dead person's spirit, with dancing and singing.

In country areas modest offerings to the spirits can often be seen by the roadside. They are intended for the god Exu and his spirits, who are the messengers of the gods and are invoked at the beginning of religious rituals to set up the connection between the worshippers and the deities.

LORDS OF THE TRANCE

A good deal of embarrassment was expressed before the Pope's arrival in Brazil in 1991 over the changes he would see since his previous visit in 1980. The percentage of those professing themselves Catholics had dropped from 95 per cent to 75 per cent, evangelical Protestant churches had been making headway and the Afro-Brazilian cults were gaining more and more middle-class supporters. One of their advantages is that in ecstatic rituals, which may go on for hours, they put the worshippers in direct contact with the deities of the religion. These then descend and take possession of devotees in trance, through whom they speak to the faithful.

William Sargant, the eminent British psychiatrist, watched a ceremony in the north-eastern town of Recife in 1964. Animals had been killed and burned in

✢

At festivals held on the beaches of Brazil devotees drum, drink and dance their way into trance to unite themselves with the deities of Afro-Christian cults. These rituals have been enjoying increasing popularity and to some extent Catholicism has taken a back seat.

✢

In Manus, in the Amazonian province of Brazil, a patient has come for treatment by a Macumba healer who has been possessed by a spirit known as the Old Black Slave. These treatments are often effective.

sacrifice to the gods before the ritual began. There was drumming and dancing as the worshippers circled the room and some of them went into trance states and behaved in the manner of the spirit which had taken them over. Some of those possessed by Ogun, for instance, dressed up in his characteristic costume with a hat and a dagger. The states of possession were violent and dramatic, with extraordinary facial contortions, trembling and shaking. They often ended in complete collapse, at which point those possessed were taken away to a private room.

✢

CHAMPAGNE FOR ONE

✢

There are spectacular festivals in honour of Iemanja at Salvador and elsewhere on the north-east coast. Buses

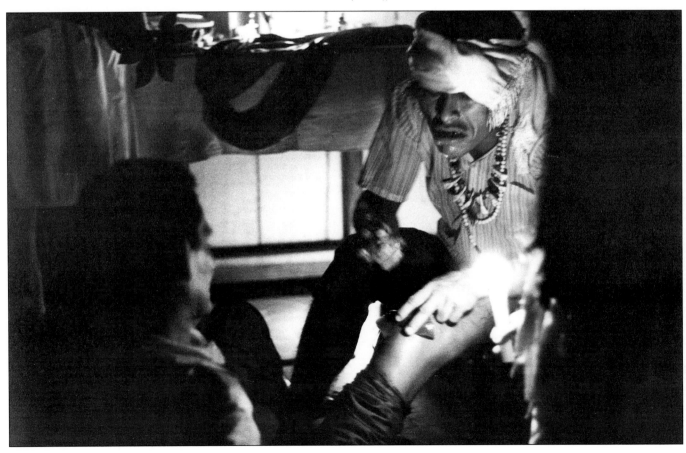

bring worshippers from hundreds of terreiros to the beach, carrying figures of the sea-goddess in her flowing blue-and-white robes. Each group establishes itself on its own area of beach to drum, drink, chant and puff clouds of cigar and pipe smoke. Priests and priestesses ('fathers-of-saints' and 'mothers-of-saints') dance their way into trance. Sometimes they cut and mutilate themselves, although they are usually prevented from hurting themselves too seriously by the other worshippers. The goddess adores all feminine wiles and accoutrements – especially jewellery, perfume, champagne and roses – which are brought as gifts to her. They may be put on little wooden rafts and pushed out to sea as evening falls, or simply thrown into the creaming surf. Sometimes they are entrusted to the fishermen, who take them out from the shore in their boats and give them to the waves.

Many Catholic families in Brazil keep a small figure of Iemanja in an honoured place in the home – she is the Virgin Mary as well, after all, despite her distinctly unvirginal characteristics – and in many a house a candle, a glass of water and a bit of greenery on an unobtrusive altar signal to the gods-cum-saints that they are welcome.

✣

FOR A BLESSING
✣

Like their equivalents in the Caribbean, the Afro-Brazilian cults – Umbanda, Macumba, Candomble, whatever the name – are not dedicated to evil supernatural powers, but to beneficent ones, though there is a deviant cult called Quimbanda, said to deal in black magic and officially outlawed. Through leaders in the group, the deities of the cult can give members much-needed help in time of trouble, or ward off dangers.

Alma Guillermoprieto, a Mexican dancer and journalist who spent some years in Rio, describes in her book, *Samba*, meeting a woman named Celina, who gave 'blessings'.

She blessed for general good luck and for emotional distress, but because her patron was the god Omolu, who assigns diseases among humankind, her blessings for health were particularly important. "She prays for lower-

A startling Indian mask from the Amazon area of Brazil. The African slaves on the plantations blended native Indian ingredients into their idiosyncratic version of the Christianity of their masters.

back problems very well", her son Sidney declared, but in the community, where there was no clinic or health post, and where infant mortality hovered around 120 deaths per 1000 live births, it was her blessings for newborns that were most often requested...When doctors failed, or simply in order to buttress medical craft, people came to her and asked that she invoke Omolu's help against their child's colic, or diarrhoea, or general jumpiness.

Celina was a 'daughter-of-a-saint', initiated years before in a month of

prayer and fasting, painting of the body and shaving of the head, to ready her for the trance state in which Omolu would enter her body and speak through her mouth. He is a frightening deity, known as 'He Who Slays and Eats'. His body, beneath a rough coat of straw, is covered with pustules and he has a hobbling gait when he takes possession of a worshipper. It is said that he was a leper from birth, thrown into the sea by his horrified mother to drown, but rescued by the compassionate goddess Iemanja. His Catholic *alter ego* is either St Lazarus, patron saint of lepers, or St Roch, who helps those stricken with plague. All three are supernatural sources of badly needed help and comfort.

THE GODS' PICTURE BOOK

Why spend years, perhaps centuries, of planning and toil to construct a vast array of pictures and patterns which cannot be appreciated at ground level, but only from up in the air? Were they intended to be seen only by the gods, and if so, were they for the gods' pleasure or what were the gods thought to want with them? Or was this curious art gallery laid out to signal to and attract visiting aliens from outer space, who may well have been mistaken for gods? Or did the people who made the lines enjoy them by hovering over them in hot-air balloons? A bushel of bizarre suggestions have been put forward to solve the enigma of the Nazca Lines.

The lines, in the Nazca Valley in Peru, cover an enormous area of some 200 square miles (500 sq km) of desert and have been preserved by the region's dry climate. They have been dated approximately to the 1st century and were made by removing the crust of small stones on the surface to reveal the yellowish-white soil beneath. There are straight lines, spirals, zig-zags and quadrangles, and more than 100 pictures of animals, fish, spiders, snakes, whales, birds and plants of gigantic dimensions. A condor, for instance, has a wingspan of 394ft (120m), and there's a lizard which is 591ft (180m) long. The

⁂

Huge pictures were drawn on the ground in Peru almost 2000 years ago for a purpose that can only be guessed at. Intriguingly, they cannot be seen properly from the ground, but only from the sky.

⁂

points at which lines converge are marked by cairns of boulders.

One of the astonishing things about 'the world's largest work of art' or 'the strangest message ever left by man' – both of which it has been called – is the straightness of the lines, which run on for miles with an average deviation of only 6.5ft (2m) per 0.6 mile (1km). In an extraordinary engineering achievement, they were laid out straighter than can be measured with modern air-survey methods, scarcely deviating from true even when they cross a gully or a low hill.

⁂

THE SKY ON THE GROUND

⁂

A Spanish chronicler in the 16th century was intrigued by the lines, which were rediscovered in the 1920s by

two men who at first thought they were irrigation channels, but later suggested that they might be sacred paths of some kind. According to Maria Reiche, a German scholar who spent 50 years studying them, they are a kind of textbook of astronomy. The animals and birds are pictures of the constellations in the southern sky, while the straight lines and spirals represent the motions of the planets. Some of the lines appear to be aligned with the positions of the sun, moon and various stars in the sky, and may have been used for determining the agricultural calendar.

A related theory links the lines with rituals connected with the calendar, the agricultural year and the stars wheeling in their courses in the sky.

⁂

A FLIGHT OF HOT AIR

⁂

In 1975 the hot-air balloon theory was tested by building one solely of materials that would have been available to the ancient Nazca people. Vegetable fibres were used to weave the ropes, the gas-bag was made of cloth and a gondola made of reeds hung beneath it. A fire was built and the balloon duly flew over the desert carrying two men.

If this was how the Nazca priests viewed the lines, it still did not explain

The Gods Look Down

Excited attention was drawn to the Nazca Lines when Erich von Däniken, the author of a succession of ludicrous bestsellers in the 1970s about godlike aliens from outer space supposedly visiting the earth in the past, seized on them to support his theories. The whole thing was obviously a gigantic airport, he said, and he pointed to a photograph showing the similarity of one section to the outlines of aircraft parking bays – not realising that the lines in the photograph were part of a condor's claws and measured only a few feet across. Maria Reiche, who had the advantage of actually knowing the area, pointed out that the ground was too soft for astronauts to have landed spacecraft on in any case.

Maria Reiche devoted most of her life to studying the Nazca Lines.

Right: a grid of lines with a single line leading miles away into the distance across the desert.
Below: a possible 'spaceman' figure, but few people take the space visitor theory seriously any more.
Middle: image of a hummingbird.
Bottom: a giant spider drawn on the desert floor centuries ago.

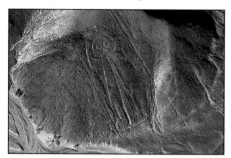

why the lines were made. A tentative theory was that dead Nazca chieftains were sent to the sun, in balloons which would soar up out of sight as they heated up in the sun's rays, and the birds and animals perhaps symbolised events in the lives of the chiefs.

Nearby tombs have yielded mummies wrapped in cloths on which are embroidered masked men who seem to be gliding or descending through the air, with ribbons round them. Could the Nazca perhaps have constructed man-carrying kites?

Another idea is that the lines were paths leading to family tombs, and yet another that they were used for athletics events. None of the answers produced so far is really convincing and the Nazca Lines keep their secret still.

THE REALMS OF GOLD

In his book *Gold of the Gods*, the egregious Erich von Däniken, the 'was God an astronaut?' author of the 1970s, announced that he had explored a gigantic system of tunnels constructed at some unknown date deep underground beneath the Andes peaks in Ecuador and Peru. It contained an astounding wealth of objects in gold as well as carvings of figures wearing 'space suits'.

The story turned out to be a total nonsense, but it is one more testimony to the enduring lure of a vast treasure of gold, said to be hidden somewhere in South America. It was this same golden magnet that drew European explorers deeper and deeper into the continent.

The Spanish settlements in the Caribbean and in Panama at the turn of the 15th and early 16th centuries buzzed with rumours of colossal wealth somewhere to the south. Expeditions went probing along the north coast of what is now Colombia, where it was whispered that an entire mountain range of gold awaited discovery. The town of Santa Marta was founded in 1525 as a base from which to prospect for it, in the Sierra Nevada de Santa Marta.

The glittering attraction of El Dorado, the lure of a treasure of gold beyond the dreams of avarice, obsessed the early European explorers of South America.

Magnificent gold mask of the sun-god of the Incas, surrounded by his beneficent rays. The Inca rulers claimed to be the descendants of the sun-god and his representatives on earth. Rumours of vast treasures of gold drew European adventurers to South America.

THE GOLDEN MAN

Other expeditions sailed down the Pacific coast, and in 1533 Francisco Pizarro and his men seized the Inca capital of Cuzco in Peru. Treasure-seekers from both the north coast and Peru now pressed on into the interior of Colombia. They had heard of El Dorado, 'the Golden Man', the cacique, or ruler, of the Muisca Indians in the area where Bogota and Tunja stand today, and of the ceremonies at Lake Guatavita, 10,000ft (3000m) up in the Andes. The lake is thought to have been created by the fall of a giant meteorite 2000 years ago. The Indians saw it as the descent of a golden god from the sky, who came down to live at the bottom of the lake. Offerings to him were thrown into the water.

On the accession of a new ruler, the Indians loaded a wooden raft with gold and emeralds. It was paddled out into the lake, carrying the new cacique whose body was oiled and then powdered with gold dust to coat his skin with gold. The gold and emeralds were thrown into the lake and the ruler dived into the water, which washed the gold dust from his body.

The Muisca and other Indian peoples of this area created superb goldwork, which can be admired today in the magnificent Museo del Oro in Bogota. The museum's collection of more than 30,000 pieces in gold includes the famous Balsa Muisca, a miniature representation of El Dorado's raft, which was found in Lake Guatavita.

The Spaniards found the lake all right, but not nearly enough gold to satisfy them, though they sent divers down into the water. In 1578 a rich merchant got official authority to drain the lake and employed an army of Indian labourers, but when the crater was emptied, little of value was found. Further large-scale attempts in the 19th century and early in this century had thoroughly disappointing results, too.

‡

A CIGARETTE FOR THE DEVIL

‡

Somehow, as time went by, the name El Dorado, which originally referred to a man, was transferred to a place – a fabulous place, a city or a kingdom of wealth beyond all imagining, which was always only just out of reach, just a little further on across the next river or the next mountain range. One more push, one more effort, would surely find it. It never did, but hope drew European explorers on across the whole continent.

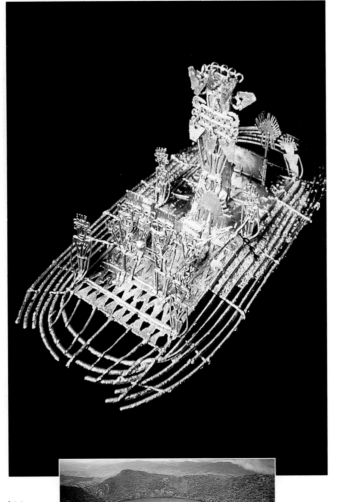

Top: in the Museo del Oro in Bogota is this gold model of the raft which carried a new ruler out on to Lake Guatavita. El Dorado, the 'golden man', and his attendants can be seen on board.
Above: Lake Guatavita, which the Spaniards eagerly drained for gold, with disappointing results.

In the 1540s an entire mountain of silver was discovered at Potosí in Bolivia, and thousands of Indian, and later African, slaves were forced to labour in the mines. Visitors today will find the little figure of El Tio, 'Uncle', standing beside the galleries, and by him small offerings of drinks, coca leaves and the butts of his cigarettes, which are lighted for him and placed in his mouth. El Tio is the Devil of Christianity, because the miners decided that the hot and hellish environment in which they worked was far closer to Satan's realm than to the open sky of God in his heaven. Since the Devil was evidently the rightful owner of the riches they were wresting from the earth, they took care to thank and placate him.

‡

FABLED RICHES

‡

No real discovery, however rich, ever matched the dream. The Spaniards were drawn to Argentina originally by rumoured treasures of silver there – hence the name they gave the country (from the Latin for silver) – but when no silver was found on the coast, the Spaniards moved inland. There were reports of a kingdom somewhere in the interior, ruled by a white king whose Indian subjects wore silver crowns. An expedition in search of this legendary realm in 1537 led to the founding of Asunción, the capital of Paraguay.

Back in the north, in 1595, an English venturer, Sir Walter Raleigh, sailed up the Orinoco in quest of 'the Inca empire of El Dorado'. He did not find it, but returned in 1618 and was told of the fabulous city of Manoa on the shores of Lake Parima. He did not find that either.

The legend has never lost its glamour, however. The town of El Dorado in Venezuela got its name when prospectors swarmed there to dig unavailingly for gold, and travellers to Bogota today arrive at the El Dorado Airport.

The Amazons

The Amazon River acquired its name because a group of Spaniards who made an astounding journey down it in the 1540s reported fighting formidable female warriors. They were described as 'very white and tall', with long, braided hair. They went 'naked, but with their privy parts covered, with their bows and arrows in their hands'. Like the Amazons of classical mythology, they were ruled by a queen and lived in their own strictly female communities, consorting with men only for breeding purposes. Modern Europeans dismiss the story, but Indian peoples in the Amazon Basin believe it and have kept alive a tradition of ferocious women warriors and all-female villages. The Amazons are said to live on an island in the Lake of the Mirror of the Moon, mating with the nearby men once a year. They keep only their female babies and hand their infant sons back to those who fathered them.

THE CROSS AND THE SUN

The great church of Santo Domingo in Cuzco, in Peru, was built on top of the Sun Hall of the Incas, the temple where the gold reserves of the empire were stored and where sacrifices were offered to Inti, the sun god, who was the chief deity of the Inca pantheon. The Incas themselves, according to a myth which they sedulously propagated, were the children of the sun. Their first ancestors appeared on the Island of the Sun in Lake Titicaca, which is still held in reverence by the Indian population of Peru and Bolivia.

Inside the church, with its images of the Bleeding Heart and St Sebastian, the altar is at the west end, an unusual location chosen to position it at the most sacred point of the Inca temple, the altar of the Almighty Sun. The arrangement is a symbolic statement of Christianity's triumph over the Inca god, but the god has had his revenge, for Cuzco's greatest fiesta today, Inti Raimi in June, is a revival of the Inca festival of the sun.

The festival is held in the ruins of the spectacular Inca fortress of Sacsahuaman. It involves the music of drums and flutes, the blowing of conch-shells, phalanxes of spear-bearing warriors and bands of young priests and maidens. The performers and the spectators drum their feet on the ground with an earth-shaking rhythm until silence falls to greet the arrival of the Inca in his litter, accompanied by high priests in feather head-dresses. All bow

The forcible introduction of Christianity to South America in the wake of European conquest generated a potent mixture of religion and magic in which Indian traditions remained alive.

The great annual feast of the sun-god is brought vividly back to life in Cuzco every year. Priests wearing lavish feather head-dresses accompany the Inca's litter.

down in reverence as the Inca raises his arms high to salute the sun. The climax comes after a llama has been released into the arena. It is stalked and caught, then tethered to a stake while performers dance round it with growing excitement. Finally the chief priest stabs it to death with a dagger, wrenches out the animal's bleeding heart and holds it up to the sun. The heart is burned on a pyre of straw as the people's offering to the god.

THE VIRGIN OF CANDELARIA

As in Mexico and Central America, the conquered people's Christian allegiance was gained by marvels and miracles. Copacabana, for example, on the shore of Lake Titicaca, was a sacred place long before the Spaniards arrived. In the temple stood a translucent blue stone, carved with the face of a goddess and greatly venerated. After the Spanish Conquest, a local aristocrat of Inca descent saw a vision of the Virgin Mary here and carved a wooden portrait of her, the famous Virgin of Candelaria, which is kept in the cathedral.

The subjugated Indians were able to identify the Virgin with the goddess of the place, and Copacabana is now a major centre of Christian pilgrimage. On Good Friday pilgrims climb to the shrine of the Sorrows of Mary on top of a nearby hill, where they buy little plastic model cars and houses. These are blessed by a priest and have beer poured over them, in the hope of securing good fortune for the family's real house or car in the year ahead.

THE DEVILS' DANCE

The Virgin of Candelaria has her own mine at Oruro, the tin-mining town further south, where she is honoured during the lively Diablada, or 'Dance of the Devils' carnival just before Lent. The

Archangel Michael and the angelic host do battle against Satan and his satraps in a series of vigorous dances which represent the battle between good and evil. Good wins, of course.

Another flourishing pilgrimage site is Chiquinquira in Colombia, where a painting of the Virgin with St Anthony and St Andrew was made in 1555. Its colours swiftly faded, but were miraculously restored by the prayers of a local lady 30 years later. Our Lady of Chiquinquira was officially appointed the patroness of Colombia in 1919 and pilgrims today enter her church on their knees to seek her blessing. At Salta in Argentina the images of Christ and the Virgin Mary in the cathedral are specially venerated because in 1692 they stopped an earthquake dead in its tracks when the townsfolk carried them through the streets.

✢

THE MARKET FOR WITCHES

✢

Meanwhile, pre-Christian traditions have survived in strength beneath the Christian surface. In La Paz, in Bolivia, the lively Alasitas Festival honours Ekeko, 'the dwarf', the little household god who brings good fortune to the house. His statues are offered coca leaves, bundles of cash, lottery tickets or chocolate to keep him sweet. Inca dances have been revived for the significantly named festival of Jesus el Gran Poder (Jesus the Great Power), which

Above: the image of the Virgin and Child is borne in solemn procession through Cuzco, once the capital of the vast empire of the Incas. The church of La Compania in the background is massive testimony to the efficiency with which Christianity was imposed on the conquered people, but it was a Christianity shot through with colourful elements from the indigenous religion.
Below: among herbs and vegetables on offer in the market in La Paz is a llama foetus for working magic.

began in 1939. Those in need of the right magical equipment for casting spells, attracting good spirits and warding off the attentions of malevolent ones can find it in La Paz at the Mercado de Hechiceria, also known as the Mercado de los Brujos (Witches' Market). Herbs and seeds to treat every known ailment are on offer, along with bones, figurines, dried llama foetuses and dubious bottles whose contents are unidentified.

In the annual Fiesta del Espiritu at Potosí, llamas are sacrificed to Pacha Mama, the earth mother and fertility goddess. The Chipaya Indians near the remote desert village of Coipasa in Bolivia honour the spirits of mountains and rivers. They especially venerate the village church tower because of its phallic shape. They do not welcome tourists, cameras or impertinent questions.

Bolivians consult a diviner (thaliri) or a magician (yatiri) to help with the problems of life. The Indians of the Sierra Nevada de Santa Marta in Colombia trust their traditional priest-magicians, called mamas, but reliance on magic, and the fear of it, is not confined to backwoods areas and slums in South America. Jose Lopez Rega, who died in Buenos Aires in 1989, was an adviser and confidant of General Perón and a writer of books on astrology and Spiritism, in one of which he acknowledged the co-authorship of the Archangel Gabriel. He was widely feared in Argentina.

ENEMY IN SIGHT

A poltergeist in Paraguay in 1973 succeeded in removing a pram, complete with peacefully sleeping baby, from inside a house to a spot beneath a tree outside, where it was found after an anxious search. The pram and baby were dry, although it had been raining the whole time that the child had been missing. This was one of the incidents reported from a farmhouse near Ponta Pora, in the remote Matto Grosso area, where a Japanese family had settled. Showers of stones fell inside the house, while outside it rained tomatoes, to the furious indignation of a redoubtable Paraguayan woman in her seventies, who was pelted while working in the tomato patch.

A journalist who went to investigate was completely sceptical about the supposed poltergeist. Or he was until he drove up in a jeep one afternoon, parked it outside and went into the house. Hearing a noise, he went back outside again and saw to his astonishment that the jeep was now standing 40yds (36.4m) away up a slope, with no tyre marks in the mud between its position and the house. In the end the disturbances ebbed away, still unexplained.

✣

SHOWING HIS CLAWS

✣

Brazil has been called 'the world's most psychic country' by the experienced British investigator Guy Lyon Playfair, who has reported a number of dramatic poltergeist outbreaks there. One of them occurred in 1972 at a house in Sorocaba, near São

✢

The influence of Roman Catholicism, Spiritism and fundamentalist Protestant churches in 'the world's most psychic country' have given a Satanic tinge to poltergeist cases.

✢

Scorch marks on the wall show where fires broke out, apparently spontaneously, in a frightening Brazilian poltergeist outbreak.

Paulo, with mysterious knocking sounds, unexplained movements of furniture and a heavy tyre rising up and hovering in the air outside in front of one of the family. A water tank was overturned which it normally took three men to lift and the mother of the family was hit by a flying brick. When the family went to stay with friends, the poltergeist went along too, and eventually they left the area altogether. The disturbances seemed to focus on their 12-year-old daughter.

The Brazilian Institute of Psychobiophysical Research reported in 1984 on a frightening poltergeist case

involving a family in Guarulhos in the suburbs of São Paulo. Objects were broken, gravel and bricks fell on the house from outside and furniture was cut, as if ripped by a pocket knife or enormous claws, sometimes when people who were watching could not see what was doing it. Members of the family and visitors, including small children, began to suffer cuts, too. The head of the family, a 55-year-old builder, saw a vision of a monstrous arm – of a wild beast, he said, not a man. 'It was very strong and big; sharp-ended claws, measuring from 5.5-6in (14-15cm), black, shiny and curved. The fur was red, thin, shiny and short as that of a cougar.'

His daughter-in-law started to see visions of a hairy creature and said she had spoken to an entity 'in the guise of Satan, of a man, with a totally distorted face, teeth outside, and throwing fire when he spoke'. A small child in the house saw frightening animals and threw fits, though the local hospital could find nothing wrong with her. These experiences were all mixed up with unavailing attempts at exorcism by the Pentecostal Church, to which the family belonged (which would predispose them to put the events down to the powers of evil).

In addition, fires broke out spontaneously. Money disappeared and sometimes a piece of paper marked with a red cross was found in its place. Sometimes the money reappeared as mysteriously as it had gone. Branches of rosemary appeared from nowhere, crossed knives and rosemary appeared under a bed and white candles, lighted,

Right: the jeep which was moved a considerable distance, without leaving any tyre marks, by some unseen force. The incident occurred on an immigrant Japanese family's farm in the remote Matto Grosso area of Paraguay in 1973. Does this constitute the world poltergeist weight-lifting record?
Below right: on the same farm the same unseen force has casually put a pair of shoes out of reach on a high beam. Both photographs were taken by an initially sceptical journalist who was sent to report on the case. Many other weird things happened on the farm, until the outbreak ebbed away as mysteriously as it began.

somehow found their own way into a bedroom.

The 21-year-old woman who said she had talked with Satan was subjected to psychological testing, which showed nothing to suggest that she was unconsciously responsible for the phenomena, and to testing for psychokinetic (mental influence on matter) ability, which proved negative. The investigation report viewed the case against the background of Umbanda (*see page 87*) and Spiritism, and found the most probable explanation in the activities of a discarnate entity, stirred to act by a sorcerer hostile to the afflicted family.

✛

THE CURSE OF THE GODDESS

✛

Brazil knows comparatively little of the secular parapsychology of North America and Western Europe, which is generally concerned to explain 'spirits' away. The Brazilian tendency is to see poltergeist cases as justification for Roman Catholic, Spiritist and fundamentalist Protestant belief in the Devil and the spirit world. These cases are also frequently interpreted as examples of black magic in action.

That a general background of unquestioning belief in supernatural entities can influence even people who regard themselves as sceptics is shown by the story of a student in her twenties at São Paulo University in 1973, as related by Guy Lyon Playfair, who called her 'Marcia'. A modern young woman, Marcia had abandoned all belief in

spirits, or so she thought. One day she was strolling along the beach at Santos, when she picked up a small plaster figurine lying on the sand, where the tide had evidently left it. It was a figure of the sea-goddess Iemanja, which had obviously been thrown into the waves as an offering. Ignoring urgent advice to leave the thing be, Marcia took it back home and stood it on her mantelpiece.

This turned out to be unwise. After a few days she began to feel thoroughly ill and then came a succession of unpleasant incidents. Her pressure cooker blew up and scalded her badly. The oven in her kitchen exploded. In the street she felt a powerful, almost irresistible impulse to throw herself under the speeding traffic, while at home she had frightening urges to throw herself out of the windows 15 floors up. The last straw came when night after

night in bed she felt the weight of a body lying on top of her and felt herself being raped by a loathsome invisible presence.

Against all her principles Marcia went to an Umbanda centre, where she was told that the whole trouble obviously stemmed from her appropriating for herself the figurine which had been meant for the goddess. She took it back to the beach and put it down as near as possible where she had found it, for the incoming waves to bear away. Needless to say, she suffered no further harm.

Did she somehow unconsciously cause it all to happen, out of a buried fear of the consequences of taking the figurine, or was there more to it? Even on the first hypothesis, the story seems to be a remarkable tribute to the powers of a human mind which can make a pressure cooker blow up and an oven explode.

ENCOUNTERS OF THE STRANGE KIND

In 1957 a 23-year-old Brazilian labourer named Antonio Villas Boas was using a tractor to plough a field on his brother's farm near São Francisco de Sales in the early hours of the morning – in the fierce heat it was best to work at night – when a strange light appeared. He had seen it the night before, when it had bothered him and his brother, but this time he was working alone. The light descended close to him and figures emerged – small creatures about 5ft tall (1.5m), in helmets and 'space suits' with breathing apparatus attached. They gripped him by the arms and marched him to their craft. Once inside it, they stripped his clothes off and left him to the tender mercies of a strange-looking naked woman with fair skin and high cheekbones, also of diminutive stature, who seized him and made love to him.

Afterwards she pointed to her belly and then to the sky, as if to signal that she was going to have his baby up in her own realm among the stars. His clothes were given back to him, and he was shown round the spacecraft, including what seemed to be the control room. He picked up a bit of equipment which looked like a clock, hoping to take it with him, but the aliens would not let him keep it. They finally let him go and he went back to the farm where he resumed his normal way of life.

Most serious students of UFOs viewed the story with a hostile eye, as wildly improbable and likely to bring the whole subject into disrepute. A doctor who examined Villas Boas the following year, however, was impressed by him and said he showed symptoms consistent with exposure to radiation.

Many reports have emerged from South America of people being abducted by mysterious visitors from outer space, who have come to study human life and conditions on earth.

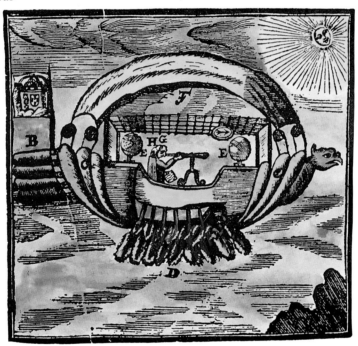

The idea of flying always fired the human imagination and stories about UFOs have a precedent in notions like this flying machine, supposedly invented by a Brazilian priest in the 18th century.

ENQUIRING MINDS

Even odder stories of encounters with UFOs have since come from Brazil, which seems to hold the record for alien abductions. In 1975, for instance, a teenage boy named Antonio, living in São Luís, was transfixed with a beam of light by a UFO, which he said had

bumped into the wall of his house. A posse of aliens, 3ft (0.9m) tall with dark hair and complexions, jumped out and hauled him on board. They took him for a ride to their planet and their leader, an alien named Croris, cross-examined him about earthlings' food and cars. The boy made a deal with them, agreeing to provide them with animals for vivisection in return for more trips around space. He gave them a dog, a cat and a parrot to cut up, and they rewarded him with all sorts of objects, including medals and statues and a ray-gun, which – surprise, surprise – he did not keep. At one point the aliens turned one of their number into an exact likeness of Antonio and sent him to the boy's home, where he completely fooled Antonio's father.

Other South American countries have had their space visitors, too. At San Pedro de los Altas, south of Caracas in Venezuela, in 1965, two respectable businessmen and a gynaecologist were looking over horses at a stables when there was a flash of light. Startled, they looked up to see a sphere emitting light and descending some distance away from them, to hover above the ground. Then a beam of light angled out from the side of the sphere like a gangplank and they saw two beings float down it. The beings were 7ft (2.1m) tall with long yellow hair and large, round, blue eyes, wearing shiny, metallic suits.

The aliens, who were perfectly friendly, explained that they had come from Orion to study humans and the possibility of a human-alien breeding programme which would create a new race. Aliens of a different kind emerged from the UFO, too, who were only 3ft

(0.9m) tall. There was a good deal of amicable philosophical discussion and the aliens went away, though the men's memory of the end of the event was hazy.

✢

WE SHALL RETURN

✢

In 1977 a patrol of six soldiers and a corporal, on duty in the early hours of the morning near the town of Putre, Chile, spotted two violet lights descending in the sky and then saw an object land not far away. The corporal, calling on the Almighty to protect him, told the young soldiers to stay where they were and walked away into the darkness in the direction of the mysterious object. The young men

This mysterious object radiating light was photographed over São Paulo, Brazil, in 1984.

waited anxiously for 15 minutes. Then the corporal returned, in a strange, trance-like state, mumbling to himself, 'You do not know who we are or where we come from, but I tell you we shall return'. At which he passed out.

When the dawn came, the soldiers were surprised to see several days' growth of beard on the corporal's face and to find that the date on his digital watch had advanced by five days. They took him down to the town, where the military authorities pulled a blanket of silence over the whole affair. When the corporal was at last allowed to talk to the media, all he would say was that he had no recollection of what had happened to him during the missing 15 minutes. The detail that the 15 minutes of earth time had apparently been equivalent to five days in the spacecraft recalls old traditions of otherworldly realms whose time-dimension is different from that on earth.

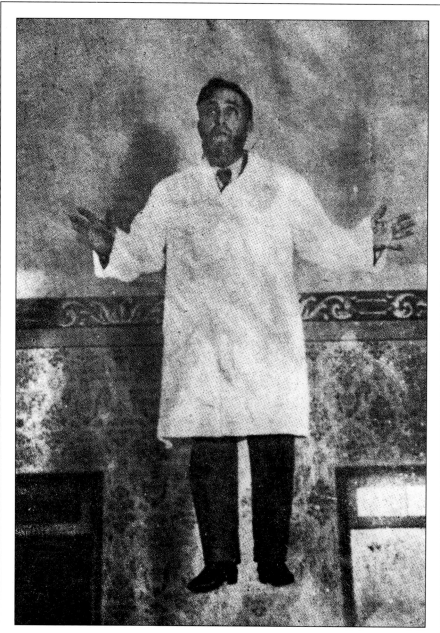

Mirabelli's Marvels

Those who saw the remarkable Brazilian medium Carmine Mirabelli at work experienced strange encounters of a different kind, as he was reputedly able to cause spirits of the dead to appear in visible form. He could also levitate in the air to a height of 8ft (2.4m), cause objects to move of their own volition and turn solid objects liquid. In addition, he produced enormous quantities of 'automatic writing' – with spirits from the beyond guiding his pen hand – in Hebrew, Arabic, Japanese and many other languages which he did not himself know. As a young man he had lost his job in a shoe shop because the boxes kept flying about.

Psychical researchers have not known what to make of him, though it now appears that a well-known photograph of him levitating was a fake. He was actually perched on a step ladder, but the photo was doctored to conceal the fact. On the other hand, the evidence that he could make small objects move about at a distance is strong and if he had genuine powers, but cheated when he thought he could get away with it, he would not be the first to do so. He was killed in a car accident in 1951.

A step-ladder has probably vanished from this mid-air picture of Mirabelli.

✦ AFRICA ✦

Africa was the birthplace of the human race, according to the currently prevailing theory, and it was from Africa that human beings spread out to settle the rest of the earth. Rock paintings of wild animals and men with bows, in the Tasili area of Algeria near Djanet, have survived from a hunting culture of more than 6000 years ago in what is now the Sahara Desert. Starting about 5000 years ago, one of the first great civilisations developed in the valley of the Nile, the sacred river of Ancient Egypt. Its majestic pyramids and temples have inspired awed fascination ever since, and the opening of Pharaoh Tutankhamun's tomb in 1923 set off whispers about 'the curse of the Pharaohs' which are still echoing.

On Mount Sinai in Egypt the spot is shown where the God of the Old Testament spoke to Moses out of the burning bush. High in the Ethiopian mountains legends grew up about King Solomon and the Queen of Sheba, and there is a persistent tradition that the Ark of the Covenant is secretly preserved there. Christianity came early to North Africa and the Coptic Church in Egypt and

Throughout the continent of Africa ancient traditions are still upheld, despite the widespread allegiance to Christianity in the south and to the Muslim faith in the north.
Above: a ceremony in South Africa.
Below: musicians at a Djerba wedding in Tunisia.

Ethiopia can trace its origins almost back to the time of Christ himself. In the 7th century, however, Arab armies stormed across Egypt and swiftly subdued the whole of North Africa for Islam, which is still the dominant religion of the north. Cities like Kairouan, Fez and Algiers became important Muslim centres and sites of pilgrimage.

Further south, powerful African kingdoms grew up in the interior. The rulers of Mali waxed rich on the control of trade routes from their capital of Timbuktu, and the mighty ruins of Great Zimbabwe would one day inspire Rider Haggard's *She*. Europeans heard vaguely of a great Christian emperor somewhere in Africa. They called him Prester John and hoped in vain for his aid against Islam.

Systematic European exploration began in the 15th century. Successive Portuguese voyages pressed down the west coast of the continent until Bartholomew Dias rounded the Cape of Good Hope in 1488. European and Arab slave-traders developed their cruelly profitable traffic in black lives, but most of 'the dark continent' remained a mystery to Europeans until the 19th century. Hostility to slaving,

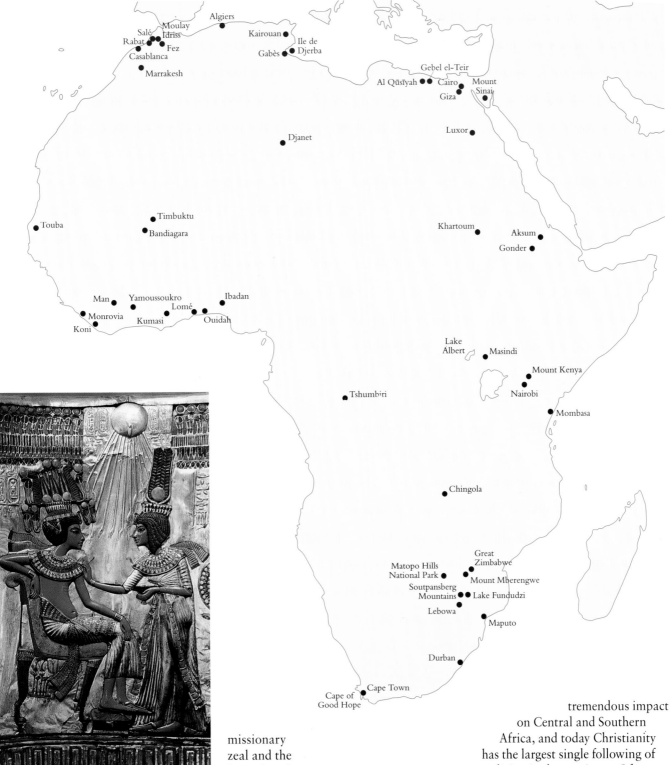

Algiers

Moulay
Idriss
Salé
Rabat
Fez
Casablanca

Marrakesh

Kairouan

Ile de
Djerba
Gabès

Gebel el-Teir

Al Qūsīyah
Cairo
Mount
Sinai
Giza

Luxor

Djanet

Touba

Timbuktu
Bandiagara

Khartoum

Aksum
Gonder

Man
Monrovia
Koni

Yamoussoukro
Lomé
Kumasi
Ouidah

Ibadan

Lake
Albert
Masindi

Mount Kenya
Nairobi

Tshumbiri

Mombasa

Chingola

Great
Zimbabwe
Matopo Hills
National Park
Mount Mberengwe
Soutpansberg
Mountains
Lake Fundudzi
Lebowa

Maputo

Durban

Cape Town
Cape of
Good Hope

*Archetypal Egyptian art. This is the
back of the throne of Tutankhamun.
It shows Queen Ankhesenamun
holding a salve-cup and spreading
perfumed oil on her husband's collar.
Incredibly, it dates from 1357-1349BC.
The fabulous treasures found in the
pharaoh's tomb indicated the
enormous wealth with which these
rulers surrounded themselves in death.*

missionary zeal and the lure of profits combined to open up the interior and at the end of the century almost the whole continent was quickly parcelled out among the European powers. In 1914 only Ethiopia and Liberia remained independent. The process was reversed again at great speed after World War II, when almost all African countries became independent.

Christian missions made a tremendous impact on Central and Southern Africa, and today Christianity has the largest single following of any religion in the continent. Of a total population approaching 700 million, some 47 per cent are classified as Christians, split between the various denominations, and 41 per cent as Muslims, with 'tribal religionists' officially numbering only about ten per cent. On the other hand, many Africans took what they wanted from Christianity and blended it with their own traditions, which are still vigorously alive.

MORE THAN MEETS THE EYE

The Hassan II Mosque, rising on the shore just outside the old city of Casablanca in Morocco, is the largest mosque in the world and has the tallest minaret in the world. A sultan of Morocco in the 12th century began to build what was planned to be the biggest mosque in creation, at Rabat, but it was never finished and little of it is left today except its minaret, now called the Tour Hassan.

Both buildings are testimony to enduring Muslim zeal in Morocco. The irresistible Arab armies which swept across North Africa in the 7th century to the war cry of Allahu akbar, 'God is most great', took Alexandria in 642, Tripoli in 644, had subdued the whole Maghreb (Tunisia, Algeria and Morocco) by 709 and stormed on into southern Spain. Kairouan in Tunisia is the fourth holiest city of the Muslim world, ranking after Mecca, Medina and Jerusalem, and it is said that seven pilgrimages to Kairouan obtain as much spiritual merit as one to Mecca. It owes its fame to the legend that when an Arab general halted his army here in 670 on his way west, a gold cup was found which he recognised as one he had lost in Mecca. Then a spring was discovered and proclaimed to be connected with the holy well of Mecca, and the general decided to found a city on this sacred spot, a kind of clone of Mecca in North Africa.

✢

Islam has dominated North Africa ever since the Arab armies stormed their conquering way across it in the 7th century, and drove on into Spain. However, older beliefs and superstitions have survived there, too.

✢

Berber menfolk celebrating the date harvest at the Saharan oasis of Erfoud, close to the foot of the Atlas Mountains. The Berbers were in North Africa before the coming of Islam and, like so many other peoples, have blended some of their own old traditions into their Muslim faith.

Far down into the 19th century Christians and Jews were not allowed into Kairouan and Muslim visitors would take off their shoes when entering the city, as if entering a mosque. The Great Mosque dates back to the 9th century and in the beautiful Mosque of the Barber is the venerated tomb of one of the companions of the Prophet Muhammad, Abu Zama el Belaoui, who always carried with him three hairs from the Prophet's beard. Confusingly, the tomb of a saint who actually was the Prophet's barber, and is much venerated, is to be found at Gabès in Tunisia.

The Berber people of North Africa, who were there before the Arabs arrived – St Augustine of Hippo, the great Christian theologian, was a Berber – though devout Muslims, have blended some of their own older beliefs and traditions into their faith. Among them is the veneration of marabouts, or holy persons, possessed of powerful baraka, a kind of holy essence or magic force which is regarded as a gift from God. Believers pray to them for help and cures of sickness at their tombs and bring them offerings and animal sacrifices, in cults which parallel the veneration of saints in Christianity.

The most famous of them is Moulay Idriss, whose tomb is in the town named after him, near Meknes in Morocco. A great-grandson of the Prophet Muhammad, he came from Damascus in the 8th century and founded the first

Land of the Lotus Eaters

The island of Djerba, off the coast of Tunisia, near Gabès, which was a major Mediterranean port far back in Phoenician and Roman times, has been identified as the idle land of the lotus-eaters, to which Odysseus came in the course of his voyage in the Odyssey. Odysseus sent three of his men to spy out the land. They met some of the natives, who gave them the fruit of the lotus to eat, which put them into a peaceful contentment in which all thoughts of their duty and the voyage vanished from their minds and all they wanted to do was stay there and go on browsing idly on the sweet fruit. The forceful Odysseus had to drag them back to the ships by force, and then he sailed hastily away. The island's beautiful sandy beaches and peaceful palm groves make a believable background for the legend.

Arab ruling dynasty of Morocco. He is held in such awe that non-Muslims are not allowed to stay overnight in his town.

Another much revered saint is Sidi Abdallah ibn Hassoun, a Sufi mystic who died in 1604. There is a candle-bearing procession to his tomb in Salé, in Morocco, every year. Worshippers anxious to have children pray to the saint buried in the Sidi Muhammad Sherif Mosque in Algiers.

The sultans of Morocco possessed particularly powerful baraka, which spread even to their cannons. Prayers for help were addressed to the muzzles of these formidable artillery pieces, which were kept sweet by being given the severed heads of the enemy as offerings after a battle.

The Berbers, especially in country areas, have preserved their old belief in many spirits, good and bad, inhabiting the world. The bad ones are the jinn, who are mentioned quite frequently in the Koran. They existed before God created human beings, and they roam in the darkness of the night. They infest lonely places and cemeteries. They fear iron and salt, which will keep them at bay, and they hate loud noises. The louder the noise, the further away the jinn will retreat. This accounts for the Berber custom of firing guns and pistols at weddings and other important occasions, to keep the malevolent spirits away. In towns this has tended to be replaced by a frightful cacophony of motor horns, as guests career about the streets in cars making as ear-piercing a racket as possible.

In the crowded markets of cities like Marrakesh in Morocco, traditional healers and diviners can be found plying their accustomed trades, along with acrobats, musicians, snake-charmers, fire-eaters and thieves. Amulets and lucky charms are often carried to attract good supernatural influences and

In the market place of Marrakesh a snake-charmer practises an ancient, subtle art which has always seemed to be almost supernatural. Today, it is as much a tourist draw as anything else.

The austerely elegant Great Mosque of Kairouan in Tunisia, dating from the 7th century, was the first major Islamic building in North Africa.

ward off bad luck, including the evil eye, which is traditionally much feared. The Touareg, the veiled warriors of the desert in southern Algeria and Libya, use the cross as a protective amulet, which is strange, as Muslims normally shun the Christian symbol. It has been suggested that their ancestors long ago may have been Christians.

THE CURSE OF THE PHARAOHS

On 4 November 1922, in the Valley of the Kings near Luxor in Egypt, a 48-year-old Egyptologist named Howard Carter made one of the greatest archaeological discoveries of all time. It was only a single step, cut in the rock, but below it there proved to be a second step, and further down a third, until a whole staircase was uncovered leading down to a doorway covered with oval seals. Behind this door lay a rubble-strewn corridor, at the end of which was a second doorway, also sealed. It was the portal of the tomb of Pharaoh Tutankhamun, who had died in 1352 BC at the age of 18, and inside it waited treasure undreamed.

For centuries Westerners had gazed in awe at the remains of the civilisation of Ancient Egypt, at the towering pyramids, the temples, the tombs with their mummified corpses preserved in elaborate wrappings and cases, the obelisks and statues and sphinxes, which testified to the wealth and sophistication of the kingdom on the Nile. There was an enticing air of secret magic and mystery about the strange animal-headed gods and goddesses, the hieroglyphs or 'sacred writing' which covered the walls and pillars of temples, the necropolises with the mummified corpses of thousands of animals – cats and dogs, crocodiles and falcons and baboons. It was all fascinating, and at the same time it felt dangerous.

BURIED IN GOLD

Howard Carter and his team of labourers were employed by the 5th Earl of Carnarvon, a rich English aristocrat

Popular belief in the powerful magic of the priests and pharaohs of Ancient Egypt seemed vindicated as the press put the death of one of the discoverers of Tutankhamun's tomb down to a curse 3000 years old.

Above: the magnificent golden death-mask of Pharaoh Tutankhamun was one of the fabulous treasures revealed when the tomb was opened.

and racehorse owner, whose weak health forced him to winter abroad. In 1903 Lord Carnarvon went to Egypt, where he quickly became obsessed with Egyptology. His discovery of a large mummified cat in a wooden coffin spurred him on, and he hired the experienced Carter to direct his digs. The two men had several successful seasons, and in 1922 came the great find in the Valley of the Kings.

As was customary in ancient Egypt, the tomb was protected by curses against anyone disturbing it, in the usually vain hope of deterring grave-robbers. It was with feelings of considerable awe, therefore, that Carnarvon and Carter broke into the inner chamber together on 17 February 1923, to discover the most astonishing treasure. It included the pharaoh's coffin of solid gold, weighing over a ton, and his mummy with a magnificent gold portrait mask, together with statues, ornaments, jewels, chariots, weapons and furniture which took three years to clear.

THE CURSE STRIKES

Carnarvon was not to live to see all this, however. Shaving one day, he grazed a mosquito bite on his face, and blood poisoning set in. His health was not strong in any case and he died of pneumonia on 5 April 1923. He was 57 years old. Almost instantly the belief sprang up, seized on with glee and promoted by the popular press, that he had been killed by the curse in the tomb. A mysterious power failure which blacked Cairo out as Carnarvon was dying added fuel to the fire, and a rumour spread that back at his stately home in Hampshire, Carnarvon's dog had started to howl inconsolably and had actually dropped dead at exactly the moment when his master expired.

The discovery of the tomb and the treasure aroused almost hysterical excitement and inspired a craze for Ancient Egyptian women's fashions and hats as well as Ancient Egyptian statuettes and ashtrays, cinema interiors, cocktail shakers and items of furniture. There was also a rash of 'mummy's curse' horror films. Taking no notice of the fact that Howard Carter and other people concerned with exploring the tomb lived serenely on, entirely unaffected by the curse, the press trumpeted the death of anyone even remotely connected with the discovery as another example of the vengeance of the pharaohs striking again. The elderly Lord Westbury, for instance, who comnfitted suicide in London, was identified as the nineteenth victim of the curse on the singularly slender grounds that his son had once been Carter's secretary.

✦

BONE OF CONTENTION

✦

There was a curious sequel to the story. In 1936 a young Scots diplomat, Sir Alexander Seton, was in Egypt with his beautiful wife Zeyla and they watched the opening of two tombs close to the Sphinx and the Great Pyramid at

Top: a modern reconstruction of the scene when Lord Carnarvon and the excavators opened one of the shrines in Tutankhamun's tomb.
Above: a photograph taken at the time shows part of the astonishing litter of objects that were in the tomb when Carnarvon and Carter broke in, defying the ancient curse directed against grave-robbers.

Giza. Lady Zeyla paid one of the locals to bring her a human bone from one of the tombs and she and her husband took it back home to Edinburgh and displayed it in a glass case in their drawing room.

Trouble followed. The Setons both fell ill and mysterious fires broke out in the house. A nine-year-old boy who came to stay said he saw someone in a strange robe walking in the drawing room. Ornaments fell off shelves and tables, and broke. There were unexplained thumping noises from the drawing room and the furniture in it began moving about by itself. Feeling a sudden desperate panic at one point, Seton rushed into the room to find the glass display case shattered on the floor. He announced that he would return the bone to the tomb in Egypt. The story inevitably aroused considerable press interest and mediums began announcing that beings from beyond the grave were demanding the bone back and would strike those who touched it blind if it was not returned.

Sir Alexander did not return the bone, but after more disturbances at home the new display case was mysteriously smashed and the bone itself was found reduced to powder. The Setons divorced, the disturbances ceased and nobody went blind. The story had fizzled out by the time Sir Alexander and his ex-wife both died in 1963. It would probably only require some marginally odd event vaguely connected with ancient Egypt to set the whole hysteria off again.

THE HOLY MOUNTAIN

The southern end of the Sinai Peninsula today is turning rapidly into a holiday and resort area, but Mount Sinai, or Gebel Musa in Arabic, above the head of the Red Sea, is a hallowed place for all the 'people of the book' – Jews, Christians and Muslims alike. All three honour Moses as a great prophet of God, and it was here, according to tradition, that God spoke to Moses out of a burning bush, which flamed but was not consumed, and told Moses to lead the Israelites out of captivity in Egypt (Exodus, chapter 3). It was through the wilderness of Sinai that they made their way after the miraculous crossing of the Red Sea, and the Chapel of Aaron today stands at the place where, it is said, the golden calf was made. It was on the summit of Mount Sinai that God gave Moses the Ten Commandments, and a spot where the Almighty subsequently spoke to the prophet Elijah is now marked by a tree.

A chapel was built on the site of the burning bush in the 4th century, on the orders of the Empress Helena, discoverer of the True Cross and mother of Constantine the Great (and somewhat improbably, according to legend, a daughter of Old King Cole of the nursery rhyme). Christian hermits were living here in the desert at that time, to find their way to God far from the busy haunts of men, and pilgrims began to make their way to this desolate area.

✛

Besides its treasures of ancient and Muslim civilisations, Egypt contains many sites linked with events of Jewish and Christian sacred history in both the Old and New Testaments.

✛

Spiritually fruitful in a barren land, the monastery of St Catherine in Sinai stands walled and guarded in a region honoured in Jewish, Christian and Muslim religions.

✛

ST CATHERINE'S FLIGHT

✛

The Chapel of the Burning Bush, with a small plate marking the exact spot where the bush stood, is now part of the monastery of St Catherine, on the lower slopes of Mount Sinai. Originally the monastery of the Transfiguration, its

history goes back to the 6th century, when the Emperor Justinian built a church here and protected it with fortifications and a guard of soldiers. One of the legends of the place is that the monastery's Muslim Bedouin staff today are descended from the original Byzantine soldiery.

After the Arab conquest the monastery generally enjoyed an amicable relationship with the Muslim authorities and in the 9th century the body of St Catherine was discovered here. A Christian of Alexandria, she had been condemned to be broken on the wheel (hence the catherine-wheel firework), but it was the wheel which broke, and her frustrated persecutors finally had to cut her head off. Her body was taken up by angels and transported to Sinai, to the summit of the mountain called Gebel Katarina, where the monks, guided by a dream, duly found it long afterwards, miraculously preserved. They gave it respectful burial in their church.

A mosque was opened for Muslim pilgrims in the 12th century. The monastery received costly presents from the kings of Christendom over the years, especially from the Russian tsars, who regarded themselves as its protectors in succession to the Byzantine emperors. It has a library full of treasures and a superb collection of icons. The bones of past generations of the Eastern

Orthodox monks can be seen in the charnel house, presided over by the black-robed skeleton of a 6th-century gate-keeper. At one time visitors to the monastery had to be hoisted up to the main door in a basket.

✢

FLIGHT INTO EGYPT

✢

Egypt was one of the first centres of Christianity outside Palestine and, according to tradition, was evangelised by St Mark, who was martyred at Alexandria, the principal early Christian base. The Coptic Christians of Egypt, the spiritual descendants of the first converts, have formed their own separate Church since the 5th century. They still celebrate Christmas according to the old calendar, on 7 January.

Coptic Christianity naturally prizes the only occasion which brought Jesus himself to Egypt, as a baby, when Joseph and Mary took him there to escape the massacre of the innocents by Herod in Bethlehem. In Cairo the church of St Sergius (Abu Serga) stands above a cave where the holy family are said to have taken shelter on their journey, and in the northern suburb of Mataria the Tree of the Virgin is a huge old braced-up trunk, descended from one which gave them shade. The spring here fed an ancient sacred pool in which, according to Egyptian mythology, the sun god Ra washed his face when he rose in splendour upon the world for the first time.

Joseph is said to have plied his trade as a carpenter in Old Cairo, the predecessor of the present city, but presently fled further up the Nile to Al Qusiyah, on the west bank near Meir, where at moments of danger the holy family used to hide in a small cave near by. Here today stands the Deir al-Muharraq, or Burned Monastery, the largest and wealthiest of all Egyptian Coptic monasteries. The church dedicated to the Virgin Mary on the site of the cave is claimed to be Egypt's earliest church.

Further north, pilgrims go up to the top of Gebel el-Teir, the mountain where the infant Jesus put his hand on a rock to stop it falling, and the print of his hand can still be seen. The little church on the summit has a reputation for healing.

✢

VIRGIN IN THE SKY

✢

The Virgin Mary returned to Egypt almost 2000 years later, or so it was believed by crowds of Coptic Christians who saw her in the sky above a church in the Zeitoun district of Cairo in 1968. She was first noticed on the church roof by some Muslim workmen, who ran to get a ladder, thinking she was a suicidally inclined nun. Then the figure rose and hovered over the church for ten days, attracting enormous crowds. In 1986 the Virgin appeared several times

Top: the Israelites adore the golden calf in the wilderness of Sinai, a favourite theme of Christian art. Above: this blurred photograph purports to show the apparition of the Virgin Mary above the Coptic church at Zeitoun in 1968.

again in the sky above another Cairo church, either with the baby Jesus in her arms or with a dove. It may be significant that this happened at a time when Coptic Christians were feeling threatened by rising antagonism from Muslim fundamentalists in Egypt.

SOLOMON AND SHEBA

The description in the Old Testament of King Solomon's vast wealth, regal grandeur and superhuman wisdom gave this king of Israel of the 10th century BC an awesome reputation in subsequent Jewish, Christian and Muslim tradition. He was claimed as the ancestor of the first Christian kingdom in Africa, high up in the mountains of Ethiopia, where Christianity was introduced from Egypt in the 4th century. The Ethiopian emperors gained ample prestige from the legend that they were descended from Solomon and the Queen of Sheba, and the story was enshrined in Ethiopian national tradition.

The legend was that Makeda, the beautiful Queen of Sheba, heard of Solomon's wisdom and went to visit him. With a vast train of camels, asses and mules laden with sumptuous presents, she journeyed in state to Jerusalem, where Solomon greeted her with honour. He craftily invited her to a splendid banquet at which she was served with food certain to make her thirsty. Then the king pressed her to stay the night with him and she agreed on condition that he would not force her. He promised, provided that in return she swore not to take anything from his house, to which

The exceedingly beautiful Queen of Sheba graciously makes her curtsey to King Solomon in a painting by a 17th-century artist, Frans Francken the Younger. The luxury and sensuality of the theme strongly appealed to European painters.

she laughingly agreed.

Later in the night she woke up, desperately thirsty, and drank from a jar of water which the wily Solomon had thoughtfully left by the bed. At this he seized her and accused her of breaking her promise, which freed him of his. Resignedly accepting defeat, the queen let him have his way with her and after her return home she bore him a son named Menelik, who grew up to be the founder of the Ethiopian royal house.

✛

The story of King Solomon and the Queen of Sheba was popular with both Christians and Muslims, but in the remote mountain stronghold of Ethiopia it became something more serious – part of the national identity.

✛

THE ARK OF THE COVENANT

✛

Where exactly Sheba was has never been established. It is usually placed in south-western Arabia, but the Ethiopian tradition is in no doubt that the queen came from Ethiopia. Her visit to Jerusalem and Solomon impressed her so deeply that she was converted to Judaism. When Menelik grew up, he went to visit his father and was crowned Emperor of Ethiopia in the Temple in Jerusalem. He then displayed a touch of the paternal cunning by contriving to steal the Ark of the Covenant, leaving a replica in its place.

The Ark was the portable shrine in which the ancient Israelites had carried their irascible deity about with them. This was before it was placed in the Holy of Holies, the innermost sanctuary of the Temple which Solomon built in Jerusalem, the dwelling place of God on earth. It also contained the original tablets on which the Ten Commandments were inscribed. Menelik brought this profoundly sacred, and by tradition intensely dangerous object – for the huge force of God inside it could kill anyone who touched it – back to Aksum, where it was hidden in a special shrine and treasured ever after.

Possession of the Ark entitled the Ethiopians to consider themselves the Chosen People. The emperors styled themselves Lions of Judah and the imperial guard wore the Star of David as their badge. The story about the Ark being concealed in Ethiopia was known to the outside world by the 13th century at least, and as late as the 1930s, when the Italians invaded the country, there is a story about two Italian soldiers forcing their way into the secret shrine of the Ark in the cathedral at Aksum, despite the attempts of the priests to stop them. Perhaps not surprisingly, the two men were never seen again.

✛
THE CRYSTAL FLOOR
✛

In Christian legend the Queen of Sheba was often depicted as a black African and the verse, 'I am black, but comely...' from the 'Song of Solomon' was linked with her. Muslim story-tellers named her Bilqis and in Islamic tradition it was Solomon who summoned her to visit him.

However, for all her loveliness, it was whispered that she had hairy legs, and Solomon tested this by having a special crystal floor built. When Bilqis came to it, she thought it was a pool of water and raised her skirts to cross it. This enabled the crafty king to see that the whisper was indeed correct. Undeterred, he invented the first depilatory known to history, and subsequently made her his wife.

✛
PRESTER JOHN
✛

In the Middle Ages, when Christian armies went to Palestine to wrest the Holy Places from Muslim control, a story began to circulate that there was a powerful Christian emperor somewhere in the east, who was a potential ally against the infidels. He was called Prester John (prester being an abbreviation of presbyter, meaning priest) and like the legendary King Solomon he was a master of magic. He owned a magic mirror in which he could see events everywhere in his country, and a glass church which expanded and contracted according to the size of the congregation.

In 1165 someone unknown forged a letter from this mysterious potentate to Frederick Barbarossa, the German emperor. In 1177 Pope Alexander III sent a letter to Prester John, but no one knows what became of it. At one stage the great Mongol warlord Genghis Khan was improbably identified as Prester John's son, while other people said that Prester John's realm had been saved from the Mongols by the miraculous intervention of the three Magi.

Marco Polo and other travellers kept an eye out for the mystery kingdom, but in vain. It was eventually identified with Ethiopia, the isolated mountain fastness which was known to have a Christian ruler.

The Black Jews

When Menelik returned from Jerusalem with the Ark, according to Ethiopian tradition, he had an escort of Jewish soldiers, provided by his father. These soldiers were the ancestors of the Falashas, the mysterious 'black Jews' who lived in Ethiopia for centuries untold, many of them in villages near Gonder. The Falashas are not ethnic Jews, in reality, but of Hamitic stock, and their Judaism is so old that they have no rabbis, but priests, regarded as descendants of Aaron. They are strict observers of the sabbath and claim to be descended from those of Menelik's guards who refused to cross a river on the sabbath day. Menelik and the others, who sinfully crossed the stream, became Christians. The Falashas survived much persecution in Ethiopia, where they were suspected of having the evil eye, and most of them were airlifted to safe refuge in Israel between 1984 and 1991.

A group of Falashas, or 'black Jews', wait to be airlifted to safety in Israel.

SPIRITS OF THE TIMES

✢

In Africa, as in South America and the Caribbean, possession cults help people to cope with the problems and sorrows of life and the stresses of a changing world.

✢

At the beginning of this century the traditional African religions held the allegiance of more than half the population. About one-third of Africans were Muslims and fewer than ten per cent were Christians. Since then, however, Christianity has made long strides. Most people in Kenya today, for example, are at least nominally Christian, belonging to denominations ranging from Roman Catholics, Methodists and Lutherans to Seventh Day Adventists. Along the coast, however, Islam is the dominant religion and the island of Lamu with its mosques and dhows is almost entirely Muslim, while there are Hindu temples in towns such as Nairobi and Mombasa.

Christianity and Islam in Africa, on the other hand, tend to have distinctly African characteristics. When white people first encountered them, many African peoples believed in a supreme and omnipotent male deity, who created the world. But they often considered him too remote to have much time for human beings and their problems. Nearer at hand were the numerous deities and spirits of the forces of nature and natural phenomena – the sun and the moon, wind and rain, animals and trees – and also the spirits of the ancestors, who were believed to take a continuing interest in the doings of their descendants. The Kikuyu, for example, regarded Mount Kenya as sacred and positioned their houses so that the doors faced the mighty peak. Rain-making rituals are held in the sacred and spectacular Matopo Hills of Zimbabwe, with their Bushman cave-paintings, while Lake Fundudzi in the Venda area of South Africa is sacred as

Masai warriors at a ceremony in Kenya. The Masai gods live remote from human beings.

the home of the python god. Outsiders are seldom allowed near it.

In Africa, as in other parts of the world, the traditional tendency is to disbelieve in chance and accident. If something occurs for which no obvious explanation is available, then it is likely to be put down to a supernatural being or to witchcraft. Many diseases, especially nervous and mental illnesses, are explained in this way and specialists in the sacred – healers, diviners, mediums – are needed to cure sickness, counteract the effects of hostile magic and act as channels between the human world and the world of spirits.

✢

THE WHITE-FACED RIDERS

✢

In Egypt, Ethiopia and the Sudan there is a deep-rooted belief in white-faced spirits called zars that, like the jinn of Muslim tradition, form a whole race of beings – some good, some bad and some mischievous and tricky – parallel to the human race. Mental illness and persistently peculiar behaviour, especially in women, may be explained as possession of a human being by a zar, which 'rides' its victim like a rider on a horse.

A professional medium is called in to conduct a ceremony of prolonged dancing, with music or hand-clapping, which works the victim up into a trance in which she behaves in the manner of the zar. If it is the English zar, for instance – a spirit instantly recognisable in Khartoum, in the Sudan – the victim will light a cigarette, brandish a walking stick and speak in caricature pidgin English. The medium may be able to persuade the possessing zar to leave its victim, perhaps in return for a gift. Alternatively, the victim may have to learn to live with the zar in reasonable harmony.

✢

IN TIME OF TROUBLE

✢

The Banyoro people of western Uganda have a traditional belief in spirits called Cwezi, who are said to have been a remarkable race of wise, fair-skinned people with miraculous powers who came to the area, governed it for a while and then disappeared into Lake Albert. (They are possibly based on a distant memory of the Portuguese.)

Some of these beings are linked with the sun, night, thunder, wild animals and other natural phenomena and all of them intervene powerfully in everyday life.

Before they vanished, the Cwezi founded the mbandwa cult, whereby contact can be made with them through persons who have become victims of a troublesome spirit. The trouble may be illness or failure of crops, a miscarriage, the loss of a job or any other misfortune. A specialist diviner is employed to identify the spirit responsible and the usual method is to throw nine cowrie shells down on a goatskin and inspect the pattern in which they fall.

Once the spirit has been identified, it 'mounts into the head' of the victim in a trance induced by drumming, singing and the shaking of gourd-rattles, and the victim behaves in the typical manner of the spirit. Only in this condition can the spirit either be persuaded to leave its victim's head or to say what it wants, so that some accommodation can be made with it and victim and spirit can achieve some measure of peaceful coexistence. As a practical therapy, it seems to work a good deal better than Western psychoanalysis.

Some of the spirits are connected with disturbing 20th-century developments in Banyoro life: like the spirit of military tanks, whose name is related to the word for the rhinoceros,

or the spirit of aircraft or the spirit of 'Polishness', which appeared after a large Polish camp had been established near Masindi during World War II. Also dangerous are ghosts, spirits of dead people who may or may not be related

Top left: seen from the Teleki Valley, Mount Kenya rises in sacred majesty. The Kikuyu people regard it as the home of the creator god.
Top right: a healer-magician in Kenya with human and animal puppets.
Above: dancers at a funeral ceremony of the Nuba people in the Sudan. A coating of ashes often represents the spirits of the dead in Africa.

to the victim. If the ghost is not closely related, it may be possible for a medicine man to expel it from its victim – while it squeaks agitatedly in falsetto protest – and catch it quickly in a pot, which can then be buried or taken and left far away in the bush.

THE GREAT CATTLE KILLING

÷

Spirit mediumship can have far-reaching political and social effects. Mediums in communication with approving ancestors played an important part in gaining popular support for the successful guerrilla campaign of the 1970s in Zimbabwe. In 1991 it was reported that the Frelimo regime in Mozambique, with its capital in Maputo, was scoring military victories against rebels with the help of a cult founded two years before by a man named Manuel Antonio. He claimed he had returned from the dead and was in touch with the spirits of his ancestors and with Jesus Christ. He 'vaccinated' his followers against enemy bullets by cutting their chests with a razor and forbade them to carry guns in battle. This filled them with self-confidence and they were surprisingly successful.

Spirit mediumship had catastrophic consequences for the Xhosa people in South Africa in 1857, when a girl named Nongqawuse was told how the people could put themselves right with the spirit world, which was allowing whites to steal their land and destroy their society. She said that the spirits required a huge sacrifice of cattle and crops, in return for which the whites would be driven into the sea. As a result, some 30,000 Xhosas died of starvation and 30,000 more were made utterly destitute.

THE HORSES OF THE GODS

West and Central Africa display a remarkable mixture of diverse peoples, religions and beliefs. The colossal new cathedral of Our Lady of Peace in Yamoussoukro, the capital of the Ivory Coast, said to be the second biggest Roman Catholic church in the world, after St Peter's in Rome, cost £100 million to build. It was consecrated by the Pope in 1990 to the thunder of African drums and the chanting of ecclesiastical Latin, but only ten per cent of the Ivory Coast's population is Roman Catholic and a few streets away journalists noticed Muslims quietly bowing in prayer in the direction of Mecca.

About half the population of West Africa is Muslim and one of the major pilgrimages of the Islamic world is the one to the tomb of Amadou Bamba, a famous marabout, or Muslim saint, in

✣

Traditional religion still has a firm grip in West and Central Africa, for all the impact of creeds from outside, and in the area from which African cults were taken to the New World they keep their vitality.

✣

Above: Dogon dancers in the fantastic masks for which they are famed.

the town of Touba in Senegal in June every year. He was kept in exile by the French for many years and the pilgrimage celebrates his return home in 1903. Meanwhile in Monrovia, the capital of Liberia, the visitor can contemplate the ruined splendour of the Masonic Temple, once the city's most

prominent building. The Masonic Order, founded by the American black pioneers who created Liberia in the 19th century, was immensely influential in Liberian politics until it was banned by President Doe after his coup in 1980.

At the same time, African traditional religions and cults are still vigorous, despite the influence of Christianity, Islam and Freemasonry. The night before the annual Mount Cameroon Race in January, for example, sacrifices are offered to smooth away any irritation the spirits of the mountain might feel as the runners in this newfangled competition tear up and down their precipitous and immemorial abode. At many village celebrations in West and Central Africa the drums and the dancers honour the local deities and spirits in traditional rituals to ensure fertility and prosperity, and the spirits of the ancestors are everywhere venerated.

GODS WALKING THE EARTH

✛

West Africa was the area that produced most of the black slaves exported to the New World and the African religions on which Voodoo and similar cults in the Caribbean and South America are based are still very much

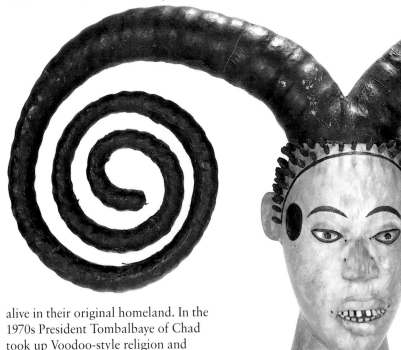

An Ekoi tribal mask from southern Nigeria, possibly made originally for an exhibition in London in 1925. Masks play a key role in many traditional African rituals.

may process through the town at the head of the worshippers, behaving in his characteristic fashion. Shango, for instance, will thrust an iron rod through his tongue and walk along like this casually for a while before removing it. Sometimes an iron spike will apparently be driven into his throat or his eye without blood or damage. The fact that

alive in their original homeland. In the 1970s President Tombalbaye of Chad took up Voodoo-style religion and introduced a cultural revolution in the name of 'Authenticity' and 'Chaditude' under the influence of Andre Vixamar, a Haitian intellectual and *éminence grise*. Everyone with a Christian name had to replace it with an African one, while all civil servants and army officers had to undergo a traditional and painful tribal initiation rite. There were numerous reports of the torture and killing of those who were reluctant to submit. Tombalbaye was assassinated in 1975.

The traditional religion of the vodun, or orisha, the gods of the Fon and Yoruba people, is still practised in Nigeria and Benin (the former Dahomey), where Ouidah, once a premier slaving port, is a centre of it. The gods 'ride' or 'climb on' their 'horses', the devotees they take possession of in trance at the culmination of rituals of drumming and dancing. Among them are Ogun, the god of warriors and blacksmiths, Shango, the thunder god, Shapana, the god of smallpox and contagious diseases, and Legba, the cynical and foul-mouthed messenger of the gods.

In the body of the devotee the god

the god seems to be visibly present and gives messages of comfort and hope to his followers is naturally a great strength to the religion. In African Christian churches in towns like Ibadan in Nigeria similar scenes of possession occur, but here the worshippers are believed to be possessed by the Holy Ghost.

✛

THE SPEAKING OF THE DRUMS

✛

Music and dancing are crucial to African religious rituals. They involve

the worshippers in the ceremony and unite them in it, create the right mood and are a means of working up and expressing emotion. As in many other societies around the world, the pulsating beat of the drums makes a bridge to the supernatural, helping to induce strange states of mind in which worshippers make a direct contact with the spirit

realm. Many a chief in West Africa in the past had his own sacred drum, which was given offerings of blood and played only at major ceremonies. When the drum was first made, a slave was sacrificed upon it so that his spirit would enter it and give it life.

The Ashanti people of the area round Kumasi in Ghana make their sacred drums out of a species of cedar tree, in which lives a spirit named Tweneboa Kadua. Each tree is cut down only after a special ritual and each drum is consecrated to Tweneboa Kadua. On ritual occasions Ashanti drums convey verbal messages from the worshippers to the gods or the ancestor spirits, like rhythmic speech, with the sound of the drums reproducing the tones of the Ashanti language.

Masks are also used in many rituals and have their own supernatural links and connections. They may be worn by dancers representing spirits, or to scare malignant spirits away, and some of them are venerated as guardians of a community's traditions, customs and values. Those which appear at the annual Fête des Masques at Man in the Ivory Coast are of this kind, and the Dogon people near Bandiagara in Mali are famous for their masks.

THE PREVALENCE OF WITCHES

In 1985 President Samuel Doe of Liberia put down an attempted coup against him and had its leader, Thomas Quiwonkpa, executed. He then paraded the castrated and disembowelled carcass of his opponent through his capital of Monrovia in a motorcade and took care to be seen in public chewing on pieces of the body, which meant that he was magically acquiring his enemy's vitality and powers.

In 1990 there was a sensational case in Liberia involving the ritual beheading of a policeman, sacrificed in a ceremony aimed at toppling President Doe, as well as a report about another police officer who acquired a magic ointment which would protect him against all harm. He asked a friend to fire a test bullet at him, the friend's aim was good and that was the end of that. Doe himself did not see the end of that year.

Belief in magic and witchcraft is prevalent all over Africa, and any harm or misfortune which does not have a simple, evident cause is liable to be put down either to a spirit or to hostile magic. This has the advantage of providing an explanation for undeserved suffering and ill luck, and also a remedy for it. Specialist medicine men and women, magicians, healers or 'masters' – anthropologists shun the old, condescending term 'witch doctor' – are on hand to deploy counter-magic, and in a society which believes that magic works, it may well be effective. Stories of African football teams retaining

Christianity, Islam and Western-style education programmes have failed to eradicate the fear of witchcraft and evil magic which runs all through African life.

A 'master' in Zambia has adopted Western promotion methods to advertise his services.

magicians as well as managers are legion, and the Cameroon side's doctor explained in 1990 that players gained confidence from a belief in their own medicine man's powers. It is also likely that successful African magic is sometimes the product of genuine psychic abilities.

THE EVIL WITHIN

Magic is used as a sanction against crime and antisocial behaviour, as in an incident reported recently from the bus station in the Zambian town of Chingola when a gang of four pickpockets jostled an old man and ran off with his money. The old man shouted after them that they had better bring it back or they would regret it. He then took a bicycle pump and an inner tube from his bag and began pumping the inner tube up. The four thieves all found their bellies swelling dramatically. They rushed back to the old man and returned the money. He counted it and then let the inner tube down, and their distended stomachs were seen to return to normal size.

Witches are believed to have an uncontrollable evil force inside them which harms other people. Witches and sorcerers also use spells, incantations and charms to project harmful magic at people, their families, farm animals and crops. Some of them can turn themselves into animals and birds to attack their victims. Accusations of witchcraft generally arise out of the ordinary tensions, jealousies and quarrels that arise among families and neighbours in small communities, and fear of being accused is a factor tending to make people behave more considerately to each other than they otherwise might.

ORACLES AND POLITICS

When a case of witchcraft is identified, a spirit medium or diviner, or 'master', is called in to discover who the witch is by consulting the ancestral spirits perhaps, or by using an oracle. Among the Azande people in the Sudan, for example, chickens were fed poison, the names of those suspected by the victim were called and their guilt or innocence depended on whether the chicken vomited the poison up or died. Deep in the jungles of the Congo suspects may be made to swallow a poisoned drink – not strong enough to be lethal – and a 'master' interprets their reactions as evidence of their guilt or innocence. Secret societies sometimes form to 'smell out' evil magicians, though they all too often turn into protection rackets.

Depending on circumstances, a convicted witch may be treated by a medicine man or may be executed. There are still reports from South Africa

Death of a Witch

The explorer H M Stanley, famous as the man who said, 'Dr Livingstone, I presume', saw an African man accused of witchcraft executed at Tshumbiri on the River Congo in 1877: 'arms tied behind and a wooden gag in his mouth, thrown into a canoe and paddled into the river and tossed overboard. As he was tossed the executioner cried out to him, "If you are a magician, cause this river to dry up and save yourself". After a few seconds he rose again and was carried down the stream about half a mile. A huge crocodile, fat with prey, followed him slowly and then rushed on him and we saw him no more.'

Below left: a phallic Ashanti fetish from Ghana. Statuettes of this kind, which are believed to be imbued with powerful magic, are needed for protection and reassurance in a world where many unwelcome events (which in the West are attributed to chance

and accident) are put down to hostile supernatural influences.
Below: part of an elaborate healing process for a sick child in Senegal. When magic is believed in by the participants in such cases, it is surprisingly effective.

of people suspected of evil magic among the Xhosa being burned to death. The Sotho people around Lebowa in South Africa call in an inyanga, or diviner, to identify witches, who may be beaten, expelled from the community or clubbed or stoned to death. There was a rash of cases in 1990-91, and it was strongly suspected that young political activists were using witchcraft accusations to get rid of conservative elders who opposed them.

✚

PIECES OF LUCK

✚

At Lomé in Togo there is a famous 'fetish market' where charms, medicines and magical equipment can be bought –

warthogs' teeth, the skulls of birds and monkeys, porcupine needles and all sorts and conditions of bones. Fetish, another term disliked by anthropologists, is derived from a Portuguese word used indiscriminately by the early explorers of the West African coast to mean a lucky charm or a religious figurine. A fetish is an object believed to have magical powers which protects its owner and wards off harm. It may be the head of a snake or a necklace of animals' teeth, or a piece of iron or steel or a small statuette. In Ghana, an Ashanti woman who wants to have a child may carry a small wooden fertility doll on her back, like a real child.

Statues of deities and other spirits are

in a different and more serious category.

Some fetishes have nails driven into them to harness the magic powers of iron. Blacksmiths, who work in iron, are widely credited with supernatural power. Among the Senoufo people of the Ivory Coast, for instance, the blacksmiths of Koni take charge of funerals because their magic protects them from harmful spirits.

Many Africans carry a small bag of protective and ritual objects with them, slung from the wrist or round the neck. Others are kept in the house. They include bones, roots, twigs, stones and things specially prepared by a medicine man. These small pieces of magic are the equivalents of a Westerner's cross or rabbit's foot or car mascot.

KING SOLOMON'S MINES

Africa's equivalent of El Dorado is the fabled land of Ophir, which is mentioned in the Old Testament (1 Kings, chapters 9,10) as a country to which King Solomon sent ships manned by Phoenician seamen to bring him treasures of gold and precious stones. Where Ophir was is not revealed, but the story of the Queen of Sheba's visit falls between two references to it and the context suggests that Ophir was somewhere to the south of Palestine. By at least the 6th century speculation had located it in Africa.

Medieval geographers identified the

✢

Generations of geographers, romantics, explorers and adventurers dreamed of and searched for a fabulous land of gold where Solomon's mines were hidden, deep in the heart of Africa.

✢

The massive ruins of Great Zimbabwe testify to the power and wealth of its medieval African kings.

Nile as one of the four rivers of paradise in Genesis, which implied that the original Garden of Eden lay somewhere in Africa to the south, and this could be connected with the fabulous, gold-rich country of Ophir. There was also a legend of a Jewish kingdom somewhere in Africa, the home of the lost tribes of Israel. The lost tribes were the ones deported from Palestine by the Assyrians in the 8th century BC, the mystery of whose disappearance has aroused much wild speculation, including the notion that the British are descended from them.

✛
THE LOST CITY
✛

The threads came together after the Portuguese rounded the Cape of Good Hope and sailed up the continent's south-eastern coast, when they began to hear rumours of a great ruined city in the interior. They eagerly connected it with the legendary Ophir and King Solomon's treasure mines, and some identified it as the city of the Queen of Sheba. The ruined city was Great Zimbabwe, whose massive stone walls, houses and fortifications, built between the 11th and 15th centuries, rise impressively from the landscape of southern Zimbabwe. Its powerful kings traded with Arabia and India, and even imported porcelain from China, and by the 12th century they were mining for gold.

In 1652 Dutch settlers founded a colony at Cape Town, and small groups began to push north. Among them were expeditions searching for Ophir and King Solomon's mines. Far down into the 19th century the Boers in South Africa believed that the Garden of Eden and the treasure-land of Ophir lay enticingly beyond the northern horizon, and in 1862 two German missionaries set off from Transvaal in search of Ophir. About five years later a white man – an American elephant hunter named Adam Render – at last cast eyes on the mighty ruins of Great Zimbabwe, but he kept the discovery to himself. It was not until the German geologist and explorer Karl Mauch arrived in 1871, guided by Render, that news of the city reached the outside world.

Mauch thought he had found the fabled Ophir, and that the city was its capital. He discovered that the most impressive building among the ruins was locally known as 'the great woman's house' and he decided that the city had been built by the Phoenicians for the Queen of Sheba on the model of the Temple and Solomon's palace in Jerusalem. The local African chief, he believed, was a descendant of the Jewish

Stewart Granger and Deborah Kerr in the 1950 film version of King Solomon's Mines, *which was based on the legend of a fabulous kingdom in the heart of Africa.*

chief priest whom Solomon had sent to accompany the Queen of Sheba home.

A British mining company moved in swiftly to exploit the discovery, but the gold had been mined out long before. Gold jewellery found in the ruins was ruthlessly melted down and sold. With their built-in attitude of superiority, Europeans were unable to believe that an African culture could have built anything as magnificent as Great Zimbabwe, and King Solomon, the Queen of Sheba and the Phoenicians were the preferred candidates.

✛

THE IMMORTAL QUEEN
✛

The greatest single influence in fastening the whole romantic legend into the consciousness of the English-speaking world was the adventure novelist Henry Rider Haggard, whose book *King Solomon's Mines* was published in 1885. It sold like hot cakes and has never been out of print since. Haggard had lived in Natal during the Zulu War and the first Boer War, and

his heroes make their way north from Durban across desert and mountains to the fictitious country of the Kukuanas, which he set in Matabeleland (now the southern part of Zimbabwe). In the sequel, *Allan Quatermain*, the same heroes journey deep into the interior in search of a lost white race and come to a great city ruled by two beautiful twin queens. In *She*, the central figure is the white queen of a remote African mountain kingdom, who is immortal and bathes in fire to keep herself eternally beautiful and young.

'She who must be obeyed' was based on the Rain Queen, who was revered by the Zulus and other peoples in southern Africa as the ruler of a land to the north, where she was worshipped as a goddess at a sacred mountain. Some said that she was white and immortal. She controlled the life-giving rain, and not even the fearsome Zulu warlord Shaka ventured to attack the Rain Queen's domain. Behind the legend is a real figure, a queen of the Lobedu people in South Africa, whose rain-making powers still descend from mother to daughter.

✛

FOLLOWING A STAR
✛

Linked with this complex of legends are the 'black Jews' of South Africa, the Lemba, whose origins are mysterious, but who claim to be descended from the Falashas of Ethiopia, and so from the Jewish escort which accompanied the Queen of Sheba on her return from Jerusalem. They maintain that their ancestors helped to build Great Zimbabwe and that they brought the Ark of the Covenant there with them and hid it in the Soutpansberg Mountains, in the Venda area of South Africa. They left Great Zimbabwe because they had sinned there, by eating mice, and followed a star sent by God to lead them to settle round Mount Mberengwe. So even today the mists of legend cloak Africa in romance.

✛ ASIA ✛

hen James Hilton's novel *Lost Horizon* was published in 1933, the story of Europeans stumbling across the secret, idyllic valley of Shangri-La in the Himalayas caught the public imagination. The fictional Shangri-La was a haven of wisdom and tranquillity, unspoiled by the corruptions of modern Western civilisation. The author drew not only on ancient Oriental traditions of a secret community of the wise somewhere in Tibet or Mongolia, but also on the deeply rooted Western awe of the mysterious and inscrutable civilisations of the East and the belief that they have discovered a deeper supernatural wisdom than the West knows.

Asia is the largest continent on the globe, covering 60 per cent of the world's land surface. It contains the highest mountains on earth, deserts from Arabia to the Gobi, huge areas of steppe and great rivers, from the Euphrates to the Indus, the Ganges and the Yangtze, in whose valleys the first human settlements and civilisations developed. Asia's people, who number more than half the population of the world, are equally diverse. So are the religions and cults they have produced, from the murderous sects of the Assassins of Persia and the Thugs of India to the courteously rule-bound celestial bureaucracy of the state religion of Imperial China, and the Shinto deities of Japanese nationalism.

Asia cradled all five of the world's major

Among Asia's numerous deities is Ganesha, the Hindu elephant god. His statue here is suitably garlanded.

religions – Hinduism and Buddhism in India, Judaism and Christianity in Palestine, Islam in Arabia. Buddhism was born in India, died out there, had its major influence in south-east Asia, Tibet, Mongolia, China and Japan, and in this century has regained a presence in India. Palestine, the mother of Judaism and Christianity, is the birthplace of stories familiar to generations in the West – of Adam and Eve, Noah's Ark, Samson and Delilah, the three Magi – which have their place in Muslim tradition as well.

Arab armies and traders carried Islam triumphantly across Palestine, Mesopotamia and Iran to Afghanistan and India, and on to China and Indonesia. Caliphs and sultans reigned in sophisticated splendour from Baghdad and Istanbul, and the Great Mogul held sway in unexampled magnificence from the Peacock Throne in Agra. The main Christian missionary drive in the East began in the 19th century. From 1917 on, Communist regimes in the USSR and China did their best to wipe out religion as 'the opium

of the people', while western Asia has seen an upsurge of Islamic fundamentalism.

Beneath the major religions, however, lies the bedrock of older traditions. People believe in many gods and spirits influencing their lives, whatever orthodoxy may demand. Trance and mediumship to communicate with the spiritual realm have played a crucial role in Asia, from ancient Israel to the whirling dervishes of Turkey, god-men in India, shamans in Siberia, China and

Istanbul

Ephesus

Konya

Antioch Mount Saphon

Mount Ararat

Marand

Kafarnaum

Nineveh

Haifa

Alamut

Tel Aviv

Sāmarrā

Gaza 5 6

Jerusalem/ Bethlehem/ Bethel

2 Baghdad

Tehran

Qom

Beer Sheva

Ecbatana

Hebron

1

Isfahan

3 4 Shuruppak

Sodom

Ur

Dead Sea

Shīrāz

Medina

1 Babylon
2 Karbala
3 Najaf
4 Al Kūfah
5 Jericho
6 Nazareth

Jeddah Mecca

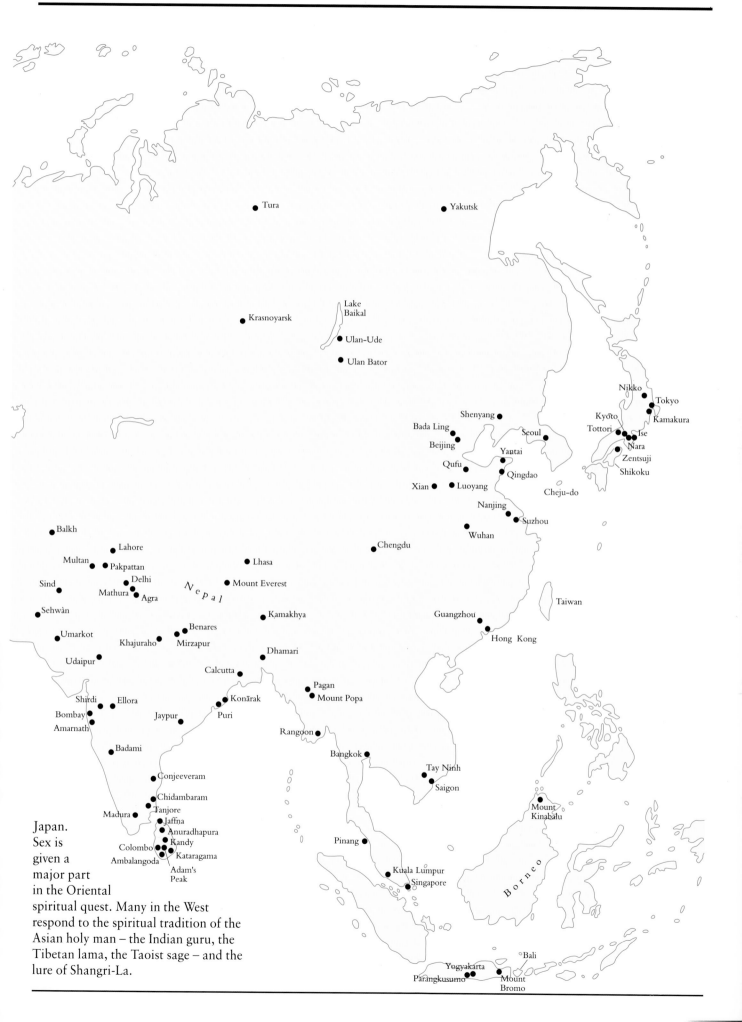

Tura

Yakutsk

Krasnoyarsk

Lake
Baikal

Ulan-Ude

Ulan Bator

Nikko

Tokyo

Shenyang

Kyoto

Kamakura

Bada Ling

Tottori

Ise

Beijing

Seoul

Nara

Zentsuji

Yantai

Qufu

Shikoku

Qingdao

Xian

Luoyang

Cheju-do

Nanjing

Balkh

Suzhou

Lahore

Wuhan

Multan

Pakpattan

Chengdu

Lhasa

Delhi

N e p a l

Mount Everest

Sind

Mathura

Agra

Sehwàn

Kamakhya

Guangzhou

Umarkot

Benares

Khajuraho

Mirzapur

Hong Kong

Udaipur

Dhamari

Taiwan

Calcutta

Shirdi

Ellora

Konārak

Pagan

Bombay

Jaypur

Puri

Mount Popa

Amarnath

Badami

Rangoon

Conjeeveram

Bangkok

Tay Ninh

Chidambaram

Saigon

Madura

Tanjore

Jaffna

Anuradhapura

Mount
Kinabalu

Kandy

Colombo

Kataragama

Pinang

Ambalangoda

Adam's
Peak

Kuala Lumpur

B o r n e o

Singapore

Bali

Yogyakarta

Parangkusumo

Mount
Bromo

Japan.
Sex is
given a
major part
in the Oriental
spiritual quest. Many in the West
respond to the spiritual tradition of the
Asian holy man – the Indian guru, the
Tibetan lama, the Taoist sage – and the
lure of Shangri-La.

THE BIBLE LANDS

From the Garden of Eden and Noah's Ark to the finding of the True Cross and the Holy Lance, south-western Asia bristles with sites famed in the legends and traditions of three major religions.

For Jews, Christians and Muslims alike, the Bible is sacred history, the record of God's creation of the world and dealings with mankind. Places of importance in the record are deeply revered in all three faiths, and many legends grew up to amplify the Bible's texts. This is especially true of some of the best-known and best-loved stories which most archaeologists and historians no longer regard as literally true.

Much ink has been spilt, for instance, on the geography of the Garden of Eden, which the book of Genesis leaves unclear. Some Jewish writers placed it on Mount Saphon (modern Jebel Akra) in Syria, others at Hebron in the most fertile valley in the south of Palestine. An alternative location was the head of the Persian Gulf, while later speculators put Eden in Africa south of the sources of the Nile, in Arabia or almost anywhere that was just beyond the bounds of known geography.

Above: pilgrims jostle excitedly as the cross is carried along the Via Dolorosa in Jerusalem, the way Christ took to Golgotha.
Right: this circular stone tower at Jericho dates from long before the time of Joshua.

Ararat in Armenia (now in Turkey) and ancient writers said that remains of the ark had been found there. The peak was long believed to be too sacred for any climber to reach, but European mountaineers conquered it in the 19th century and after World War II an American party reported finding semi-fossilised timbers on Ararat, dated to about 1500 BC. Local people claimed many connections with Noah and his family. His wife was said to be buried at Marand and the site where he planted the first vineyard was shown at Arghuri.

The story in the Bible was based on a much older myth from ancient Mesopotamia, and in the Epic of Gilgamesh the hero, who is named Utnapishtim, comes from the city of Shuruppak on the banks of the Euphrates. The story of the Tower of Babel in Genesis was probably inspired by the ziggurats, or temple-towers, of Mesopotamia, and perhaps specifically by the ziggurat of the god Marduk in Babylon.

NOAH'S ARK

Genesis is clear about the spot on which Noah's Ark came to rest when the waters of the Great Flood began to recede. It was on snow-capped Mount

AND THE WALLS CAME TUMBLING DOWN

Abraham, the first of the Hebrew patriarchs, also came from Mesopotamia, perhaps in the 19th century BC, from the city of Ur on the Euphrates, now a ruined site in Iraq. Abraham settled at Beersheba (modern Beer Sheva), today the capital of Israel's southern district. His nephew Lot lived in Sodom, which with Gomorrah became a byword for its sexual practices and was destroyed by a rain of fire and brimstone. The 'cities of the plain' were close to the southern end of the Dead Sea, which the Arabs called 'the sea of Lot'. Because Lot's wife looked back when escaping, she was turned into a pillar of salt, which is solemnly pointed out by today's tour guides.

North of the Dead Sea is Jericho, one of the world's oldest towns, famous for the story of the walls falling flat when the Israelites under Joshua marched round them carrying the Ark of the Covenant and blowing the ram's horn trumpets. After the Crusaders took Jericho, Christian pilgrims came to visit the spot near by, where Jesus was baptised by St John the Baptist in the River Jordan. Also close by is the peak where Jesus was tempted by the Devil, and in Muslim tradition the tomb of Moses is in the mosque of Nabi Musa.

The legend of Samson and his temptress wife Delilah, who wormed the secret of his strength out of him and betrayed him to the Philistines, reaches its climax at Gaza, on the Mediterranean coast of Palestine, where the blinded hero pulls down the temple on himself and his tormentors. Elijah called down fire from heaven to rout the prophets of Baal on Mount Carmel, above Haifa, another site revered by Jews, Christians and Muslims. Also on the coast, Jaffa (modern Tel Aviv) has a role in Greek mythology as the place where Perseus rescued Andromeda from the dragon: the rock to which she was chained is still pointed out.

✣

THE CROSS AND THE LANCE
✣

The holiest place in the Holy Land is Jerusalem, long believed to stand at the

A 12th-century view of the world's first lifeboat, with the animals packed neatly in by twos. In 1994 investigators claimed to have discovered a huge wooden vessel of the right dimensions buried near Ararat, the traditional site.

exact centre of the earth. It is the site of Solomon's Temple and the Holy of Holies, which in the Old Testament is the dwelling place of God on earth. Jerusalem is also the scene of Christ's trial and crucifixion, and the third of Islam's sacred cities (after Mecca and Medina). The Dome of the Rock stands on the site of the Temple, the Wailing Wall is part of the Second Temple and the Via Dolorosa follows the footsteps of Christ carrying his cross to Golgotha. It is not surprising that the Jerusalem

police have a special branch to deal with visitors suffering from religious over-excitement.

It was on Golgotha, or Mount Calvary, in the year 335 that the actual cross on which Christ died was discovered by the Empress Helena – or so it was claimed – during excavations for the building of the Church of the Holy Sepulchre. Helena was the mother of Constantine the Great (and British legend makes her a daughter of Old King Cole, of nursery rhyme fame). Buried directly beneath the spot on which the cross stood, the skull of Adam was found – appropriately, since Christ was 'the second Adam', who came to rescue mankind from the sin of the first. Slivers of the wood of the True Cross, which was believed to have miraculous power, were eventually distributed all over the Christian world, in such quantities as to arouse scepticism. As well as the Cross were found the inscription mocking Jesus as King of the Jews, the nails which pierced him and the crown of thorns.

Another great Christian relic was found in 1098 by the crusaders at Antioch. This was the Holy Lance, with which the Roman centurion pierced Christ's side as he hung on the cross. The crusaders had taken Antioch by storm, but then found themselves besieged in the town by a Saracen army. Food and water ran desperately short and morale was at rock bottom when a priest claimed he had seen in a vision where the Holy Lance was buried in the church of St Peter. The sacred relic was duly found and the discovery so heartened the Christian warriors that they sallied out and routed the enemy.

MINISTERS OF GRACE

Perhaps the two most familiar appearances of angels in Christian tradition are those of the Archangel Gabriel to the Virgin Mary in Nazareth, to tell her she was to give birth to Jesus, and of another angel to announce the Saviour's birth to the shepherds watching their flocks by night at Bethlehem.

Judaism, Christianity and Islam have only one God, but they also believe in lesser spiritual beings, 'the heavenly host', who are the angels of God's court. Because angels lived in the sky, they were imagined with wings. Because they were linked with the stars, there were believed to be enormous numbers of

⊹

The angels familiar in Christian art, carols and traditional Christmas cards go back to early Jewish traditions, while successful cures of possession cases helped to spread the early Christian message.

⊹

Below left: Islamic angels in a 16th-century Turkish miniature. Below right: angels dancing, from Fra Angelico's Last Judgement.

them – 3,472,000 according to one computation. Beautiful, as befits God's attendants, they are principally occupied in hymning God's praises. In the Old Testament, the idea of the heavenly court seems to have been modelled on the courts of powerful human kings with their attendants and royal servants, and one of the functions of angels is to communicate with human beings.

⊹

JACOB'S LADDER

⊹

The writers of the Old Testament evidently felt the need for divine intermediaries less terrifying than God

himself to speak to men, and the English word angel translates the Hebrew for 'messenger'. Jacob fell asleep and dreamed of a ladder set up between heaven and earth, with angels going up and down it, in a way clearly symbolic of their role in communicating between God's realm and the human world. Awed, he called the place Bethel, 'house of God' (Genesis, chapter 28). In some passages, 'the angel of the Lord' is not so much a separate being as God's presence. It was the angel of the Lord, for instance, who appeared to Moses as a flame of fire in the burning bush, but it was God who spoke from it.

The angels also made useful scapegoats for God's more dubious actions, as in the scene when the Almighty is seen by the prophet Micaiah, sitting on his throne, 'and all the host of heaven standing beside him on his right hand and on his left' (1 Kings 22. 19). God needed a spirit to trap the wicked King Ahab and entice him to his death, and after the heavenly host had shifted their feet uneasily and mumbled one thing and another, one of them stepped forward and volunteered to be a lying spirit in the mouths of the king's diviners and mediums, and so lead him astray. This scene, with the responsibility for a morally questionable action shifted from God himself to an angel, is a step in the development which eventually led to the idea of the Devil, the great archangel and principle of evil who rebelled against God.

The use of spirit mediums in ancient Israel to discover the future and obtain advice is also illustrated in the well-known story of Saul, at a crisis in his affairs, consulting the witch of Endor, a medium who summons up the spirit of his dead adviser, Samuel. It brings Saul no comfort, for the ghost of Samuel predicts his imminent death (1 Samuel, chapter 28).

✢

CHERUBIM AND SERAPHIM

✢

Other angelic beings in the Old Testament are the cherubim, which God set to guard the gate of Eden after the expulsion of Adam and Eve – apparently imagined on the model of the winged bulls of Assyrian sculpture – and the seraphim, the fiery, six-winged entities

seen by Isaiah. Later Jewish and Christian speculation conceived of a whole hierarchy of orders and ranks of angels and gave the greatest of them personal names. Michael was the guardian archangel of Israel and the

Top: many artists have been drawn to the story of the war in heaven, when Satan and his angels rebelled against God and were driven from the sky by Michael and the good angels. This wood-graving illustrating Milton's 'Paradise Lost' is by Gustave Doré. Above: the fiery seraphim are seen on this Greek amulet case dating from the 19th century.

leader of the angels who fought for God against the Devil and his followers in the war in heaven, as recounted in the Book of Revelation, which accounts for his connection with 'high places' in medieval Europe (*see page 33*).

The archangel Raphael appears engagingly in the apocryphal Book of Tobit, where in human disguise he guides the young hero, Tobias, through his adventures. Together they go from the exiled Jewish community at Nineveh in Assyria to Ecbatana in Persia, where Tobias is to seek the beautiful Sarah's hand in marriage. She is the victim of a powerful evil spirit, named Asmodeus, who has jealously killed Sarah's seven husbands in succession, each on his wedding night. With Raphael's help Tobias routs the fiend and all ends happily.

Islam accepted the angelic 'messengers' or 'envoys', too, and gives each person a pair of angels who record his deeds in life. It was through the angel Jibril (Gabriel) that God revealed the Koran to Muhammad, and he was also the divine messenger who told Noah to build the Ark. Later he lured the army of Pharaoh to destruction in the Red Sea. Izrail is the Angel of Death who parts the soul from the body and Israfil will sound the last trump when the world ends.

✢

EVIL EXPELLED

✢

Parallel to the good angels, in Jewish and Christian tradition, were armies of evil spirits, led by the Devil and his sinister satraps. At the time of Jesus, diseases were often attributed to evil spirits and the successes of Jesus and his early followers in healing disease and exorcising people apparently possessed by demons were a powerful factor in drawing attention to Jesus and his teaching. This is emphasised in the very first chapter of the earliest Christian gospel, which describes how at Capernaum (modern Kafarnaum) Jesus cured a possessed man and people brought him 'all who were sick or possessed with demons' (Mark 1.32). Later, St Paul made a great impression at Ephesus, when the mere touch of his handkerchiefs cured the sick, 'and diseases left them and the evil spirits came out of them' (Acts 19. 12).

FROM ARABIA TO THE CASPIAN

Arabia is the motherland of Islam, whose two holiest cities – Mecca and Medina – are in Saudi Arabia. The Prophet Muhammad was born in Mecca and spent most of his life there. All Muslims turn towards Mecca to pray and each year many thousands of faithful pilgrims make the journey there from every corner of the Muslim world. The rites and observations culminate at the Kaaba, a building in the Great Mosque, in whose wall is set the Black Stone, which pilgrims kiss. Thought to be a meteorite, it was already revered in Muhammad's time. Medina 'the radiant' is the city to which he was forced to escape in AD622, and it is there that he lies buried. Both cities are forbidden to non-Muslims.

Many traditions and legends grew up about the holy places. After Adam and Eve were hurled bodily out of the Garden of Eden, Adam fell on Adam's Peak in Sri Lanka, where his footprint is still to be seen in the rock. Eve landed at Jeddah on the Red Sea coast, and the wicked serpent at Isfahan in Iran. After many years God sent the repentant Adam to Mecca, to live in the Kaaba, and there he and Eve were reunited. She was buried at Jeddah when she died. Long afterwards Abraham arrived, with his son Ishmael, the ancestor of the Arabs, and rebuilt the Kaaba, which had been destroyed in the Great Flood.

✢

THE JOURNEY TO PARADISE

✢

Jerusalem is the third of Islam's holy cities. Muhammad made his famous night journey from Mecca to Jerusalem on the winged horse al-Buraq, which then carried him up through the seven heavens to Paradise and the presence of God. They took off from the rock which is today at the heart of the magnificent Dome of the Rock on the Temple Mount in Jerusalem.

✢

Holy cities and the shrines of venerated holy men are marked on the map of Islamic culture in the Middle East, with the ruins of an Assassin stronghold.

✢

Above: the summit of Moriah inside the Dome of the Rock.

In Jewish, Christian and Muslim tradition, this was the rock on the summit of Mount Moriah, on which Abraham was about to sacrifice his only son Isaac when God stayed his hand. The angel Jibril (Gabriel) held the rock steady for the horse to take flight and his fingerprints are shown in the Dome.

Visiting Jerusalem in the 1930s, H V Morton described the huge, uncanny slab of black rock at the centre of the building, 'as if the sharp top of a mountain were pushing its way through the floor of a house'. One of the buildings near by is called Solomon's Throne and, according to legend, Solomon was found dead there. Not wanting the jinn, whom he controlled by magic art, to realise that he was dying, he propped himself up on his throne with his staff. The dim-witted jinn were duly deceived, until eventually worms gnawed through the staff and Solomon's corpse fell to the floor.

A copy of the Kaaba was built in the old mosque at Shiraz in Iran, a city famed for its beauty, its gardens and its wine. The three Magi, the wise men from the east who took gifts to the infant Christ, are said to have started their journey from Shiraz, following the star.

✢

MURDERERS AND MARTYRS

✢

A religious sect in Persia gave the world the word 'assassin'. It comes from the Order of Assassins led by the legendary Old Man of the Mountains, who held sway at the fortress of Alamut in the Elburz Mountains, between Tehran and the Caspian Sea. Their name comes from the Arabic for hashish. Founded by Hassan-i Sabbah, a fanatical 11th-century ascetic from Qom, who had both his easy-going sons executed for not living up to his standards, they were early specialists in terrorist murder. The Order's trained killers were buoyed up by the belief that they were sure of a place in Paradise after death. To reinforce their confidence, they were drugged with hashish and then left to come round in a beautiful garden of trees, fountains and delectable girls as a foretaste of what was in store.

The Assassins were an offshoot of Shiism, the second largest division of Islam. Today concentrated mainly in Iran

Right: procession in commemoration of the martyrdom of Hussein, in Karachi in Pakistan.

and southern Iraq, the Shiites differ from the Sunnis, the majority branch of Islam, about the correct line of succession to Muhammad, which they maintain should have run through the Prophet's son-in-law, Ali, who was murdered at Al Kufah in Iraq in 661. His son, Hussein, was defeated in battle at Karbala on the Euphrates in 680, captured and beheaded. Shiites believe in a succession of Imams, or semi-divine and sinless spiritual leaders, who followed the martyred Hussein. The last Imam was Muhammad al-Muntazar, who mysteriously disappeared at Samarra, north of Baghdad, in 874, when he was only a small boy. He is the Mahdi, the Expected One, whose return is confidently awaited.

The Shia holy city of Najaf in Iraq grew up round the great golden-domed mosque, barred to all infidels, which was built over Ali's tomb. The bodies of the dead have been brought from as far away as India to be buried in this hallowed earth. Hussein was buried at Karbala, where a mosque houses his remains. Sacred earth from Karbala is distributed to Shia communities in small tablets, which the devout touch with their foreheads when praying.

A PASSION OF GRIEF

✢

The martyrdom of Hussein is commemorated every year by the Shia with mourning and tears, and great processions which include groups flagellating themselves and cutting their heads. Little models of the Karbala tomb are carried in the procession and a passion play re-enacts Hussein's death.

The scenes at the funeral of the Ayatollah Khomeini in 1989 testified to the Shiite reverence for holy men. Huge numbers of weeping, black-clad mourners beating their breasts and heads in sorrow made the planned funeral parade from Tehran impossible and the body was flown to the cemetery by helicopter. On arrival, the bier was jostled by thousands of people desperately snatching pieces of the shroud, so that the corpse was exposed, and eventually it had to be put in a metal coffin and surrounded by armed guards.

The Power of the Dance

Many of the Sufi mystics of Islam are venerated as saints at their tombs. The 'whirling dervishes', 'dancing dervishes' and 'howling dervishes', of whom disapproving Western 19th-century travellers wrote, are members of Sufi brotherhoods which seek ecstatic union with the divine through dancing, leaping and stamping. They are believed to attain paranormal powers, including the ability to read minds and to be in two places at once. The Mevlevi Order, with its technique of whirling round faster and faster to induce a state of trance, was founded by the 13th-century poet and mystic Jalal al-Din Rumi, who came from Balkh in Afghanistan and spent most of his life in Turkey. 'He who knows the power of the dance', he said, 'dwells in God'. The Order was closed down by the modernising Turkish regime of the 1920s, but still has adherents, who gather for ritual dancing and music each year at Rumi's tomb in Konya.

Whirling dervishes from Konya appeared at London's Albert Hall in 1990.

FATAL ATTRACTIONS

The Indian sub-continent resembles a huge and colourful tapestry whose threads are a multitude of diverse peoples, languages, shades of skin colour and religions. The Republic of India itself has a population of more than 700 million, speaking 15 major languages. Over 80 per cent of this number are Hindus, with substantial minorities of Muslims, Christians, Sikhs, Buddhists and Jains, while Islam is the dominant religion in Pakistan and Bangladesh, and aboriginal tribes in remote areas still uphold their ancestral cults.

Hinduism, the oldest of the Indian religious traditions, has room for innumerable different gods, cults and practices. Some Hindus believe in one God, most often Krishna or Shiva, some in many, and besides the major deities known all over the country there are local gods and goddesses, spirits of trees and animals, ancestor spirits and deities of forests and mountains. Cows are sacred, of course, and must never be harmed. Rivers are sacred, too, as the veins of Mother Earth, especially the Ganges, and a devout Hindu may confer a certain sanctity on his bath-water by imagining it as the Ganges.

So numerous and varied are the Hindu sects that it is doubtful if any religious belief or activity known to mankind has not occurred in some form somewhere among them.

A huge and lavishly decorated 'juggernaut' rumbles through the crowded streets of Madurai in southern India during the Chitrai festival, when the Hindu deities of the vast Meenakshi temple make a stately progress. The temple is one of the finest in the country.

✛

THE LADY IS FOR BURNING

✛

Under British influence, educated Indian opinion turned against the custom of suttee, by which a widow was expected to ascend her husband's funeral pyre and burn herself to death – as a mark of faithful love – to accompany him to the next world and to obtain spiritual merit for herself and him. She was entrusted with messages for the family's dead relations and then seated herself on the pyre, with her husband's head in her lap, before it was lit. Sometimes she was mercifully drugged, sometimes she was tied down to stop her jumping out of the flames. Some women went voluntarily and bravely to a horrible death, but many were forced into it. If the widow was pregnant, she was allowed to wait until her child was two months old before immolating herself.

When a king died, all his wives and concubines might be sacrificed in this way. The British did their best to wipe suttee out, and when the Maharana of Udaipur died in 1861, none of his wives could be persuaded to mount his pyre, so a slave girl was burned instead. Suttee is now illegal in India, but occasional instances of it are still reported.

Human sacrifice was offered to the gods in India from very early times and one text describes a victim being knocked out before his eyes were gouged out and his entrails pulled out and draped like a garland over the branches of a tree. Human victims tended to be offered especially to goddesses. At the dedication of a temple to the love goddess who gave her name to Kamakhya, in Assam, in 1565, 140 men were slaughtered and their severed heads were presented to her on copper plates. As late as 1861 the ruler of Joipur, near Vizagapattam, sacrificed a girl to the goddess Durga.

MERCHANTS OF DEATH

The Thugs, the professional assassins and robbers who preyed on travellers in Central India, strangled their victims as sacrifices to the black and blood-smeared goddess Kali, under her name of Bhavani. They believed that the goddess herself had founded their cult and taught them their skills, which they handed down to their children generation by generation. Creeping up on a victim from behind, the Thug would whip a length of cloth tightly round his neck and relax it, and tighten it and relax it several more times to throttle the victim slowly and agonisingly, while calling on the goddess to come and share the enjoyment. The Thugs never killed women and the temple of Kali at Mirzapur was their principal sanctuary.

The British authorities declared virtual war on the Thugs and wiped them out, but the memory of them has survived among the dacoits of the Chambal Valley south of Agra, who live by professional banditry. They worship Kali, too, and believe she is present in their guns, which they decorate elaborately and hold in special awe.

Above: this graphic Indian ceramic piece shows a band of Thugs who have caught an unwary victim and are strangling him. Below: an unfortunate widow is burned alive in this 19th-century Indian depiction of suttee.

THE JUGGERNAUT

British observers were also horrified by the death toll at the festivals of the god Jagannatha, a form of Krishna worshipped at Puri and elsewhere in eastern India. The giant image of the god was placed on a colossal 16-wheeled, elaborately decorated wooden car, the size of a house, which the British called the Juggernaut. It was drawn through the city on ropes by 4200 men, and excited devotees used to hurl themselves to their deaths beneath the huge creaking wheels in the belief that they would go straight to paradise.

This has been stopped, but the festival continues: worshippers dance to the beat of drums and go into trance, women bring tresses of their hair as offerings, musicians on the sacred car beat drums and clash cymbals as it is pelted with marigolds and rice by the enraptured crowds, who scoop up the dust behind the wheels as they pass and rub it on their faces. There is a similar celebration at Dhamrai, a Hindu village in Bangladesh, where a giant 32-wheeler chariot of Jagannath is dragged through the streets.

GOD-MEN OF INDIA

At Lahore in 1838 the British consul, an English army colonel and a European doctor all kept a sharp eye on the proceedings as an Indian yogi named Haridas went into a trance while sitting cross-legged on a white cloth. The cloth was wrapped round his body, which was as rigid as a board, and he was placed in a large box, which was then locked. It was put into a grave dug inside a garden pavilion, whose doors and windows were locked and sealed. The pavilion was watched day and night by relays of British soldiers for a month to prevent any trickery. The box was then dug up and opened. To the astonishment of the onlookers, Haridas was not dead. Far from it, after his assistant had washed him with warm water and massaged him with butter for half an hour, the holy man was as lively as a cricket.

All religions believe that there is a divine element or ingredient of some kind in human nature, but Hinduism teaches that human beings can realise the divine in themselves in this life and this world, can become deities walking the earth. Numerous gurus, or spiritual teachers, are treated as living gods in India, by anything from a handful of followers to many thousands. Images of the teacher are venerated, hymns are sung to him and incense burned in his presence; offerings of money and flowers are placed at his feet and his followers bow down before him. Worshippers may drink the water in which his feet have been washed or with which he has rinsed his mouth. In earlier times the guru often

Nowhere on earth has the pursuit of spiritual perfection and paranormal powers been carried on with greater determination and intelligence than in India, whose holy men have been famous for centuries for their remarkable feats.

had his pick of his followers' womenfolk, but modern Hindu reformers frowned on this practice.

CHAITANYA AND GANDHI

Great gurus of the past are worshipped, too. An example is the famous spiritual teacher Chaitanya, who founded a popular ecstatic sect in eastern India devoted to the god Krishna, and was regarded by his followers as an embodiment of the deity. The fact that he was frequently seized by fits in which he foamed at the mouth, wept or laughed crazily, shinned up trees or ran about shouting before collapsing in a stupor strengthened this impression. He spent the last years of his life at Puri, on the Bay of Bengal, and died in 1534 when he was taken with an ecstatic fit while bathing in the sea. The sect has worshipped him ever since.

In this century, Mahatma Gandhi, the great Indian reformer and political leader, was treated as divine by multitudes of admirers who swarmed over him whenever he appeared in public, jostling to get near him and clawing at his body and clothes,

The ascetics of India fascinated the early European explorers and settlers. This one has held his arms above his head for so long that they are immovable.

to his intense embarrassment. The title Mahatma means 'great soul' and to be close to such a one is to acquire some of his holiness. When Gandhi began to campaign for Indian self-rule in the 1920s, the word spread among his simpler followers that he would expel the British from India by magic, and that the authorities would never be able to seize him, because he would simply fly away. One of the reasons why he was so cheerful when he was arrested was his hope that these myths would be exploded, but they went too deep for that.

✢

SAINTLY FATHER, BLISSFUL MOTHER

✢

Gandhi claimed no miraculous powers, but the followers of Sai Baba (Saintly Father) treat him as a divine avatar, or incarnation, the reincarnation of a famous holy man who died in 1918. His remarkable powers include producing things out of thin air – flowers, sweets, religious medals, crucifixes for his Christian admirers and photographs of deities. Numerous miraculous healings are attributed to him and he is said to have restored the dead to life. His predecessor or previous self lived at Shirdi in a broken-down mosque for some 60 years. Wildly eccentric and unpredictable, he beat his followers in rages and screamed abuse at invisible entities, smoked a peculiarly repellent clay pipe, tended a fire whose ashes appeared to have healing properties and in 1886 'died' for three days, saying he was going to visit God, before returning to life again.

Indian society is traditionally male-dominated and most spiritual teachers and mystics are men, but there have been holy women too. Anandamyi Ma (Blissful Mother), for example, born in 1896, was venerated for her spiritual radiance, her healing powers, her strange trance-states – in which she rolled on the ground, changed size and

Above: a fakir has had himself buried in the ground, his hands clasped in prayer.
Below: this holy man with his snake and prayer beads at Patan in Nepal is a devotee of the goddess Kali, once the divine patron of the Thugs.

bounced up and down like a rubber ball – and her ability to assume the personality and appearance of various Hindu gods and goddesses. Many of her followers regarded her as an incarnation of the great goddess Kali. She had ashrams, or spiritual centres, in Delhi, Calcutta, Benares and elsewhere. Arthur Koestler visited her Calcutta ashram and asked, through an interpreter, whether she approved of her followers saying she was divine. She replied impatiently, 'Everybody sees in me what he likes'.

✢

ASCETICS AND SAINTS

✢

Hindu sadhus and yogis are credited with supernatural powers ranging from the ability to levitate, to fly, to read minds and see into the future, to insensibility to pain or the power of being in more than one place at the same time. These ascetics and wonder-workers make a living by begging, by making and selling lucky charms and astrological talismans, by casting spells for clients, by conjuring and snake-charming. Some live alone, some in small monastic communities, some are wanderers. They subject themselves to ferocious mortifications of the flesh. Some lie on beds of nails or stay motionless for so long that birds nest in their hair.

Their Muslim equivalents are called pirs or fakirs, and renowned saints of the past are venerated at their tombs. Snake-charmers gather at the shrine of Pir Namana Shah in Umarkot and fakirs laden with chains swarm at the tomb of Hazrat Sakhi Qadir in Pakpattan. There is a cluster of saints' shrines at Multan in Pakistan and ragged ascetics dance themselves into trance to the rhythm of drums in the oasis of Sehwān in Sind, at the 13th-century shrine of Lal Qalander Shah Baz, a saint whom the awed locals sometimes saw flying through the air like an eagle, riding on a lion or using a snake as a walking stick.

SEX AND THE SACRED

Perhaps the best-loved and most worshipped deity in India is the god Krishna. According to his mythology he was born at Mathura and grew up – hidden away from enemies who wanted to kill him – among the cow-herding people of the Jumna region north of Agra, at the village of Vrindavana. A handsome and mischievous youth, he made many conquests among the local milkmaids and farmers' wives. His special love was the beautiful Radha, the wife of one of the farmers, but he was said to have enjoyed more than 16,000 women altogether during his time on earth.

Far from being regarded with disapproval, the tales of the god's lusty sexual exploits were relished and helped to inspire the Hindu ideal of bhakti, or devoted love, in relationships between human beings and the divine. The women's longing for Krishna's embraces was translated into spiritual terms as the devotee's longing for the god.

✧

LORD OF CREATION

✧

More direct and down-to-earth is the veneration paid to the linga (phallus) of the next most popular Hindu god – Shiva, the Lord of the Dance, the maker and destroyer of worlds. From very early times he was typically represented squatting in the position of a meditating yogi and with a huge erect phallus. This is the symbol of the god's colossal creative power. In mythology his erect linga is the central pillar which supports the entire universe and keeps it in being. Early religious poems were addressed to it, and a linga of stone, wood or metal has a prominent and honoured place in Shiva's temples, as at the Walkeshwar temple in Bombay and the linga shrines at Badami. Male and female members of the Lingayat sect of Shiva-worshippers carry a small stone phallus in a silver box round the neck.

The Aryan invaders who conquered northern India in the 2nd millennium BC

✧

The Kamasutra is the world's best-known erotic manual and sex has long been regarded as a pathway to the divine and to supernatural power in the Indian religious tradition.

✧

were disconcerted by the phallic cults of the local people, but the same strain invaded their own religious tradition before long. Phallic-shaped natural stones and other objects are venerated today in India, including a notorious phallic block of ice which is formed by water dripping from the roof of a cave at Amarnath in Kashmir. There is a famous shrine at Chidambaram in South India which is said to be the site of the akasha-linga, the great ethereal and invisible organ of Shiva.

✧

SENSUALITY AND RITUAL

✧

Riotous celebration of sex and sensuality is one of the characteristics of Indian cave art, with its sculptures of amorous deities and voluptuous nymphs in erotic poses. There are celebrated examples in the cave-temples at Ellora, while at Khajuraho and at the Black Pagoda at Konarak – a huge temple to the sun-god which is shaped like the sun's chariot – varieties of sexual play are elaborately delineated.

Ellora was a Tantric centre. Tantrism is a powerful current of ideas which has attracted followers among Hindus, Buddhists and Jains in India and Tibet, and has parallels in Chinese Taoism, which may have influenced it. The central Tantric principle is that everything in human experience is formed of pairs of opposites – positive and negative, light and dark, good and evil, male and female, and many more – which are expressions of a fundamental polarity running through the entire universe. The way to union with the divine is to unite the opposites, symbolised as a god and a

The god Shiva as a personified linga, which symbolises the colossal creative force of the divine, the power that generates and sustains all life throughout the world.

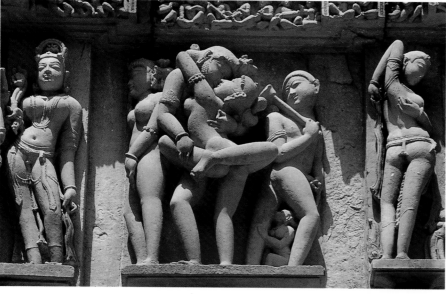

Above: Krishna and his favourite mistress, the beautiful Radha, in a 15th-century painting. The god's sexual prowess was much admired. Left: erotic sculpture of the 10th century on the façade of the Lakshmana Temple of Khajuraho.

goddess, who are usually Shiva and his consort Shakti (who is not only his partner, but also the femininity which is half of his being), or in Buddhist contexts the Buddha and the goddess Tara. This is also the way to the acquisition of magical and paranormal powers.

Uniting the opposites has an obvious sexual connotation. Women are deeply revered in Tantrism, for only through the female can the male find spiritual completeness and salvation, and so ritual sexual intercourse becomes an act of worship. In many Tantric cults this was carried out only symbolically, but the 'left-hand' Tantrics did not limit themselves to symbolism. Some of them went further and violated conventional taboos to break free of the opposites of good and evil. According to one Tantric text, 'Perfection can be gained by satisfying all one's desires'. The Kapalikas, who worship Shiva as Lord of Skulls, are said to have practised human sacrifice, cannibalism and necrophilia in pursuit of this ideal.

Slaves of the Gods

Sacred prostitution was widespread in India until late in the 19th century. The devadasis, or 'god's slaves', earned money for the temples which they staffed and were often dedicated to this service as little girls of seven or eight by their families, who acquired spiritual merit by marrying a daughter to the god as well as ridding themselves of the expense of keeping her (the birth of too many daughters has always been a catastrophe for poor families in India). They were taught the arts of love and were deflowered either by a favoured customer or by the artificial phallus of the god. Temple prostitutes were respected and no stigma attached to the profession. The temple at Tanjore had 400 dancing girls and those at Conjeeveram and Madurai were virtually brothels.

THE LAND OF SNOWS

Before the Chinese Communists conquered Tibet in 1950 and began a brutal campaign to destroy the country's institutions and character, its leading spiritual and political figures were the abbots of the great Buddhist monasteries. As they were celibates, they had no children and the system of succession to their office was perhaps the strangest in all human experience – by reincarnation. When an abbot died, a search was made for his successor, a young child, who by certain signs could be recognised as the abbot reborn. This was the method used to identify each of the Dalai Lamas, the rulers of Tibet, who were considered to be incarnations of the Boddhisattva Avalokitesvara, a great spiritual being of Buddhist belief who is widely regarded as the Tibetan national god.

The present Dalai Lama was born in a tiny, remote Tibetan village in 1935. The 13th Dalai Lama had died two years before and when the little boy was two a deputation arrived in search of his successor, following indications which had come to a senior lama (monk) in a dream. They showed the child a collection of objects. Some of them had belonged to the 13th Dalai Lama and some had not. He unerringly picked out the right ones, each time saying, 'It's mine, it's mine'. Certain marks on his body were thought to clinch the matter and he was identified

Remote and inaccessible among its mighty, snow-crowned peaks, Tibet has long been a land of mystery to the outside world, with an awesome reputation for magic and paranormal powers.

as the reincarnation and taken away from his family to be trained. He was subsequently enthroned in the vast Potala Palace in Lhasa at the age of five.

BY MAGIC ART

Tibetan lamas, hermits and ascetics, devoting themselves to meditation and the things of the spirit – not just over many years but over many lives, as it was believed – gained an immense reputation for paranormal powers. They were believed able to control demons and communicate with the spirits of the dead, control the weather, cure or kill at a distance, change their appearance at will, levitate and fly. They were able to move about with supernatural rapidity and they had amazing powers of endurance, including the ability to remain warm in the iciest conditions – crouched naked in snow, for instance, or in a freezing cave 18,000ft (548m) up. They could make themselves so light, it was said, that they could sit on a barley stalk without bending it.

As long ago as the 13th century, Marco Polo reported that Tibetan lamas at the court of the Mongol rulers of China were able by magic art to make the Great Khan's drinking cup rise spontaneously to his lips – a feat which naturally impressed him.

THE MERCILESS BLOOD-HEAD

Buddhism spread into Tibet from the 7th century on and took over the indigenous religion, known as Bon, many of whose beliefs and practices survived under a Buddhist cloak. Both lamas and lay magicians are traditionally called in to secure a good harvest, cure disease, cast out evil spirits and ward off hostile influences. They are also needed to placate local deities and spirits. These are legion and include gods of mountains and glaciers, snake-deities in lakes, plague spirits and evil-tempered entities under the command of a being called 'The Merciless Blood-Head', who lives in a nine-storey black fortress.

Specialist mediums deal with unhappy ghosts, who appear to their families in dreams or cause poltergeist-style disturbances in their former homes. The medium chants and dances his (or her) way into trance, to the music of a drum and a bell, until the spirit of the dead person takes possession of him and speaks through his mouth to explain what the matter is. It may have been seized by an evil spirit, in which case the medium must track the demon to its lair in the spirit world and rescue the captive ghost, dragging it away from the furious spirit. This is accompanied by frightful contortions of the medium's body and broken, incomprehensible words from his mouth, until at last he returns to normal and announces success, to the relief of the fascinated onlookers.

THE GRISLY FEAST

Behind all this lie the traditions of Central Asiatic shamanism, which probably also inspired the weird and terrifying rite called Chod, undertaken by monks. Alexandra David-Neel, who explored Tibet earlier this century, described it in her book *Magic and Mystery in Tibet*. After long and arduous preparations, the monk goes alone to a graveyard or any wild and forbidding spot and summons the evil spirits to attend a banquet. Then he vividly imagines a goddess, who personifies his own will, standing before

him, sword in hand. With one stroke she cuts off his head and as the hordes of demons crowd gleefully round, she cuts him up, skins him and rips his belly open. The spirits noisily gnaw on the lumps of his dismembered carcass, smacking their lips, as he recites a formula in which he offers himself to all living beings, his body to the hungry, his blood to the thirsty, his skin to clothe the naked, his bones to warm the cold, his happiness to the unhappy, his breath to the dying.

After this, he visualises himself as a little pile of bones in the mud – the mud of all the faults and shortcomings of his numerous past lives. He must understand that he has nothing to sacrifice, nothing to give, because he is nothing. Some lamas undertook to perform this rite at 108 lakes and 108 cemeteries, and spent years carrying out the vow.

Opposite page: prayer flags flutter in the wind to honour spirits in the high places of Tibet, while monks in their traditional robes and head-dresses sound trumpets.
Top: a cheerful little boy is confirmed as a reincarnated lama at the Dalai Lama's headquarters in northern India. Beside him are his rosary and a furry toy. On the wall behind him hangs a photograph of himself in his previous life.
Above: grotesque skull masks at a Tibetan butter festival. Many gods and spirits of popular pre-Buddhist belief were absorbed into Buddhism in Tibet and are honoured in Buddhist ceremonies today.

SPIRITS AND WITCHES

The traditional beliefs of the Sherpas, the mountain people of Nepal, are very similar to those of Tibet. The abbots of monasteries like Tengboche, in the shadow of Mount Everest, succeed to office by reincarnation. Lamas and spirit mediums are needed to provide protection against hordes of evil spirits called shrindi, which are generally blamed for illness and misfortune.

Anyone can train as a lama, but only a person of psychic gifts can be a medium, through whom ghosts and spirits speak and show themselves. The medium goes into a trance, usually assisted by drumming and chanting, and the possessing spirit explains what it wants and what must be done to appease it. The medium may also be possessed by an animal, such as a yak or a monkey, or by a living witch, which enables villagers to take precautions against offending the witch and attracting her malevolent attentions.

A DISTANT DRUM

The word 'shaman' comes by way of Russian from the Tungus-speaking peoples of Siberia, who used it for their specialists in the sacred. The background to shamanism was the belief that parallel to the human world is a plane peopled by numerous deities and spirits, invisible but powerful, who inhabit all the phenomena of nature from thunder and earthquake to rocks and trees, lakes and pools, animals and birds. These spirits could not be seen in any normal state of mind, but there were certain people who could put themselves into an abnormal state of mind, a trance or altered state of consciousness, in which they were able to see spirits, talk with them and go on long journeys of exploration into their world.

Soviet Communism disapproved of shamanism and eventually snuffed it out. Within living memory, however, such peoples as the Yakuts of eastern Siberia, with their capital at Yakutsk, and the Buriats, the horsemen of Ulan-Ude, the Lake Baikal region and Mongolia, valued their shamans as healers, diviners and intermediaries between humans and spirits.

‡

The shamanism of Siberia and central Asia has attracted eager attention in the West, while dying out in its old home ground between the Urals and the Pacific.

‡

RIDING TO THE SKY

‡

The trances and curious states of mind in which the shaman operated might be induced by fasting and self-torture, chanting and dancing, and especially the violent beating of a drum, in the form of a kind of tambourine, which was the Siberian shaman's most characteristic accessory. The drum was often called a 'horse' and it was on it that the shaman 'mounted' into the sky when he went travelling in the spirit world.

The shaman's tasks were to visit the gods with offerings from the people, to bring back from the spirit world news of the future weather or the prospects for the harvest, to guide the souls of the dead to the next world, and to track and bring back the soul of a sick person who had either wandered off into the spirit world and got lost or had been carried away by evil spirits. Since he could leave his body in trance, the shaman was credited with remarkable powers – the ability to fly, to make himself invisible, to turn into an animal, to

Fire From Heaven

Far fewer reports of visitors from outer space have come from Asia and Africa than from the Americas and Europe, but one explanation of the colossal and mysterious explosion which occurred in the depths of Siberia in 1908 attributes it to interplanetary astronauts. The explosion occurred on 30 June that year, at soon after 7am, near a small trading post named Vanavara, some 406 miles (650km) north of Krasnoyarsk. A flash of light was seen, as bright as a million suns and followed by a huge fireball in the sky. The heat was almost intolerable 37 miles (60km) away, where a farmer was blown off the porch of his house by the blast. An area the size of St Petersburg was devastated, as trees for miles around were hurled down or stripped of their branches. Subsequent investigation showed that the explosion was not caused by a meteorite hitting the earth, as was at first assumed. Among alternative theories are a black hole entering the earth's atmosphere or a nuclear explosion in a spaceship which crashed in this remote spot.

see things happening far away. He was impervious to heat and cold, and shamans often demonstrated the ability to handle live coals without being burned, which greatly impressed their audiences.

The Chukchi shamans in north-eastern Siberia claimed the power to turn into wolves and many Siberian and Mongolian shamans felt a close spiritual kinship with animals and birds – bears or bulls, eagles, owls or geese – which came promptly when summoned and helped them work their magic.

✛

THE GIFT OF LONELY POWER

✛

A shaman might inherit his office or might feel a vocation for it. In either case he would need a long training. A man might also turn into a shaman after some extraordinary and traumatic experience like being struck by lightning or falling out of a tree. A young man destined to be a shaman was often marked out by being different from everyone else – nervous and highly strung, solitary and moody, introspective, the prey of mysterious illnesses and strange dreams. He would be given to temper tantrums and fainting fits, headaches and attacks of vomiting, and was liable to sing in his sleep.

A liking for being alone was an important symptom. Potential Yakut shamans used to run wild in the forest, eating the bark of trees and slashing themselves with a knife. Among the Evenki, the reindeer herdsmen of the area round Tura, a young shaman would run away alone into the mountains for a week or more, hunting animals and tearing them to bits with his teeth and returning to his village filthy, blood-streaked and raving.

Shamans went through curious rites of initiation which qualified them for their office. For instance, the shaman might 'die' and lie motionless in his tent or in some solitary place for anything from three to seven days.

Opposite page: traditional shaman's head-dress, mask and robe from a village in Siberia.
Top: Yakhut shamans dance, in a print of the 1850s. The drum, or tambourine, was the typical shaman's instrument and the 'horse' on which he rode into the spirit realm.
Above: Siberian shaman's costume, of about 1890.

During this time, he would feel the agonising sensations of being dismembered by spirits. His flesh would be scraped or boiled from his bones, his eyes would be torn out and the blood and all the fluids of his body poured away. The spirits might cut off the shaman's head, hack his body to bits and parcel out the pieces among the spirits of disease, before putting his bones back together again and furnishing him with new flesh and new blood.

✛

THE ORACLE OF BLOOD

✛

The resemblance to the Chod rite in Tibet (*see page 133*) is obvious, and there are strong similarities between the shamanism of Siberia and Central Asia and beliefs and traditions in Tibet, China, Korea and Japan. There was a close spiritual connection for centuries between Tibet and Mongolia, where numerous Buddhist lamaseries flourished. Travelling in Mongolia in the 1840s, a French priest, Abbé Huc, watched with a large, excited crowd as a lama, seated on an altar, worked himself into a frenzy while his fellow-monks chanted, their invocations rising to high-pitched yells as the lama seized a long knife and slit his stomach open. Blood and guts poured out as the lama replied to a hail of questions about future events, which in this condition he could infallibly predict, or so it was believed. At the end, exhausted, he passed his hand over the terrible wound in his belly and it closed up, leaving no mark, but for the blood stains on the altar.

Things changed after the Mongolian revolution of 1921, however, and scenes of this kind could no longer be witnessed. Tens of thousands of monks were drafted to work in factories and co-operatives, and only the great Gandan Lamasery in Ulan Bator was allowed to remain open. Predicting the future was entrusted to the latest Five Year Plan.

THE CHINESE WAY

Before the Communist takeover in 1949, China had long been a powerful, centralised state, run by a highly trained elite of civil servants. The state religion ingeniously conceived of a parallel bureaucracy in the sky, with gods and godlings neatly organised in their pecking order in departments and committees. At their head was the Jade Emperor, the chief god. He was the heavenly counterpart of the Chinese emperor, who was the religion's chief priest and carried out the great state rituals which preserved order and harmony on earth. Below the Jade Emperor were the various ministries and boards which meticulously supervised every last detail of life on earth.

City gods and village gods formed one ministry. All occupations, businesses, shops and crafts, from the most respectable to thieves and prostitutes, had their own supervisory gods. In the home the figurines or paper images of the household gods were given offerings of incense and all the family news was told to the ancestors, whose tablets were kept in their own shrine and who could be asked to intercede with the divine bureaucrats in time of need. Once a year the kitchen god went up to the sky to report on each family's

It was once a common saying that the three major religions of China – Confucianism, Taoism and Buddhism – were really all one religion, because most Chinese people took whatever they wanted from all of them.

Above: the Eight Immortals, seen on this delightful 19th-century tile, were great Taoist adepts who had discovered the secret of eternal life. Right: a modern protective Taoist necklace, with each bead separately marked with a magic symbol.

behaviour. Before he went he was given honey, to sweeten his tongue, or if necessary to stick his lips together so that he could not speak at all.

PUNISHING THE GODS

If a celestial bureaucrat fell down on his job, he was punished by the senior earthly mandarins. A god who failed to bring rain to his district or halt an epidemic might have his statue whipped or he might be demoted ignominiously and another god appointed, to see if he could do better – which he usually could, since the rain does fall eventually and epidemics do stop. The system had the great advantage of explaining disasters and calamities as divine bureaucratic mistakes and providing for their punishment and amendment, and it took a firm hold on Chinese loyalty.

A human being, meanwhile, could rise through the system to become a god. A notable example was Confucius himself. The great sage was honoured as divine, especially at his home, Qufu (formerly Chufu), where generations of his descendants revered him until the Red Guards came and smashed the statues in his temple, burned the ancestral tablets and looted the family tombs.

'I LOSE ME'

The state religion was needed for social cohesion in a huge country, with a population of different racial origins, speaking different languages and believing in myriads of different gods and spirits – local deities, gods of fertility and nature, spirits of hills and rivers, evil spirits and disease spirits. In very early times their cults were in the hands of priest-magicians and shamans, male and female, who worked themselves up into states of ecstasy and trance in which deities and the spirits of ancestors spoke through their mouths.

Religious fervour of this kind had no place in the state religion, but it survived in Taoism, which is still alive on Taiwan, in Hong Kong and in Chinese communities in Singapore and south-east Asia. Taoist mystics aimed through meditation and trance to attain a state in which, as they said, 'I lose me', in becoming one with the Tao (the Way) itself, the ultimate Unity underlying all diversity.

At this high level, Taoism was an elevated system of mystical philosophy, whose supposed founder, Lao Tzu, was revered as a god. At the popular level, however, Taoism was an earthy peasant religion which worshipped numerous gods and goddesses whose favour was needed for prosperity and success. Taoist leaders were believed to control all spirits and protect their followers from supernatural evil. In its early days the religion encouraged orgiastic sexual rites, but these fell away when Taoism began to coalesce with Buddhism, which established itself in China in the early centuries AD.

✤

THE QUEST FOR IMMORTALITY
✤

Taoists made determined efforts to achieve immortality. A group of adepts said to have succeeded were revered as the Eight Immortals, seven men and one woman, who lived alone in mountain caves in various remote places until they achieved magical powers and eternal life. They gathered at the Penglai Pavilion in Yantai, where they all got merrily drunk and tried to fly across the Yellow Sea to Japan. They now live in the Laoshan Mountains, outside Qingdao (Tsingtao).

Several of the Tang emperors were

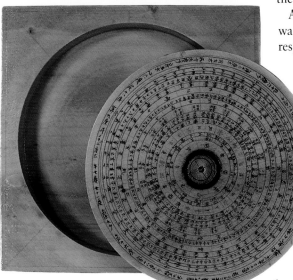

Top: the symbols of Yin and Yang, the two great opposite cosmic forces of traditional Chinese belief, are joined at the heart of the circle and surrounded by the eight trigrams which are the key to knowledge. This amulet would have been hung on a door to keep evil influences out.
Above: a compass of the type used by the masters of feng-shui, the art of sacred geometry.

enthusiastic Taoists and some were said to have achieved immortality (or from a cynical viewpoint, poisoned themselves) by drinking magical elixirs.

✤

BALANCE OF FORCES
✤

The four most important Taoist monasteries were at Beijing (Peking), Chengdu, Shenyang (Mukden) and Suzhou (Soochow), and important cities like Nanjing (Nanking), Guangzhou (Canton), Luoyang, Wuhan and Xian all had Confucian, Taoist and Buddhist temples. Most ordinary Chinese people felt no need to belong to only one religion, and paid homage to whatever permutation of supernatural beings seemed most adequately to provide prosperity and good fortune. The merciful goddess Kuan Yin, for example, was originally a male Buddhist saviour (the same as the one incarnated by the Dalai Lamas), but changed sex and became popular with non-Buddhists as well. One of the objections to Christianity in China was the missionaries' insistence that theirs was the only truth.

Another objection to Westerners was their failure to understand and respect the rules of Chinese sacred geometry (feng-shui), which was used to determine the positioning and orientation of temples, tombs and other structures, and even the layout of fields and the course of roads, so as to tap the subtle and beneficent energy in the earth, the atmosphere and the sky. The impressive tombs of the Ming emperors near Bada Ling, for example, were all sited in accordance with feng-shui. When the British in Hong Kong built the road called The Gap from the town to the Happy Valley, the Chinese were horrified by the breach of feng-shui principles involved, and their misgivings were confirmed when many of the labourers went down with malaria. The railway was not allowed near Qufu, in case it disturbed the balance of forces at the tomb of Confucius. Today feng-shui is part of the architecture course at Singapore University.

THE RISING SUN

Japan is the only leading country in the world with a monarch still regarded by millions of his subjects as a god. When Emperor Hirohito died in 1989, the government was seriously alarmed by the possibility that thousands of people might follow the ancient tradition of committing suicide at the death of one's lord. A few elderly people did. At the funeral, attendants carrying gold and white banners represented the eight million deities of Shinto, the native Japanese religion, and an official bore a box in which was a new pair of shoes for Hirohito to wear in the next world. A curtain was discreetly lowered during those of the rites which directly related to the dead emperor's status as a god.

According to Shinto tradition, the Japanese emperors are the descendants of the sun goddess Amaterasu, the chief Shinto deity, whose symbol of the rising sun is the national emblem. The Meiji regime of 1868 to 1912 put a special emphasis on this tradition as part of a policy of enhancing imperial authority and it played a powerful role in the aggressive Japanese nationalism of the 1930s and 1940s. The emperor, who is his people's chief priest, lives hedged by taboos in a secluded palace at the centre of 125 acres (50ha) of grounds in Tokyo – a piece of real estate said to be worth more than the entire state of California. At his accession, temporary buildings of wood from specially grown trees are constructed in the grounds, priests and priestesses dance and sing as hallowed by the tradition of centuries, the lamps are lighted from

Emperor worship is an ancient cult which has played a powerful role in Japanese nationalism. Older still are the shamanistic traditions which remain alive in Japan and Korea.

The traditional Japanese religions lost ground after World War II, when they were no longer allowed state subsidy. However, spectacularly colourful old-style ceremonies and processions still bring out the crowds, as at this festival in Hiratsaka.

a flame kindled by rubbing two sticks together and the new emperor, incarnating the rice god, goes through a secret rite of sacred marriage with the goddess.

DIVINITY IN DUST

The emperors are by no means the only human beings to be accorded divine status in Japan. As in Chinese tradition, people of exceptional gifts and achievement are honoured as gods. The patron deity of sumo wrestling, for instance, is Sunuke, a great champion wrestler of the 1st century. Shinto has maintained the ancient belief in multitudes of kami, or supernatural entities, inherent in people and animals, in trees, rocks, caves, rivers, mountains and all the phenomena of nature. Over the centuries it has co-existed with, and often blended with, Buddhism, which spread to Japan from China by way of Korea.

The great homosexual 9th-century teacher Kukai, or Kobo Daishi, for example, created a mixture of the two religions in which the entire world is the body of the cosmic Buddha, so that everything in it, down to every least particle of dust, has a spiritual component. According to tradition, Kukai emerged from the womb with his hands clasped in an attitude of prayer, travelled about as a beggar performing miracles and drove away innumerable evil spirits, dragons and monsters which tried to interrupt his meditations. He is venerated to this day at his birthplace, Zentsuji, and his tomb on Mount Koya in Shikoku.

Shinto shrines and Buddhist temples lie cheek by jowl at places like Nara, once the imperial capital, where the powerful Fujiwara family built both the Kasuga Shrine, where ritual dances are performed in honour of

The Divine Winds

The kamikaze pilots who crashed their bomb-laden planes on American and Allied warships in the Pacific during World War II were examples of emperor worship and patriotism carried to suicidal lengths. They were told that in losing their lives they would become gods. Kamikaze means 'the divine winds' and the reference was to storms, believed to be sent by the gods, which defeated a Mongol invasion in the 13th century. The code of the samurai warrior-class put a fighting man's life in his superior's hands without reservation. Following the death of the Emperor Meiji in 1912, a distinguished general, Count Nogi, committed hara-kiri, with his wife, apparently to continue to serve his emperor in death as he had all his life.

Amaterasu, and the Kofukiji, 'the Temple Providing Happiness', with its Buddha statues and graceful pagodas. The sun goddess has her major shrine at Ise, the war-god Hachiman at Kamakura, and the other principal Shinto centres are at Kyoto and Nikko.

POSSESSED BY FOXES

By-products of the belief that everything has a soul are the evil or mischievous supernatural animals of Japanese tradition. There is a typical story about a man catching a badger, pinioning it and telling his wife to make soup of it. The badger cajoled the wife to untie its bonds by saying it would help her do the cooking. It then promptly killed her, assumed her appearance, dressed in her clothes and made her into soup, which it served to her husband when he returned. After he had eaten it with every appearance of enjoyment, the badger returned to its normal form, jeeringly told

Top: wooden blocks to write a wish on are sold at Shinto shrines. Above left: telephones are blessed at a Buddhist ceremony. The Japanese believe that everything has a spirit. Above right: a festival at the great temple of the goddess Kannon in Tokyo.

him what it had done and ran off.

In the more remote areas of Japan, illnesses may still be put down to evil spirits, which have taken possession of the patient and which are either angry ghosts or spectral animals. Westernised attitudes are spreading, but in some villages, until recently, evil supernatural foxes, controlled by witches and sorcerers, were held responsible for almost every sickness and misfortune. Specialist exorcists would cast the invading spirits out. The temple of Taikyuji, near Tottori, was still a functioning exorcism centre for fox-possessed patients in the 1960s.

In her book *The Catalpa Bow*, in 1975, Carmen Blacker revealed that despite the

rising tide of secularism and materialism, shamans were still practising here and there in Japan. These were people who in trance were still believed to penetrate the spirit world, go on journeys there and speak to the spirits, returning with powers of healing and clairvoyance. Some of them acted as the mouthpieces of spirits which took possession of them.

The same tradition is still alive in country places in Korea, especially on the island of Cheju-do. Korean religion is mainly a blend of Confucianism and Buddhism, but its oldest strand is the belief in a vast multitude of spirits, many of which are inimical to mankind. Temples in Seoul and other cities have shrines to the Mountain Spirit and the Spirit of the Seven Stars (the Plough). Korean shamans, who are now always women, act as go-betweens in trance with the inhabitants of the spirit world and demonstrate curious acrobatic feats like dancing barefoot on sharp knife blades or walking over a paper bridge without breaking it.

SURROUNDED BY SPIRITS

Two of Buddhism's most revered relics are preserved in Sri Lanka, which boasts a longer continuous Buddhist tradition than India itself. One of them is the Buddha's left eyetooth. It is kept in the Temple of the Tooth at Kandy in a golden casket, which every year is paraded in state on the back of a magnificent elephant at the climax of the Esala Perahera festival in August. The elephant, splendidly

In south-east Asia the major religions have been forced to accommodate the multitudes of spirits believed by ordinary people to affect everyday life, health and happiness.

DEVIL DANCING

Juggernaut-like cars rumble through the streets of Colombo and Jaffna at Hindu festivals and the Hindu temples at Kataragama witness spectacular fire-walking, as devotees from small children to elderly people walk along a bed of glowing embers without the slightest sign of discomfort or injury. Some

tusked and caparisoned in colourful cloth fringed with electric light bulbs, dominates a tremendous procession of 100 or more elephants escorting four Hindu deities and their consorts in palanquins, with hordes of dancers, acrobats and whip crackers.

Profoundly sacred also is the venerable bo tree (*ficus religiosa*) at Anuradhapura, which is claimed to be 2300 years old. Bowed with age and supported on crutches, it has grown from a shoot of the tree beneath which the Buddha attained enlightenment, brought to Sri Lanka in the 3rd century BC and revered here ever since.

Above left: all over south-east Asia devotees mutilate themselves at festivals of their deities.
Above: the magnificent Temple of the Emerald Buddha in Bangkok is one of Thailand's finest buildings, but older, pre-Buddhist beliefs still permeate daily life.

worshippers thrust skewers through their tongues and cheeks or hang from hooks piercing their bodies, while the beating of drums, blowing of conch shells and chanting of pilgrims fills the air.

In Sri Lanka the major faiths have been infiltrated by each other and by the old nature deities. Evil spirits are widely believed to cause disease and other misfortunes, and traditional rites are performed to expel them from their victims. To the beating of a special 'demon drum' the exorcist summons the spirit to speak through a patient's mouth and reveal what it wants. At 'devil dancing' ceremonies performers leap and cavort as evil spirits in fearsome masks. The spirit of madness is especially frightening, roaring and shinning up the timbers of the building. The leading exorcist is dressed as Vesamuni, the lord of demons, so that he can control the others. These rites have evolved into spectacular folk theatre (and a tourist attraction), but they are also still believed to cure sick patients. Ambalangoda on the south coast is especially celebrated for its devil dancers and masks.

✢

NATS, PHIS AND LENIN

✢

When Buddhism became the state religion of Burma in the 11th century, King Anawrahta took care to include the native Burmese deities, called nats, in the religion. Figures of them were placed in magnificent Buddhist temples like the Shwezigon Pagoda in Pagan and the Shwedagon Pagoda in Rangoon so that the people, going to worship them, would learn the new faith. The 'inner' nats are the ones allowed inside Buddhist pagodas, and there are thousands of 'outer' ones as well. Their traditional home is on Mount Popa.

Signs of respect for the nats are everywhere, for they can cause bad luck if they are neglected. The house nat has his shrine in each home and a coconut adorned with red and yellow streamers in his honour often hangs on the south wall. Miniature bamboo nat shrines stand by the road or look out from trees and the sprig of blossom in a Burmese girl's hair is a precautionary nod to the nats.

In Thailand, similarly, Buddhism is the country's dominant religion, as the ravishing Temple of the Emerald

Buddha in Bangkok bears witness, but the crowds which bring eggs, flowers, cigarettes and bottles of Coca Cola as offerings bring them not only for the Buddha but for Hindu and native Thai deities. Little shrines of the innumerable minor spirits, called phis, are everywhere, even in the brashest new Western-style hotels.

The situation is much the same in Vietnam, though the Communist regime

Ways of death in south-east Asia. Top: crumbling coffins dangling from a cliff in Sulawesi (Celebes) have deposited skulls and bones. Above: in Bali the traditional ritual involves burning the corpse on an ornate pyre.

disapproves of all doctrines other than its own. Some two million people belong to the syncretistic Caodai faith, founded in 1926 as a blend of Buddhism, Hinduism, Christianity, Islam and Spiritualism, with its headquarters at Tay Ninh, north-west of Saigon. Worshippers communicate with spirits

at seances and Caodai 'saints' include Lenin, Shakespeare and Joan of Arc.

✢

SHAMANS AND SEVERED HEADS

✢

In Malaysia, Islam holds sway and the National Mosque stands in Kuala Lumpur, the capital, but the temple of the merciful Buddhist goddess Kuan Yin in Pinang draws worshippers from all faiths and the old animist conviction that everything in the world contains a spirit is still a factor in everyday life. When a new house is built, a medium will be summoned to go into trance and persuade any evil spirits to leave before people will live there. Mentally ill patients are exorcised by a bomoh, or medicine man, who may beat them or cut them to drive the possessing spirit out, and many Malays who fall ill consult both a Western-style doctor and a bomoh to be on the safe side. In 1993 the murder of a politician who had called in bomohs to help his career by magic made headlines.

There are shamans still in Indonesia, another Muslim country, and ceremonies are held to placate the spirits of active volcanoes – including Mount Bromo in Java. A procession goes from Yogyakarta once a year to the coast at Parangkusumo, where a set of the Sultan's old clothes are pushed out into the waves on a raft as an offering to the sea-goddess.

On Bali the dramatic dance ritual called the Sanghyang carries the performers into trance in which spirits are summoned up and exorcised. Red-haired tourists may be eyed askance here, incidentally, as red hair is a traditional mark of a witch.

In Borneo the Dyaks were zealous head-hunters and no young man could expect to gain a girl's favour until he had harvested an adequate number. The heads were hung up in the longhouses and it was through them that contact was made with the spirit world. Head-hunting finally died out in the 1940s, but peaceable offerings are still made to the spirits on Mount Kinabalu, whose name means 'place of the dead'.

✦ AUSTRALASIA ✦ AND THE PACIFIC

In 1961, when an American went missing on the south shore of New Guinea, there was a strong suspicion that he had ended up in the stomachs of the locals and rumours spread about a white man's skull and a pair of spectacles being in the possession of some of the tribespeople. In that year a Dutch Protestant mission was founded in the Yali-mo Valley and six years later the local people burned the mission down, then killed and ate the preacher and 12 assistants. Though Christian missionaries of fiercely competing denominations have converted thousands of Pacific islanders, older traditions linger on.

The Pacific Ocean covers about one-third of the surface of the globe, a vast waste of heaving waters dotted with islands which were among the last places on earth to be conquered and exploited by Europeans. Long before any white

Above: an aborigine elder in front of Uluru, or Ayers Rock. This whale-like mass of red rock deep in the Australian outback is a sacred place. It was visited by many of the mythological ancestors on their journeys across the land, for like their descendants, the aborigines, they were nomads and hunters.
Below: men of the Asaro Highlands of Papua New Guinea, coated in mud to represent spirits. The long fingers made from bamboo and weird woven masks evoke fear.

man set eyes on the Pacific, however, people from south-east Asia had ranged across the trackless ocean in voyages of astonishing seamanship and skill, in canoes 100ft (30m) long which could undertake journeys of thousands of miles.

All the peoples of Australasia and the Pacific were still living in the Stone Age when whites first discovered them. They believed in a great multitude of spirits, including the revered spirits of the primordial ancestors – the ones who first arrived in a given territory, settled it and established the way of life there, which had been followed ever since. Rituals united the people with their ancestors in trances or elevated states of mind and repeated the mythological doings of the ancestors, so as to preserve the order of the world which they had created. Among the Australian aborigines, for

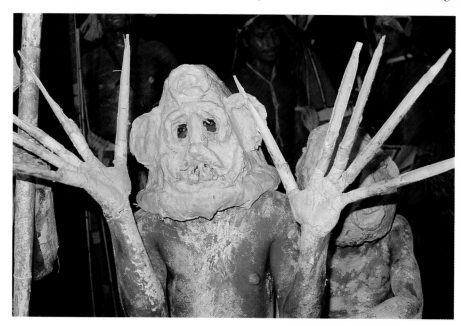

example, rituals of chanting and dancing gave access to the special time-plane in which the primal ancestors moved.

Many Pacific islanders accepted the twin principles of mana and tapu: that a spiritual energy, called mana, exists in all the phenomena of nature, in human beings, animals, trees and rocks and even whole islands, which means that everything in the whole world is sacred; and that this energy is inherently dangerous as well as vigorously creative – like a powerful charge of electricity – and so requires a system of rules and restrictions called tapu (the origin of the English word taboo). There is a report on record of a Maori priest in New Zealand, for instance, whose personal mana was so potent that he was never allowed to walk on any public path in case he made it unsafe for everyone else.

When the whites appeared, the people of the Pacific fell prey to the twin plagues of

Western diseases and Christian missionary work. For example, Ferdinand Magellan arrived in Guam in 1521. Between that date and 1695 smallpox and influenza are estimated to have reduced the population from 100,000 to below 5000, virtually all of whom meekly accepted Christianity.

Christian missionaries were shocked by the islanders' casual approach to sexual matters, and often failed to understand their charges' ancestral beliefs and patterns of behaviour. Though Christianity remains a powerful force in the South Seas, however, a rising tide of nationalism since the 1970s has brought a strong revival of interest in the older, pre-Christian beliefs and ways.

One of the mysterious statues on Easter Island, which have intrigued the outside world ever since the island was first discovered by the captain and crew of a Dutch ship in 1722.

IN THE DREAMTIME

For many centuries before the white men came, the aboriginal people of Australia lived in close harmony with the natural world that surrounded them, each small group of hunter-gatherers ranging its recognised territory. In their Stone Age world they saw far more than met the eye, for they viewed the whole landscape as sacred and populated by innumerable spirits. Among them were the spirits of animals and birds, of plants and rocks, the spirits of their own dead predecessors and the great mythological ancestors who long ago created the world and everything in it.

These beings inhabited their own time-sphere, which anthropologists have christened the Dreamtime, in which the mythological creative events were still occurring. In an altered state of consciousness human beings could enter that sphere to experience the events and repeat them, and so be at one with the gods and keep the world-order in being. The songs which they sang in the rituals at their sacred sites were the same as those which the ancestors sang in the Dreamtime, and the dances re-enacted their adventures. Chanting and singing with rising excitement, sometimes cutting themselves in frenzy till the blood ran, the performers became one with the ancestors.

Figures of mythology in an aboriginal bark painting. Aboriginal art is interwoven with religion, magic and mythology, and is primarily used to keep the great creative figures which feature in aboriginal belief alive and vigorous.

✢

In remote regions of Australia aborigine elders still hand down generation by generation the secrets of rituals in which the sacred mythological past is brought fruitfully into the present.

✢

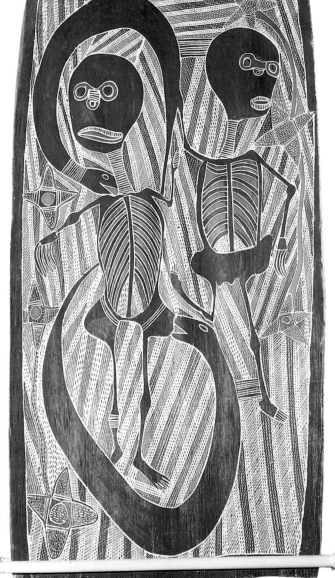

✢

SACRED LAND, SACRED ART

✢

To represent the dead in ritual the aborigines painted themselves white, which was one reason why they treated white explorers and settlers with reserve. Whites were sometimes identified as dead aborigines and sometimes as evil spirits. Aboriginal culture has been destroyed in most of Australia, but survives in remote places in the centre and north of the continent. The most famous of its sacred sites is Ayers Rock (Uluru to the aborigines), that massive whale-like hump which rises dramatically from Australia's central plain. In aboriginal tradition it is a myth made manifest, embodying and preserving a titanic battle fought in the Dreamtime by two rival groups of ancestors. Thousands and thousands of tourists go there every year, hoping to experience something of a primordial sacredness which their presence inevitably destroys.

Another sacred place is Wilpena Pound, a deep natural amphitheatre in the mountains where in mythology people were attacked and killed by two giant snakes, which then gave themselves up to death to make the towering walls. On the rocks at Mootwingee in New South Wales aborigines painted and carved men, emus and kangaroos, boomerangs and snakes and the outlines of human hands and feet. There are more examples in the Kakadu National Park in Arnhem Land, south-east of Darwin, while the art galleries in Alice Springs are stocked with aboriginal mythological paintings of today's Papunya School.

The Kimberley area of north-western Australia is known for cave-paintings of the Wandjina spirits, ancestors who created the landscape, made the paintings and disappeared underground. Today their descendants must retouch and renew the paintings every year, to make sure that the rain will fall and life be renewed in full vigour and abundance, as it was in the days when the Wandjina trod the earth.

✣

POINTING THE BONE

✣

Things in the aboriginal world did not happen by chance. Premature death, serious illness, harm and misfortune with no evident cause were put down to a spirit or the malevolent magic of an enemy. Aboriginal magicians knew how to strike a victim at a distance by 'pointing the bone' – jerking a pointed bone or stick in the victim's direction

Above: mythological snake and witchetty grubs.
Below right: aborigines at a painting ceremony.
Below: the Ayers Rock Skull is linked with the Dreamtime.

while chanting and propelling a current of murderous hatred at him. In a society where magic is believed in, it works, and there are many reports of aborigines falling ill and even dying when they knew that a curse had been put on them.

In an example reported by an American anthropologist, a man fell sick when he discovered that a magician had pointed the bone at him, though a mission doctor who examined the victim could find nothing physically wrong with him. When the doctor threatened to have the magician and his people driven away, the magician convinced the victim that he had not cursed him at all, and the victim promptly recovered.

Equally, a 'clever man' could cure a victim by magically extracting the 'badness' which had entered his body and ostentatiously throwing it away, or he could go in pursuit of the departing soul

Family in the Bush

In his *Journey Through Australia*, the novelist and poet Rodney Hall recalled walking in the bush with an elderly aboriginal under the blazing sun when the old man suddenly put his hand out to bring them to a halt and signalled urgently with his eyes towards some tufts of grass. Hard as Hall stared, he could see nothing there. A breath of cool breeze blew in and the old man relaxed and said, 'Did you see him there?' Hall asked, 'Who?' 'That was my Uncle Jack', he said, and then apologetically, 'Oh, you would have called it the shadow of those leaves in the grass. The wind blew him away.' 'Whatever else was in question,' Hall comments, 'there was no doubt the spirit of his uncle had been with us. He told me later that the whole bush was alive with his relatives, but that Uncle Jack was his favourite uncle and the one who had taught him most.'

of a dying man and bring it back. Again confidence in the magic would often bring about the desired result.

Accounts of the initiation of 'clever men' recall the shamanism of Siberia. In one example the novice 'clever man' goes to the mouth of a special cave where he is seen by the spirits of the Dreamtime. They hurl two invisible spears at him which kill him. Then they carry his corpse into the cave and take all his internal organs out, replacing them with new ones and also with magic quartz crystals from the sky, from which he will draw his healing and supernatural power.

MYSTERIES DOWN UNDER

On the white side of the fence in Australia poltergeists and other paranormal phenomena make their appearances, and sometimes the fence between white and aboriginal is intriguingly crossed. At a farm near Pumphrey Bridge in 1957 stones began falling out of a clear blue sky. The farmer called the police, who came and made an unavailing search while yet more rocks dropped from above. The aboriginal farm workers put the trouble down to a young black stockman named Cyril Penny, who had been put under a curse. The farmer sent Penny away from the farm on an errand for a whole day, during which no stones fell and all was calm. When he returned the stones started raining down again, though it was clear that he was not throwing them, nor did anyone else seem to be throwing them. A sceptical reporter came out from Pumphrey Bridge to sneer at the whole business, but changed his tune when a shower of stones fell round him.

The biggest of the stones were about the size of a man's fist. They were dusty, but showed no fingerprints, and they seemed to materialise in the air a few feet above people's heads. The aborigines demanded that Cyril Penny be dismissed, and he left, but the falls continued and when some of the workers went to other farms the stones followed them, until the whole thing stopped as inexplicably as it had begun.

⁑

Poltergeists, ghosts, mysterious lights which chase or even assault people, dangerous UFOs and alien invaders have all been reported from Australia in recent years.

⁑

Another infestation that ended for no apparent reason occurred at a restaurant called the Drunken Admiral, on the waterfront in Hobart, Tasmania, where a ghost kept trying to strangle people in the loo. The spectre was thought to be that of a Chinese man who had hanged himself there in 1880. Mediums reported that he refused to believe he was dead and that he enjoyed frightening people. He went away eventually.

Below: a Cessna Skylane aircraft of the type Valentich was piloting. Opposite page: simulation of the mysterious disappearance.

LIGHT FANTASTIC

Mischievous and sometimes frightening are the mysterious 'min-min lights' reported from the area near Boulia in the outback in western Queensland and also around Lake Manchester, near Brisbane. They are globes of light which hover in the air or sometimes roll, bounce and move about. People have chased them on horseback and in cars, but without success and on occasion have found themselves being chased in turn.

In 1912 a hotel-owner from Boulia was riding in the outback in the early hours of the morning when he saw a greenish light floating in the air. It came so close to him that he could see the hairs on his arm by its light and then it suddenly went out – 'phut! just like that'. Another sighting was reported in 1916 by a stockman who was passing the Boulia graveyard when he saw a strange glowing light hovering above it. Not caring for it much, he spurred his horse to a gallop, at which the light pursued him for a time before disappearing. In 1981 a policeman reported seeing a mysterious light near Boulia. He watched as it dived towards the ground and went out. In the morning no evidence was found of anything hitting the ground.

Something altogether more alarming happened in 1988, when a family driving along the

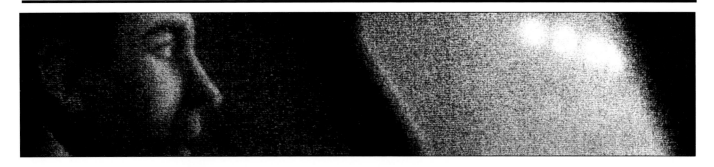

road from Perth 25 miles (40km) west of Mundrabilla was pursued by a bright light which swooped down on to the roof of the car and lifted the vehicle up in the air, while members of the screaming family heard their own voices alter and distort. The car fell back on to the road, with its roof-rack torn off, and a tyre blew out. The family ran and hid in bushes until they were sure the light had gone away. The car was coated with black ash which the police laboratory reported to be burned rubber. The crew of a trawler fishing off the coast said that a shining white light had hung over their boat and while it was there they had not been able to speak normally. By coincidence or not, the worst series of earthquakes in Australian history began within 24 hours of these events.

✢

DARK SHADOW

✢

Some researchers connect weird light phenomena like this with geological, seismic or electromagnetic currents of some kind. Others link them with UFOs, of which there have been quite a few Australian reports. A celebrated one occurred in 1944, when the crew of a Royal Australian Air Force bomber flying over the Bass Strait, between Melbourne and Tasmania, saw something they called a 'dark shadow', with flame belching out from its back end, flying beside them and keeping pace not more than 150ft (45m) away. During the 20 minutes or so it was there the bomber's radio and direction-finding equipment went completely dead. The mysterious craft then accelerated away at great pace, leaving the bomber standing.

In 1953 film was shot of a peculiar unidentified flying 'missile' at Port Moresby, but the film went mysteriously missing and there were whispers that the security service had confiscated it. In 1973 'a large black, airborne object' was seen from the North West Cape communications station, hovering in the sky before accelerating 'at unbelievable speed' and disappearing to the north.

✢

DANGEROUS GAMES

✢

A few suspected alien abductions have also been reported. In 1967 a man from Mayanup in Western Australia was out driving one night when his car lost power and stopped as a ring of blue light encircled it from an oval object in the sky. Suddenly the light went out and the car started again. The man drove on, but his watch proved unaccountably to be several minutes slow and he suffered from severe headaches for the next two weeks. His doctor could find nothing particularly wrong with him.

In 1978 there came the strange and troubling case of the disappearing pilot. His name was Frederick Valentich, aged 20, and he was flying his blue-and-white Cessna 182 on an October evening from Melbourne over the Bass Strait to King Island, off the coast. There were numerous UFO sightings in the area that day and night. Other pilots in the air heard Valentich radioing that he seemed to be flying beneath 'a large aircraft' with four bright lights, like landing lights, travelling at tremendous speed. It flew over him and away and back again, as if it was playing a game with him. Then he said it was 'not an aircraft', but 'a long shape', shiny on the outside, with a green light. His last words were, 'It is hovering and it's not an aircraft'. Nothing more was ever heard of Valentich or his aircraft and no trace of them has ever been found.

THE LAND UPLIFTED HIGH

It was the Dutch explorer Abel Tasman who sighted and named New Zealand in 1642, calling it 'a great land uplifted high'. The Maori people, who had arrived there several centuries before after a formidable voyage across the Pacific, named it Aotearoa, 'Land of the Long White Cloud', which was how it looked on the horizon as their ocean-going canoes approached it. Long before Tasman's day, according to Maori tradition, the first discoverer of New Zealand was a great Polynesian navigator named Kupe, who sailed down the west coast of the two islands 1000 years ago. He reported his discovery when he returned home and the first migrants set out following his sailing directions, 'to the left of the setting sun in the month of November', to reach their new home. They brought the dog and the rat and the sweet potato with them and settled down to live there.

Going much further back still, into the far reaches of mythological time, the North Island of New Zealand, according to the Maori account, was originally a giant fish, in the form of a stingray, which was drawn up out of the ocean by the demi-god Maui, who had superhuman powers. The 'head of the fish' is to the south, where today's capital city of Wellington stands. The East Cape and Cape Egmont are 'the wings of the fish', while the elongated Northland Peninsula makes the whip-like 'tail of the fish'. Maui went away to

‡

The first National Park in New Zealand was founded by a Maori chief as his last hope of preserving his people's sacred mountains from despoliation.

‡

Above: a preserved Maori head, from a museum in Basle. These heads were often brought back to Europe from New Zealand by sailors.

give thanks to his celestial ancestors for his magnificent catch, but while he was gone his brothers, who were greedy and quarrelsome, began hacking the fish to pieces. It writhed and squirmed in its death throes, which is why New Zealand

is a mountainous country.

The South Island, or Te Wahi-pounamu, the place of greenstone, is in the shape of Maui's canoe, and Rakiura, now known as Stewart's Island, was the stone which Maui used as an anchor. On the other hand, the Uepohatu tribe, on the east coast of the North Island, believe that Maui's canoe lies in a petrified state on the sacred summit of Mount Hikurangi.

‡

CANNIBALISM AND WITCHCRAFT

‡

The Maori believed in numerous gods who controlled the principal forces and departments of nature – the forest, the sea, the wind and rain, earthquakes and the rest. Closer to ordinary people and ordinary daily life, however, were the many local spirits and the spirits of the ancestors who took a lively interest in the doings of their descendants and the fortunes of the tribe. According to tradition, the souls of the Maori dead leave the mortal sphere by way of Cape Reinaga, the headland at the northernmost tip of the North Island, where an ancient tree juts out from the cliff. Here the dead leap out into the water and go down to the underworld.

Down to the 19th century and the time of European colonisation, tribal wars were endemic among the Maori. This involved cannibalism, as the bodies of defeated enemies were consumed to debase their mana, or spiritual force, and strengthen that of the victors. The heads of chiefs were cut off and smoke-dried to preserve them as trophies of war. European sailors not infrequently bought these trophies and took them home to sell, and many of the heads are now in European museums. Some of them have now been returned to New Zealand and their tribe of origin.

The Maori also deployed magic

swarms of geologists, botanists and mountaineers at bay indefinitely, and in 1887 the local chieftain presented the area to the crown to be a national park – New Zealand's first – so as to keep it as unspoiled as possible.

Taranaki (Mount Egmont), another volcano, was also sacred and Maori chiefs were buried there. A naturalist

The focus of traditional Maori community life today is the marae, a ceremonial area which is used for greeting visitors, cultural activities, weddings, funerals and educational and political meetings. Each settlement has an elaborately carved meeting house, which is traditionally thought of as a living thing, with a mask below the gable as its head, the ridgepole as its spine and the interior as its belly. There are fine examples at Rotorua and Poverty Bay, among many others in New Zealand. The presence of meeting houses in towns, at schools and on university campuses bears witness to the renaissance of the Maori tradition today.

Left: interior of the Waitangi Meeting House. Each meeting house is a repository of tribal lore and identity. Below: a Maori hei-tiki, or amulet, carved in jade.

against enemies. They believed that their life-force was protected against malevolent spirits by the gods, but that protection was withdrawn if certain laws were broken or a shaman cast a spell against them. The victim of the spell would grow weak and, in serious cases, would even fade away and die. The only recourse was for a high priest to work counter-magic against the shaman's spell.

✢

IN HIGH PLACES
✢

New Zealand's impressive mountain peaks and volcanoes were often held sacred by the Maori. In the Tongariro National Park, North Island, the three volcanoes of Mount Tongariro, Mount Ruapeho and Mount Ngaurohoe were taboo and the local people tried to prevent whites from climbing them. When Sir George Grey climbed Mount Ruapeho in 1851, he had to hide from the local people because they were so upset, but the Maori could not keep the

named Ernest Dieffenbach arrived in 1839 and insisted on climbing the mountain in defiance of local sentiment, but his Maori guides would not accompany him above the snowline.

✢

LIVING TRADITION
✢

Under British rule from 1840, the Maori were converted to Christianity and the tribal wars came to an end. Today, three-quarters of the Maori people live in towns and cities, outside their tribal territories. There has been extensive intermarriage with Pakeha (Anglo-Europeans), but much of Maori culture has remained alive, the Maori language is taught at schools and used in the universities and the Maori remain a distinctive element of the population.

THE PRESENCE OF THE DEAD

The geography of the huge island of New Guinea, which is long enough to stretch from London to Moscow, splits it up among high mountains, swamps and deep valleys where some 800 languages are spoken and each little village jealously preserved its independence before the white men came. The western part, Irian Jaya, is today part of Indonesia, while the rest is independent as Papua New Guinea (PNG). The principal Christian denominations have made zealous missionary efforts, and when a hitherto unexplored valley and hitherto unknown people are discovered – which happens every so often – the Churches vie with each other to rush in, convert them and sabotage their belief system.

Traditional religion in New Guinea involves a host of spirits, whose sympathy is needed for prosperity and good fortune. As among the Australian aborigines, rituals need to be carried out regularly to keep the world in being, in its due and accustomed order. This order was created by gods and spirits, and religious rituals repeat the actions of these supernatural beings to perpetuate the original creation.

Rock paintings of the great ancestral spirits, partly human and partly animal in form, who laid down the order of nature are admired today by tourists along the coast of the Bomberai Peninsula, between Kokas and Goras, in mountain caves inland and near Kaimana. There are pictures of birds and fish, too, stencils of human hands and geometric designs.

✢

The Church of England cathedral of St Peter and St Paul in Dogura, Papua New Guinea, stands peacefully on the local people's traditional fighting ground, but the various competing missionaries have not found it entirely easy to replace ancient indigenous traditions with Christianity.

✢

COUNTING HEADS

✢

Part of the order of the world as understood from time immemorial in New Guinea was petty warfare, with constant skirmishing, raiding and ambushing going on between one village and another. Heads of slaughtered enemies were brought back and hung up in the men's cult houses and sometimes a whole enemy corpse would be brought back and ceremonially eaten.

In the Menyamya area of PNG the dead were smoked until their bodies were dried and hard, and then propped in a seated position on platforms overlooking their old homes: these kippered bodies can still be found among the mountains. In other areas it was the custom to eat one's own dead and corpses were respectfully consumed by relatives and privileged friends. Eating a dead person is a way of magically acquiring that person's strength, courage and good qualities.

✢

A GIFT OF TWO FINGERS

✢

The dead and the ancestors were important spirits. The ghosts of the dead were thought to linger round their old homes and watch the behaviour of the living, not always with a kindly eye. They could cause disease and misfortune, and frighten people. They could sometimes be persuaded to mark an enemy for death, which would soon follow in a skirmish. The more distant dead, the ancestors, were regarded as generally benevolent. On some of the offshore islands, including Biak and Yapen, venerated carvings of the ancestors were consulted, before a war party set out, by a man who went into trance to speak with them and ask them to protect the warriors. Fire-walking was also a tradition here as part of

‡

MEN IN COMMAND

‡

It was men, not women, who dressed up to the nines and carried out the religious rituals, and they did this with the maximum of ostentation and display in large cult houses, specially built, or in the mountain areas on special dancing

In the area north of Port Moresby, PNG, people still build their traditional 'dancing villages', which are created specially for feasts and ceremonies. Impressive ceremonies are also staged by the Asmat people of Irian Jaya, notorious head-hunters in the past, whose capital is at Agats on the south coast. They are famous for their wood carvings, which

religious festivals, and is still sometimes performed for tourists.

The goodwill of supernatural beings was sought by offering them the spirit of a butchered pig or a reaped crop. In some areas it was customary to offer them two or more fingers chopped off a young girl's hand, left out to dry and then burned. Adult women might have only four to six fingers left if much propitiation had been needed. Displays of wealth, ornate and impressive body decoration, costumes and masks, giant feathered head-dresses, elaborate carvings and paintings were also believed to please spirits and gain their sympathy and approval.

Opposite page: Okapa man in an impressive wooden mask.
Above left: a barkcloth and grass mask.
Above right: smoke-drying corpses is a traditional procedure in some parts of Papua New Guinea.

grounds. It was the spirits, they believed, who had originated the rites and ceremonies down to the tiniest details, and in the drumming and dancing of the rituals the men impersonated and became the spirits they hoped to impress, while the ostentatiousness of the displays had an additional purpose, to overawe the people of other villages who came as guests.

were traditionally produced to represent and to gratify ghosts, ancestors and other spirits. The heads they took in war were hung up by the sago fields to encourage fertility. At a time of crisis, such as an epidemic or a devastating enemy raid, the Asmat staged orgiastic sexual ceremonies to work up a powerful tide of vital energy which would steer the course of events in a favourable direction.

Women were kept at a distance from masculine preserves which their presence might pollute. To this day in the more remote areas of New Guinea a woman does not sleep in the same building as a man, eat at a man's table or speak to any man outside the family circle.

THE CARGO CULTS

Although Christian missionaries have gathered many converts in the Pacific, they have sometimes been fiercely resisted – with spears and showers of arrows – and their efforts have not always led to quite the desired results. In New Guinea, for instance, their pale white skins suggested that they were ghosts or spirits, and in the early days many of the indigenous people assumed that these white strangers with their enviable supplies of worldly goods and their magical ability to cure disease (with penicillin shots, for example) must be powerful beings from the spirit world, whose rituals should be carefully studied and copied.

The white people wore peculiar clothes unsuited to the climate. They sat at tables to eat, they seemed to attach great importance to writing things on pieces of paper and they performed odd ceremonies in churches. They also spoke into little boxes which caused boats or planes or helicopters to appear as if by magic, bringing fresh supplies of food and equipment, which the whites had done nothing to grow or to make. The locals, much impressed, did their best to copy these powerfully effective rituals in the hope of achieving the same rewarding results.

CONSUMER PARADISE

In various Pacific islands, at least as far back as the 1880s in Fiji, cults developed which focused on obtaining the white man's goods and lifestyle by magical means. Prophets arose among the people and proclaimed that their ancestors would soon return to the island in a ship loaded to the gunwales with tinned food, furniture, radios, refrigerators and other desirable consumer items. The islanders would obediently build a quay where the boat could tie up and a warehouse to store the goods. The prophet might order them to throw all their money into the sea or kill all their livestock to bring on the great day, but of course the day never

These curious modern religious movements, which use magic to try to bring ships or planes loaded with Western goods ('cargo') to Pacific islanders, are a consequence of white influence and also a rebellion against it.

came and the islanders merely suffered.

World War II gave a powerful stimulus to this type of cult, because it brought American transport aircraft to the Pacific islands, loaded with Coca Cola, jeeps and trucks, canned food, cigarettes, moving pictures and other treasures in what to the islanders was an astonishing and overwhelming display of wealth. In local tradition, ostentatious wealth of this sort belonged to dominating leaders gifted with supernatural powers, and so offers were made to buy President Franklin D Roosevelt, and later President Lyndon B Johnson, so as to bring them and their supernatural influence to the Pacific. Islanders laid out airstrips and made miniature dummy planes to bring real planes to the scene.

THE COMING OF JON FRUM

One of the cults flourishes on the island of Tanna in Vanuatu (formerly the New Hebrides), which was an important staging area for American and Anzac forces in World War II. It looks for the arrival of a white-faced leader named Jon Frum, who will bring the expected 'cargo' in a red aircraft and a fleet of ships and drive all the whites away. Figures of Jon Frum and his plane are erected at shrines, with red crosses and gates. The red cross symbol comes from the Red Cross flights which brought free medical supplies to the islands during the war.

Jon Frum's identity is uncertain. Some say that the name simply stands for 'John from America', some that he is John the Baptist, some that his name is derived from the famous American abolitionist John Brown (of 'John Brown's body' fame). Some believers have made themselves imitation radio aerials out of empty tins and wire, through which to receive the news of Jon Frum's arrival. Wharves where his ships will unload have been constructed. A visitor who recently enquired why the cultists were still waiting for John Frum after all these years was firmly told that they had not been waiting anything like as long as the Christians have been hanging on for the Second Coming of Christ.

MARCHING RULE

Another cargo cult appeared after the war in the Solomon Islands, which had also enjoyed the open-handed generosity of American troops and where the islanders had noticed that black American personnel ate the same food and used the same equipment as the white personnel did, and seemed just as rich. A movement which looked for the Americans to return was called Marching Rule, and many villagers moved from inland to new 'towns' which they built on the coast. Rows of huts were constructed to store the expected cargo and look-outs were posted to watch for ships. Some of them would hold an empty bottle to each eye in magical imitation of the binoculars that American soldiers had been seen using.

Anthropologists have pointed out that these strange-seeming cults were a form of rebellion against the dominance of colonial officials and missionaries. At first the locals tried to gain equality in the new white world that had been imposed on them by becoming Christians and climbing their way up the white man's ladder. When that failed to bring them the consumer desirables they

wanted, some of them claimed that the whites were deliberately keeping the way to their wealth secret, left the white churches and founded religio-magical cults of their own. In parts of Papua New Guinea, for instance, a cult grew up which claimed that the secret of the white man's riches depended on knowing the secret names of the Supreme God and Christ, both of whom in reality were important native New Guinea gods.

As Pacific islanders have gradually become better educated and more emancipated from white rule, more conventional paths to white-style success have opened up, through politics, business and the civil service. The pulling-power of the cargo cults has consequently weakened.

The arrival of huge American airplanes at island strips during the war in the Pacific, bringing quantities of consumer goods – cigarettes, Coca Cola, tinned food, jeeps and so on – to supply the needs of Allied troops, played a powerful role in stimulating native religious movements which aimed to bring the islanders the white man's long-desired wealth.

SPIRITS OF THE SOUTH SEAS

Spread over an immense area and living often at great distances from other communities, the Pacific islanders developed a wide variety of languages, customs and beliefs about the supernatural. Some of them cherished traditional myths of powerful gods of the sea, the forest, agriculture, war and other departments of nature and life, who might be represented by statues or symbolised by clubs or canoe paddles. They took possession of their priests in trance and spoke through their mouths, and they were consulted before important decisions were taken or major enterprises set in train.

The Hawaiian islanders worshipped their war god, Ku, and other deities in walled stone enclosures called heiau, inside which were temple buildings of wood and grass. Dogs, chickens and fish, and human victims on occasion, were offered to the gods on stone altars. Figures of the deities were made of stone, wood and feathers, with human hair, the teeth of dogs and eyes made of pearl shells, and sometimes with sharpened bases so that they could be stuck into the ground.

The ferocious goddess Pele lived in the crater of the great Kilauea volcano, which looms above Honolulu, her eruptive wrath mollified by offerings of juniper berries and the occasional pig or man. A surprising number of today's tourists pick up lava samples to take home with them and subsequently send the rocks back to the local post office with apologetic notes explaining that they

Visitors to Hawaii today still go in some awe of the goddess of the Kilauea volcano, whose traditional offerings of juniper berries have been replaced by regular donations of gin.

have experienced nothing but bad luck ever since. Park rangers return the lava to the goddess with propitiatory bottles of gin, to which she is known to be partial.

A WATCHFUL SKULL

Much of the time, however, these great divine beings were considered too superior and far away to take an interest in ordinary people's life and happiness. These were more the concern of a multitude of lesser spirits, guardian spirits of families, gods of crafts, spirits of trees or rocks or pools or animals, the ghosts of the dead and the spirits of the ancestors. In the Bismarck Archipelago, off New Guinea, for instance, when the male head of a household died he became the family's guardian deity. His skull was put up over the entrance to the house, to keep the guardian spirits of other families away, watch the doings of his own family members and dole out rewards and punishments to them accordingly.

The Trobriand islanders believed that the spirits of the dead helped their descendants, especially in connection with the fertility of crops, so long as good relations with them were maintained. The dead returned to their ancestral villages at annual feasts where they were entertained by their relatives. They also showed themselves in dreams, and specialist mediums could put themselves into trance and go into the world of spirits to communicate with them.

✣

GUARDIANS OF MORALITY

✣

Carvings and masks were used to represent spirits and men dressed up as spirits in ceremonies. The women would believe, or pretend to, that the men had really become the spirits, and the men felt a strong sense of identity with them. Spirits enjoyed feasts and celebrations in the same way that human beings did. In Tahiti certain rituals worked up a powerful erotic charge through drumming and dancing, and culminated in a general orgy, to please the spirits and magically promote the fertility of nature. Harvest time in the Hawaiian Islands was celebrated with feasting, drinking and orgiastic sex, as well as surfing and boxing contests, to honour the god of the rain and vigorously promote fertility.

There was not necessarily a clear distinction between the spirits of ancestors and the dead, and those of animals or places. A man-eating shark could be identified as the spirit of a particularly formidable dead person, and if the shark caught a man and the man managed to escape, he might be thrown back to it, out of respect for the spirit and to avoid antagonising it.

Spirits were conservative by temperament and were much concerned with the due observance of tradition and custom. Rituals and ceremonies had to be performed exactly as they had always been, down to every last detail. Traditional rules of fishing or agriculture had to be obeyed or the spirits would be angry, and the spirits were equally offended by any breach of the traditional moral rules and the conventional principles of people's behaviour to each other. This was a powerful sanction and the weakening or destruction of belief in the traditional spirits by Christian missionaries often turned out to have seriously damaging and antisocial effects.

Opposite page: a wooden figure of Pele, the goddess of the Kilauea volcano in Hawaii. She has human hair and her eyes are made of shells. Right: Captain Cook, the great British explorer of the Pacific in the 18th century, is present at a human sacrifice carried out on the island of Tahiti.

Elders in Stone

Silent on their tiny speck of ground in the Pacific, almost 2500 miles (4000km) from the nearest landmass of any size, the enigmatic statues of Easter Island gaze stonily into space. Carved from the living rock in quarries in an extinct volcano, they stand up to about 20ft (6m) high and weigh up to 20 tons or so apiece. They have heads grotesquely too large for their bodies, with long ears and chins, and no legs. Some of them are crowned with 'hats' or 'topknots' of red rock from a different volcano. They are arranged in rows on stone platforms near the shore of the island and have inspired awe and curiosity in Western sailors and explorers since a Dutch ship stumbled on the island in the 18th century. When Captain Cook called at Easter Island in 1774, he was told that each statue had its own name, which often included the native word for 'chief', so it seems likely that these huge figures are among the world's most remarkable and dramatic expressions of the veneration of a people's ancestors.

The tradition on the island is that the statues walked to their places.

ISLANDS IN THE SUN

Sir Arthur Grimble, who spent years as a colonial administrator in the Gilbert Islands of the Central Pacific earlier this century, described in his famously delightful book, *A Pattern of Islands*, how he 'felt queer' when he was informed that a death-curse had been laid on him by an island magician with a fearsome reputation as a sorcerer. The magician was boasting that the white man would fall sick in a week and be dead in three.

Fortunately, Grimble had just been made a member of one of the island clans and he was now hastily taught the protective prayers to the ancestors of the clan, which would infallibly work if used correctly and ended with the comforting words, 'Blessings and Peace are mine. Blessings and Peace.'

This did much to calm his nerves, but two days later he saw the sorcerer's face in his sleep and woke up with agonising stomach pains. He doctored himself rigorously with a diet of milk, olive oil and bicarbonate of soda, told himself firmly that the curse could not work, and managed to withstand it. This information was received with great glee by most of the islanders, who were terrified of the sorcerer and relieved to see him thwarted.

Magic was always deeply feared in the South Seas and the concept of mana lay behind head-hunting, cannibalism and human sacrifice.

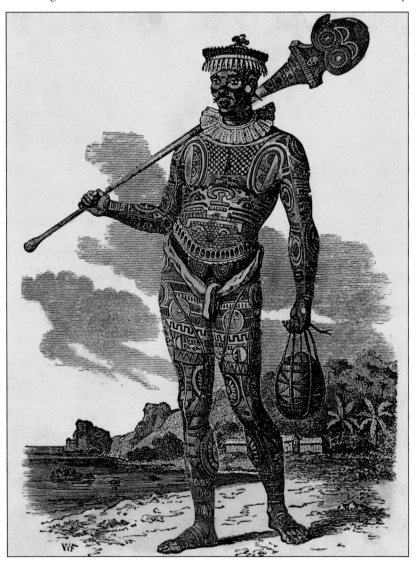

The warriors of the Marquesas Islands enjoyed a particularly ferocious appearance. They were tattooed from head to foot.

MURDER BY MAGIC

There was a deep fear of hostile magic everywhere in the South Seas, and it was well known that a magician could injure people by using their hair or nail-cuttings or left-over food fragments against them. He could take a lizard and starve it slowly to death, and as it weakened and failed, so would his victim weaken and die. Or he could employ the mana inherent in an object to strike a victim. The power in a man's fish-hook could be manipulated to spoil his catch, or the power of his cooking-oven perverted to drive him to madness. Every sorcerer had his familiar spirit, which might be a beetle or a bird or a fish or some horrible bodiless thing, which he could send to spy on his victims and bring them harm. Where magic is believed in, it frequently works, by auto-suggestion, but white men usually did not believe in it and acquired a useful reputation for immunity to native sorcery.

The sorcerers of Hawaii had a particularly evil reputation for stealing a dead body, preserving its bones and hair, and then making sacrifices to it which would build up its power and bring it to deadly life. It could then be sent against the sorcerer's victims. This procedure was dangerous, however, because if the sorcerer did not keep the reanimated corpse happy with constant sacrifices, it might turn against him.

✢

A CANNIBAL SNACK
✢

The idea of mana underlies the head-hunting, cannibalism and human sacrifices which so shocked white explorers and missionaries. The people of the Marquesas Islands had a reputation to match their ferocious appearance, tattooed from head to foot, the warriors' ears artificially stretched to touch their shoulders, the sides of their heads shaved. The Fijians enjoyed cutting off a captive's tongue or fingers, roasting them and offering them to him as a nutritious snack as a preliminary to killing him and cooking the rest of him.

Heads were taken in war and enemy corpses eaten to acquire the victim's personal supply of spiritual and magical energy. Whites had strong mana and when a missionary named Baker was murdered in Fiji in 1867, pieces of his cooked body were sent to all the local villages, though the people who tried manfully to eat his shoes gave them up as too tough. When some important occasion required a charge of extra mana, a human victim might be sacrificed to provide it. This was done when a war party set out in Tahiti and the Marquesas, and at the launch of a new war canoe in Hawaii, where human victims were also buried under the foundations of the sacred enclosures, to infuse mana into them.

✢

TEA IN PARADISE
✢

Christian missionaries and colonial administrators suppressed head-hunting, cannibalism and human

A land-diving platform on Pentecost Island in the Vanuatu group. This pagan and spectacularly dangerous sport was banned by Christian missionaries, but has been revived. It was believed to encourage the growth of the yam crop.

sacrifice almost completely. Unfortunately, by proscribing the indigenous gods and spirits, consigning much of the art which represented them to the bonfire and lauding Western ways, they also destroyed much of their converts' identity. The London Missionary Society, which arrived in Tahiti in 1797, persuaded the pleasure-loving population of that tropical paradise to drink tea, eat their meals with knives and forks, wear Western dress and hats, and live in solid stone houses where they sat on chairs and slept in beds.

Whites often imposed the grimmer aspects of their own moral code on the islands, including the famous 'missionary position' for sex and the Presbyterian Sunday. In Tonga and Western Samoa, for instance, no games are played or dances danced on a Sunday, no one goes fishing and no ships, planes, buses or taxis stir.

On the other hand, old beliefs and customs have survived here and there, separately from or mingled with Christianity. The Philippines, for instance, are predominantly Roman Catholic, but great tribal feasts of the old kind have survived in the mountain areas and pagan elements have infiltrated Christian festivals. In May people go to pray for a child or healing or a good crop at Obando, where ancient fertility rites are cloaked in homage to the Virgin of Salambao, a miracle-working image which, according to legend, a fisherman of the area found in his fish-trap. In Kalibo and Ibajay in January carnival dancers blacken themselves with soot to celebrate a pre-Christian festival now dedicated to the Child Jesus.

On Pentecost Island in the Vanuatu group, the spectacular and far more openly pagan custom of land diving, which the missionaries banned, has been revived. A tower is erected, up to 90ft (27m) high. (Women are not allowed near it while it is being built.) Then, as the spectators dance and sing, young men plummet off the tower head first after tying vines round their ankles. If the vines are too long, the diver crashes to the ground, perhaps fatally, and if they are too short he is snapped painfully back against the platform and breaks his bones, but if the length is right, his hair brushes the earth at ground level. This is a tourist attraction, of course, but it is also a traditional way of securing a plentiful yam harvest and the revival of land diving is a mark of a renaissance of ancestral customs among the South Sea islands.

INDEX